Capacity to Change

Understanding and Assessing a Parent's Capacity to Change within the Timescales of the Child

Capacity to Change

Understanding and Assessing a Parent's Capacity to Change within the Timescales of the Child

Dr Bryn Williams
Dr Emma Peart
Dr Roger Young
Dr David Briggs

With specialist contributions by

Alastair Barnett
Sarah Birch
Louise Michelle Bombér
Kari Carstairs
John Castleton
Helen Dent
Judy Eaton
Michelle Flynn
Siobhan F Kelly
Roger Morgan OBE
Caroline Pipe
Ursula Rice
Kathy Richardson

Family Law

Published by Family Law
A publishing imprint of Jordan Publishing Limited
21 St Thomas Street
Bristol BS1 6JS

Whilst the publishers and the author have taken every care in preparing the material included in this work, any statements made as to the legal or other implications of particular transactions are made in good faith purely for general guidance and cannot be regarded as a substitute for professional advice. Consequently, no liability can be accepted for loss or expense incurred as a result of relying in particular circumstances on statements made in this work.

British Library Cataloguing-in-Publication Data

A catalogue record for this book is available from the British Library.

ISBN 978 1 84661 919 9

Typeset by Letterpart Limited, Caterham on the Hill, Surrey CR3 5XL

Printed in Great Britain by Hobbs the Printers Limited, Totton, Hampshire SO40 3WX

DEDICATION

*Dedicated to Nat and Beatrice and
in loving memory of Margaret Peart*

ACKNOWLEDGMENTS

As well as the tremendous work by the authors who have contributed to this book there are a number of others who have played an important role in shaping its content. The most important person to extend thanks to is Jennifer Smith, our secretary, who has not only kept us all on time, but used her amazing skills to organise the book.

It is also with thanks to Ursula Scott, Sue Vaughan and the team of safeguarders and social workers in Guernsey, Madge Booth from Windows, Gerard Drennan, William and Cecilia White, Julie Crocker, Martin Shotbolt and colleagues who have offered thoughts over time about the content. The team at Jordan Publishing has been very supportive and encouraging and it has been a pleasure working with them. On a more personal level our very great thanks to Lucy, Raffael, Jackie, Huw, Jenny, Chris, Angie, Jess, Ashley, Faith and 'the current Mrs Briggs'.

So much of what we have learned has been hugely influenced by our dealings with solicitors, barristers and advocates. Equally, our involvement with social workers, family support workers, guardians and other mental health practitioners, who have channelled our thoughts. We would like to extend our gratitude to the courts and the many judges who have required us to explain psychology in a way that assists in making such difficult decisions about children's lives. A special mention should be given to Judge Cherry McMillen and our thanks to the Royal Courts of Guernsey and Jersey.

The adults and children with whom we work are often very hurt and in terrible crisis. We want to acknowledge the role they have played in shaping our thoughts and fuelling our passion for doing a good job. We hope our efforts will help protect children and families in the future.

Dr Bryn Williams
Dr Emma Peart
Dr Roger Young
Dr David Briggs

February 2015

BIOGRAPHICAL DETAILS

Alastair Barnett

After gaining an MA in Child Psychology at Nottingham University, Alastair trained as a Clinical Psychologist at Oxford, qualifying in 1992. Following qualification, he has held a number of posts within NHS CAMHS, working clinically with a broad range of child, adolescent and family problems. In 2010 Alastair formed Conatus Child Psychology, a specialist independent child psychology practice, based in Warwickshire. His clinical interests include attachment difficulties/relationship trauma, autism spectrum conditions, anxiety difficulties and psychological aspects of soiling and wetting problems. Alastair is particularly interested in working with 'sub-clinical' presentations of child mental health conditions; those children and young people whose problems have not met the criteria for formal diagnosis and yet give rise to significant concerns and impairment for the individuals concerned.

Sarah Birch

Sarah Birch is a clinical psychologist who has been working as an expert witness in child proceedings cases for the last 8 years. She has a particular interest in cases of non-accidental injury to children and failure to thrive. She also worked in the NHS in a forensic service for women until 2012, and she is experienced in working with people who have attracted a diagnosis of personality disorder and with people who have a diagnosis of post-traumatic stress disorder. She is currently training in eye movement desensitisation reprocessing (EMDR) and has previously been in training as a psychoanalytic psychotherapist.

Louise Michelle Bombér

Louise has had over 20 years' experience of working with children and families in a wide range of settings. Renowned in the area of working therapeutically with attachment and developmental trauma, Louise is both a qualified, specialist teacher and a child-young adult therapist. She has provided therapy, specialist assessments, consultations and training 1:1, to groups of staff, whole school settings, fostering and adoption providers, social services and health. She also works with individual children and families. Alongside her therapeutic work with Beacon House Trauma Clinic, Louise works out in Brighton and Hove schools under TouchBase and speaks every week both nationally and internationally under The Yellow Kite (www.theyellowkite.co.uk). She also runs The Attachment Lead Network which promotes a comprehensive training programme to enable schools become attachment aware (www. attachmentleadnetwork.net).

Kari Carstairs

Kari has an undergraduate degree in experimental psychology from the University of Oxford and a Doctorate in clinical psychology from Widener University in the USA, graduating with distinction in 1991. She worked in adult mental health in the NHS, leaving in 1998 for full-time private practice. Kari is the director of Carstairs Psychological Associates, a company that provides court reports in family, civil and criminal cases. She has carried out research in psychological testing and teaches and supervise other psychologists. She obtained the Certificate of Expert Witness Accreditation from Cardiff University/Bond Solon in 2004. In 2011, Kari gained diplomat status with the American Board of Assessment Psychology, with a specialty in forensic assessment. Kari started training in psychoanalysis at The Site for Contemporary Psychoanalysis in 2013, offering long term insight oriented psychotherapy to adults.

John Castleton

John Castleton is a counselling psychologist (BPS Chartered and HCPC Registered), with a special interest in substance misuse. Since 1982, he has provided psychosocial services to a variety of clients (individuals, couples, families and groups; ages 12–70; people of different cultures and abilities) who have presented with a range of difficulties (substance misuse, anxiety, depression, stress, PTSD, phobias, bereavement). He has worked as a practitioner, manager and consultant, in the statutory, voluntary and commercial sectors. He has been in independent practice since 2000 (including acting as an expert witness and completing the Bond Solon Expert Witness Certificate). He also works in an NHS community mental health team.

Helen Dent

Helen Dent is Professor of Clinical and Forensic Psychology and Programme Director of the Professional Doctorate in Clinical Psychology at Staffordshire University. She is registered as a practitioner psychologist with the Health and Care Professions Council and is an Associate Fellow of the British Psychological Society. She works one day a week as a consultant clinical psychologist in a specialist NHS team for looked after children. She has previous experience of working clinically in various services for both adults and children. Helen's research focus is mostly with vulnerable children and young people. She currently supervises a number of Doctoral research projects and is jointly conducting research into the perceived causes of attrition in cases involving child victims. She has considerable experience acting as an expert witness in cases involving child protection issues, including the assessment of children's allegations made during 'ABE' interviews.

Judy Eaton

Judy Eaton is employed as the lead consultant clinical psychologist in an independent CAMHS Tier Four hospital which assesses and treats adolescents with highly complex and challenging behaviour. She also leads on the assessment and diagnosis of Autism Spectrum Conditions across the Group. Prior to this she was the clinical lead for an NHS Tier Three CAMHS team in the West Midlands. She was an integral part of the West Midlands Criminal Justice forum which developed the first 'Attention Card' for young people with autism who came into contact with the criminal justice system. She has acted as an expert witness in criminal cases where the defendant has autism and in care proceedings cases when young parents have neurodevelopmental difficulties. Her particular area of interest is girls with autism and she has taught, presented and published in this area with specific focus on pathological demand avoidance (a form of autism).

Michelle Flynn

Michelle Flynn is a partner at Wilson Solicitors in Tottenham, London. She has been a member of the Law Society's Children Panel since 2007. She has extensive experience in representing parents in both public law care proceedings and private law proceedings. She is regularly instructed by guardians to represent children and has on many occasions separately represented young people. Michelle has experience of complex non-accidental injury cases and sexual abuse cases and is a respected and effective advocate. She is a mother of two and her interests include watching the mighty Tottenham Hotspur, running and taking part in the occasional obstacle mud race!

Siobhan Kelly

Siobhan F Kelly is a specialist family barrister and a member of Coram Chambers in London. She has extensive experience in all aspects of the law relating to children. Her main area of practice lies in acting for parents and children in public law proceedings. She is frequently instructed to represent young mothers within care proceedings and also has a particular familiarity with representing children in private law applications. She is regularly instructed on highly complex matters including those involving the death of children, extensive medical evidence, allegations of non-accidental injury and extreme sexual abuse. Her down time is devoted to good friends, good holidays and good wine.

Roger Morgan, OBE

Roger is the former Children's Rights Director for England. In that post he was responsible for statutory consultation with children on rights and welfare issues. Previously he developed Paired Reading and treatments for bedwetting, and managed social care services. Now retired, he runs Pupils 2 Parliament, securing children's views for government consultations.

Caroline Pipe

Caroline Pipe is a social worker and systemic psychotherapist with over 20 years' experience of working with children and families in statutory settings. After qualifying as a systemic psychotherapist Caroline enjoyed a 6 year career in the London Borough of Hackney where her role focussed on embedding systemic practice in a social care context. Caroline continues to be involved in a number of projects dedicated to promoting connections between social work and systemic practice and has recently commenced her role as Head of Clinical Practice for the London Borough of Hammersmith and Fulham.

Ursula Rice

Ursula is a solicitor and solicitor-advocate, practising in the field of family law. She is a director and shareholder of Family First Solicitors Limited, a firm specialising in family work. She regularly conducts final hearings in Children Act and Family Law Act matters. She writes and speaks on legal matters as well as business development for Resolution, SJ Live and various other publications and local radio. She has lectured for the University of West of England on the LPC. She takes a particular interest in the mentoring and development of young lawyers. She is founder of the Family Duty Clinic, an Oxford Court based Law Works Pro Bono clinic, and winner of the inaugural National Pro Bono Centre Award 2013. She can be found at http://www.linkedin.com/pub/ursula-rice/29/750/333 or through http://www.familyfirstsolicitors.co.uk/.

Kathy Richardson

Kathy Richardson is a senior social worker whose career has encompassed frontline practice in a number of areas including residential settings, child protection and court directed assessment services. Whilst working in the London Borough of Hackney, Kathy developed her interest in using systemic approaches in her work with children and families, specifically relating to risk management. Kathy has acquired a reputation as a robust and highly skilled practitioner, with specific expertise in working cross-culturally in cases involving 'honour'-based violence and witchcraft and spirit possession.

Emma Peart

Emma Peart is a clinical psychologist registered with the Health and Care Professions Council and British Psychological Society. She currently works for WIPC UK Ltd, an independent consultancy providing therapeutic and expert witness services. Until 2014 she worked for a child protection team in Guernsey, where her role was to establish and develop the provision of a clinical psychology service to support social work assessments and families where the children were at risk of significant harm. A particular emphasis was on the development of the use of evidence based methods for assessing risk and intervening to increase parents' protective capacity. She previously worked within mental health and medium secure forensic services within the UK. She has a particular interest in the assessment of attachment across the lifespan, relational trauma and how this relates to parenting capacity.

David Briggs

David Briggs works as a forensic clinical psychologist throughout the UK and Channel Islands. David's background was originally in practice as a child psychologist though over the past years he has been drawn into attempts at prevention, and hence work with adults, extended family members and community systems. Much of his current practice is within the family court system whereupon he is called to assess those who maltreat children, as well as the partners and family members of significance to those abusers. He has a particular interest in difficult to engage clients and has developed interventions to enhance and sustain precursors to change.

Bryn Williams

Bryn Williams is a consultant clinical psychologist and a director of WIPC, an independent psychological consultancy. After working in the NHS and for the States of Jersey he joined with other independent colleagues to offer assessment and therapy services, teaching and consultation as well as expert witness work in public and private law. Bryn has an interest in the interface between child abuse and children with developmental disorders and disability. He also works with children who have been exposed to emotional harm as a result of family breakdown and divorce. He has a practice based in Oxfordshire and Jersey, as well as providing consultancy in the United Arab Emirates. He lives in Oxfordshire with his wife Lucy and his children, Beatrice, Nat, Jess and Ashley.

Roger Young

Roger Young trained as a clinical psychologist in South Wales; his clinical experience is mostly with children and young people. For 9 years Roger was the Head of the Child and Adolescent Psychology Service for what was then the Gwent Health Authority area. He contributed to the Department for International Development (DFID) funded 'Link Project in Clinical Psychology' designed to establish clinical training in Dhaka, Bangladesh. In 1986 Roger joined the staff of the South Wales Clinical Psychology Training Programme becoming Joint Course Director in 1994 and Programme Director (and Honorary Professor of Psychology, Cardiff University) in 2003 until 2007. During his time in clinical psychology training Roger maintained some direct work with children and their carers and he continues to practise as an independent clinical psychologist; currently the majority of his work involves the assessment of children who are subject to public law/child care proceedings.

CONTENTS

CHAPTER 1

INTRODUCTION

Bryn Williams, Emma Peart and Roger Young

> In his introduction to a poem, Rumi asks why is the melody of the flute so piercingly sad? Then he answers his own question, 'because the flute started out as reed, growing by the riverbank, rooted in soil. When it was made into a flute, it was severed from its root. The sorrow keening in its song is the reed's wistful memory of its lost connection to the source.'
> *Jalal Udin-i Rumi*

1.1   A boy of 9, who we will call Michael, said as he was preparing to move to his fifth foster carer 'people keep telling me I'm special, that I need a special family, so if I'm so special why doesn't anyone want to keep me?'. His 7 year old sister Denise commented some weeks later 'now they've found us a new family we have to move our love to someone else and start again'. This was delivered in such a defended and avoidant way as to make it seem as though she were talking about something as banal as a change in routine for swimming lessons.

1.2   The loss and profound sadness is captured so powerfully in Rumi's poem above and illustrates the significance of human emotion for many children and parents when separated permanently as a result of legal proceedings, possibly not realised for many years. In our work with young people and adults we also observe the long-term devastating impact of being separated from the birth family alongside the horror of developmental trauma experienced by children through abuse and neglect by their family. It is therefore not surprising that we need take our responsibility for being involved in such proceedings very seriously, but with compassion. Our primary responsibility should be a commitment to keep the family together, but not at all costs.

1.3   Whilst working towards protecting children and young people we also recognise that our task is not to engineer 'perfection', but simply to do our best to mitigate the risks of significant harm; what is often referred to as 'good enough'.[1] Whilst protecting the rights of the child and family, as enshrined in law[2] and our diverse social and cultural beliefs, we also struggle with the consequences of failing to provide a better alternative within the care system, a system that is riddled with a history of contributing to harm and now struggling

---

[1]   Winnicott *The Family and Individual Development* (Tavistock Publications, 1965).
[2]   Human Rights Act 1998, Art 8 of ECHR.

to provide foster carers, adoptive families[3] and with ever limited resources, despite the often positive outcomes for looked after children.[4]

1.4   In order to take what Lord Justice McFarlane[5] described as the 'most draconian' decision when removing a child from the birth parents, professionals are required to exercise a collective decision making process. One that brings together social workers, teachers, health professionals, other child care specialists, solicitors and barristers to assist the 'decision maker' in determining whether a child's experience within their family is safe and, if not, whether change can occur so that the child is safe. The subject of this book emerged from hearing the repeated 'echo' of legal and social care professionals asking the question 'do you consider that the parent has the capacity to change in order to be an adequate parent, and to do so in the timescales necessary for the child?' when being invited to offer a psychological opinion, often in the role as an 'expert witness'.

1.5   As health and social care practitioners we have been mindful that we have provided our opinion based on a coherent and thought-out position using well referenced assessment tools, but also wondered whether there was a need to be more transparent in our methodology. Given the demise of the role of the 'expert witness' as part of the team involved in thinking about the needs of children and families in public and private law cases, one important contribution of this book is a hope of sharing the internal machinations of the expert witnesses formulation process that guides the evidence provided to the court. Moreover we consider the parent and the child to have the right to understand the process through which the evidence is collated and formulated before making recommendations about their family. It is expected that making such a process transparent might assist those required to interpret psychological evaluations, other psychologists wishing to provide assessments for the courts and, when there is an absence of an expert in proceedings, other professionals who may wish to incorporate some psychological thinking into their decision making process.

1.6   A few words about *formulation* may be helpful before embarking on this endeavour. It is a term all too familiar to psychologists who approach explaining human behaviour using a theoretical position, often from an integrated perspective, employing a range of psychological paradigms, theories, models and tools to deliver an evidence-based conceptualisation of a presenting

---

[3]   Social Care Institute for Excellence (SCIE) *Briefing: Recruiting foster carers* (2014); The Fostering Network Why do we need more foster carers? Retrieved from: http://www.fostering. net/could-you-foster/who-needs-fostering/why-do-we-need-more-foster-carers#.VG3jWb5N3zI (2014, November 20).

[4]   Boddy *Understanding permanence for looked after children. A review of research for the care enquiry* (School of Education and Social Work, University of Sussex, 2013); Cleaver et al *Children's Needs – Parenting Capacity – Child Abuse: Parental Mental Illness, Learning Disability, Substance Misuse and Domestic Violence* (DoE, 2nd edn, 2011).

[5]   Lord Justice McFarlane in *Re G (a child)* [2013] EWCA Civ 965, paras 49–50.

problem.[6] At the heart of a psychological formulation is the scientific principle that we are seeking towards a meaningful understanding of a problem by excluding possible factors and/or causes. Hopefully this meaning is a collaborative construction that is shared between the practitioner and the family, although sadly this is often not the case in forensic assessments. To give an example, in an assessment of a parent we may wish to explore their poor mood regulation by excluding the role that drug or alcohol might play in a person's functioning. Similarly for a child we may want to exclude the possibility that they have a language disorder before making assumptions that they have autism. We would advocate the need to remain actively critical about what is known (or thought to be known), balancing the reality of what is observed and experienced during the assessment. Even as an expert witness with the cloud of confidentiality even tighter than we might have in a therapeutic role, we can only act responsibly in our role if we seek and use supervision to explore our experience of the child and their family. Unequivocally observing, spending time with, and gaining a respectful and meaningful therapeutic/assessment relationship with the family have repeatedly proven to be the most important part in delivering a balanced and meaningful formulation.

1.7 Unfortunately, the move towards limiting the hours for assessments in family law cases therefore raises important clinical issues, some of which may render expert assessments as less robust. It is not only unethical but simply unjust to contribute to such a 'draconian' step of removing a child from their family without getting to know them first, although we often do. This book has been written at a time of change in the English and Welsh court systems and the authors appreciate this has become ever more difficult as systems seek to limit time on cases due to resource issues. However, it does raise the question as to whether or not we should be interfering in peoples' lives, unless we are willing to do it 'properly'.

1.8 For some practitioners the compromise has become too great and the work has therefore possibly been considered unethical, something commented on by a judge who was clearly concerned that in one case that the expert witness had cut too many corners. Complacency has no room in this important process, and it works both ways as 'expert witnesses' remove themselves from public law cases because they find it unethical and contrary to their own professional standards to work under such artificial rules limiting hours.

1.9 The contributing authors in this book have come together to share their knowledge, experience and reflections about the 'process' that they go through in their work with vulnerable families. There is a range of issues regarding the needs of the child alongside the needs of the parent. Each chapter stands independently and allows the reader to select a particular issue, such as 'drug and alcohol misuse' or 'child abuse and neglect'. The authors have been free to

---

6 Johnstone and Dallos 'Introduction to Formulation' in Johnstone and Dallos (eds) *Formulation in Psychology and Psychotherapy. Making sense of people's problems* (Routledge, 2006), pp 1–16.

choose whether they are talking in the singular or plural, male or female when
discussing and describing the child, adult and family. Each chapter is intended
as being relevant whether a case involves a single parent, male or female parent,
married or cohabiting, or same sex couple. Where issues are important they are
specifically highlighted. The complex issues impacting on families by virtue of
race, culture and religion are also considered where necessary and appropriate
by the authors.

1.10 To try and bring some structure and thought to this assessment process,
the substantive aim of this collection of chapters is to provide those involved in
child and family law with a framework for formulating the direction of
assessment in such a way as may be useful to work through when asking the
capacity and timescale question. We have been mindful of the maturing
evidence base concerning what we know about the risk and protective factors
impacting on children at risk of significant harm, and as such we have
attempted to guide the reader, as and when required, through the chapters that
follow. In addition, in we have provided some guidance on the most commonly
referenced 'models' that are recommended when undertaking assessments
around vulnerable families. Our aim in this book was to introduce greater
transparency into the assessment process that seeks to resolve the question:
Does the parent have the capacity to change within the timescales for the child?

1.11 The chapters are structured around the needs of the child and take a
developmental perspective, starting from the assumption that parenting is a
'developmental trajectory' which is linked to the resolution of the adults own
attachment and trauma history, and their readiness to become an adequate
attachment figure. It is acknowledged that this follows an expected
chronological trajectory that fits within the bounds of most societies, but for
others, their childhoods do not prepare them adequately for adulthood.

1.12 In Chapter 2 Alastair Barnett provides an overview of 'attachment
behaviour' and how this may support the understanding of child and adult
functioning. It is an important chapter and places attachment and the
consequences of insensitive caregiving and misattunement at the heart of the
child's experience. In Chapter 3 Helen Dent then presents a discussion of the
consequences of abuse and neglect, reason for and impact of delay in the system
and raises some important questions for practitioners to ask. Dr Roger
Morgan, formerly the Children's Rights Director for England, takes a very
different but vital perspective on the issue of timescales in Chapter 4. His focus
is from the perspective of the child and young person and reminds us to make
the impact on the children central to our decision making. Louise Bombér in
Chapter 5 starts to move this collection of chapters into more specific areas to
be considered in our work. She considers the presentation of children in schools
when their needs for safety, security and stability are not met at home and how
this impacts their functioning in the education system. Judy Eaton in Chapter 6
introduces the issues for children and young people with neurodevelopmental
conditions and associated conditions and how this impacts on parenting
capacity.

1.13 Focusing on the adult, Sarah Birch in Chapter 7 explores how we know change has occurred, and introduces the extremely important issue of reflective capacity and motivation to change. Kari Carstairs and Sarah Birch in Chapter 8 then go on to discuss the place of assessment approaches when assessing an individual's capacity to change, illustrated with reference to two particular models. John Castleton later in Chapter 9 opens up the issue of substance and alcohol misuse and considers the likelihood of change.

1.14 Turning to the 'process' issues, in Chapter 10 Caroline Pipe and Kathy Richardson describe the challenges faced with regards to social work assessment in child protection and how systemic practice has influenced the working model in Hackney. The relatively recent introduction of a 26-week time limit on care proceedings in the English and Welsh court system is introduced. They also emphasise the significance of the relationship between the family and the professionals, and highlight how this influences the process of change. This chapter also reminds us about the significance of the role of intervention in our assessment of capacity to change. In order to explore the structures in which we work and the legal issues arising, Michelle Flynn and Siobhan Kelly in Chapter 11 discuss public law and Ursula Rice in Chapter 12 draws upon the private law arena.

1.15 To bring the book to a close, Chapter 14 discusses the process of bringing together the information collated during the assessment process into a formulation that will usefully influence the provision of treatment, the development of hypothesis around whether someone might be able to engage in treatment and the conclusions that will influence the final decision as to whether change is possible within the child's timescales. An algorithm of the important issues to consider for the child, parent and by the professionals is presented.

1.16 Working as we do in different legal jurisdictions, whilst making reference largely to the English and Welsh system, we consider our discussion to be as relevant in other part of the United Kingdom, the Crown Dependencies and Territories, and the Commonwealth countries and other jurisdictions that seek to ameliorate the risks of abuse and neglect for children and young people. We hope that by sharing our experience of this important area of work we can help our legal colleagues and those who are learning to work as child care professionals, perhaps even the families and young people, gain some useful ideas in being part of a process that is arguably one of the most important tasks in our society, namely working towards the protection and the long term well being of a child.

CHAPTER 2

ATTACHMENT THEORY AS A FRAMEWORK FOR UNDERSTANDING CHILDREN'S BEHAVIOUR IN THEIR MOST IMPORTANT RELATIONSHIPS

Alastair Barnett

'Invisible threads are the strongest ties'
Friedrich Nietzsche

2.1   Attachment theory is often used by clinicians as a framework to guide their attempts to understand and explain the behaviour of children and adolescents who have experienced forms of adversity in their close relationships and family environment, and are presenting with concerning behaviour. Whilst helpful in many ways through offering a taxonomy of relationship-oriented behaviour, there is still some level of controversy in relation to the descriptions used to formulate an understanding of children who present with concerns, and the basis of the formulation.[1]

2.2   This chapter aims to offer the reader an outline of attachment theory and how the theory attempts to account for relationship behaviour that is often observed in children and adolescents who have experienced early adversity.

ORIGINS OF ATTACHMENT THEORY

2.3   The paediatrician and psychoanalyst John Bowlby (1907–1990) is credited as the originator of attachment theory, after his work in studying the interactions between young infants and parents. Attachment theory was different to the psychological theories that had been dominant during the early to mid-twentieth century to explain children's needs and actions (which were largely based on psychodynamic or behavioural theories) and that were prevalent up to that point. The theory postulates that the prime drive of infant behaviour is to seek security and protection from suspected danger and that this is obtained primarily through achieving proximity to the primary caregiver. The

---

[1]   Allen 'The Use and Abuse of Attachment Theory in Clinical Practice With Maltreated Children, Part 1: Diagnosis and Assessment' [2011] *Trauma, Violence, & Abuse*, 12(1), 3–12.

pattern of caregiver responding elicited by the infant's efforts to gain proximity determines future behaviour towards this goal.

2.4   Bowlby's seminal works *Attachment*,[2] *Separation*[3] and *Loss*[4] sought to place his clinical observations from both his work with young children who had been separated from or bereaved of a parent, as well as his work with young offenders who had also lost a parent-figure, into a wider framework that would apply to typical as well as abnormal child development. Bowlby asserted that much could be learned from studying the behaviour of mammals, and in particular the higher primates, whose behaviour seemed to be driven primarily by proximity to their parent/caregiver and gaining what seemed to be the sense of security thus provided. He concluded that human infants are instinctively disposed towards maintaining closeness to the caregiver and that these behaviours related primarily to the evolutionary instinct for survival.

2.5   In applying these observations to humans, Bowlby theorised that the parent/caregiver's responses to the infant's attempts to seek close proximity would have an influence on the infant's subsequent attempts to seek closeness and a sense of security. A particular feature of this perspective was that the developing relationship with the caregiver was selective; the importance for the infant of maintaining a relationship with a specific individual caregiver (at the time, the biological mother) is a distinctive feature. This was quite a novel proposition at the time. Bowlby also highlighted the detrimental effect of extended separations, as well as loss of the relationship altogether, on a child's emotional functioning – parental death being an extreme example or, highly relevant at the time of Bowlby's initial papers, military service. Present day separation contexts also include loss through divorce or as a consequence of care proceedings. These understandings eventually exerted significant influence over public and healthcare childcare practices and policies[5] including the liberalisation of parent visitation hours for children in hospital[6] and a recognition of the limitations of residential care environments (such as orphanages and residential nurseries) for young children.[7]

2.6   An attachment relationship is characterised by specific behaviours that are oriented towards the caregiver:

- *Proximity-seeking*: The child seeks the closeness of the attachment figure in order to reduce anxiety and to promote feelings of safety and security.

---

[2]   Bowlby *Attachment and Loss, Vol 2. Separation: Anxiety & Anger* (Hogarth Press, 1973).
[3]   Ibid.
[4]   Bowlby *Attachment and Loss, Vol 3. Loss: Sadness and Depression* (Hogarth Press, 1980).
[5]   Rutter and O'Connor 'Are there biological programming effects for psychological development? Findings from a study of Romanian adoptees' [2004] Dev Psychol, 40(1).
[6]   Robertson and Robertson 'Young children in brief separation' [1971] Psychoanal Study Child, 26, 264–312.
[7]   Tizard and Rees 'The effect of early institutional rearing on the behaviour problems and affectional relationships of four-year-old children' [1975] J Child Psychol Psychiat, 16(1) 61–73.

- *Secure base effect*: When the child is in the presence of the attachment-figure, the child experiences a reduction in anxiety and the focus on potential dangers is diminished. This promotes an increase in confidence and the capacity to play and explore away from the attachment figure.

- *Separation protest*: When the child becomes aware that the attachment figure is becoming inaccessible in some way (such as leaving the room or the caregiver becomes deeply involved in another activity or conversation) then the child will actively attempt to reduce this separation and to promote proximity once more.

2.7   These three behaviours constitute the Attachment Behavioural System, and are activated when the child perceives they need reassurance or comfort by their attachment figure.[8]

2.8   The pioneering work of Bowlby was then taken up by Mary Ainsworth and colleagues, who took the concepts of attachment security and insecurity into a structured research context to examine for the relative incidence of such patterns in the general population. To standardise the assessment protocol Ainsworth developed the strange situation procedure, a method for categorising infant behaviour during separation from, and reunion to, the caregiver.[9] This is a timed and carefully-managed sequence of interactions, whereby the infant spends time in the company of their caregiver in a room and, after a time, they are joined by a stranger (an adult unknown to the child). The stranger shows interest in the child and the caregiver, joining them in their play/interaction. After a pre-set interval, the caregiver leaves the room and the stranger attempts to continue the interaction with the infant. After a further interval, the caregiver returns to the room and recommences their interaction with the child. Throughout this sequence of events, the infant and caregiver's responses are carefully recorded (usually using video-media) and are subsequently analysed and coded to determine the predominant pattern of responding.

2.9   In their studies of infant behaviour it was found that a majority of children would protest both on separation and reunion, but would very quickly settle back down again in the presence of the caregiver. This was taken as the typical behaviour of an infant with the confidence in the availability and predictability in their caregiver, and categorised as type B, secure attachment.

2.10   A smaller percentage of children respond to the events of the strange situation procedure quite differently. These infants tend to remain distanced from their parent, both physically and emotionally. They remain preoccupied with toys and show a greatly diminished degree (or an absence of) the tearfulness and protest behaviours that are characteristic of the type B children as they endeavour to attract or demand a comforting reunion with their carer.

---

[8]   Golding *Nurturing attachments: Supporting children who are fostered or adopted* (Jessica Kingsley, 2008).

[9]   Ainsworth and Bell 'Attachment, exploration, and separation: Illustrated by the behaviour of one-year-olds in a strange situation' [1970] *Child Development*, 41, 49–67.

The group of children who seem to minimise the role of emotions in the separation and reunion are described as being *avoidant* in their pattern of relating to their caregiver.

2.11 Further, other infants respond to the artificial separation experience by displaying significantly more emotion, both anger and anxiety, and a pressing desire for comfort and physical contact. After their caregiver returns, these infants are then extremely difficult to control and settle again. They respond to the separation through excessive clinging to the caregiver on their return with fierce, angry protest and/or anxiety. The behaviour of these infants is oriented much more towards maintaining forms of emotional contact with their caregiver. These infants are experiencing an intensification of their emotions in response to the caregiver's presence, and their pattern of attachment to their caregiver is described as having an *ambivalent-resistant* quality.

2.12 Attachment theory suggests that if the infant's attempts to obtain comfort and security are met with acceptance and sensitivity from the caregiver, the child develops trust that the caregiver will be available at times when security and soothing are sought. When an individual has a sense of trust in the availability of an important person when approached – the *secure base effect* - they are bolstered to be able to explore both new experiences and their environment with increasing confidence such that, if the child seeks it, the caregiver will offer them a safe haven to which they may return. Over time and with increasing experience, the child generalises this trust such that other caregivers and important figures in the child's day to day relationships will also be reliable and responsive to their needs.

Sensitive caregiving

2.13 Secure attachment is promoted through the availability and reliability of the caregiver to meet the child's many needs, particularly when the caregiver is providing what Siegel and Hartzell[10] termed the ABC's of attachment:

2.14 *Attunement* – A state of emotional connection whereby a caregiver's internal states (thoughts, feelings) become harmonious with those of their child. It is often achieved through contingent exchanges of non-verbal communications (such as facial expressions, emotional intensity, tone of voice, body posture and timing). When the caregiver takes responsibility for establishing attunement with their child, the child is likely to feel understood.

2.15 *Balance* – Through attunement with the parent/caregiver, the child is facilitated to regulate their physical self (body) as well as their emotions and thoughts. A secure attachment allows the child to tune in to the caregiver's sense of balance, and this is called co-regulation.

---

[10]   Siegel and Hartzell *Parenting from the inside out* (Penguin, 2003).

2.16 *Coherence* – This is a sense of meaning that children come to acquire through their relationship with a sensitive and present caregiver, 'in which they are able to come to feel both internally integrated and interpersonally connected to others'.[11]

2.17 A principal characteristic of sensitive caregiving is that of *contingent communication*: the parent/caregiver and the child are engaged in a moment-to-moment 'dance of attunement'[12] whereby the signals of the infant are understood, reacted to, and given meaning by the caregiver such that the child experiences feeling understood and an active agent in the myriad of exchanges that constitute the relationship. However, sensitive caregiving does not mean parents must achieve parenting *perfection*. In the 1960s the paediatrician and psychotherapist Dr Donald Winnicott offered the concept of the good-enough parent[13] to reassure parents that striving for faultless perfection was unrealistic, and indeed undermined the efforts of typical parents who were more than able to meet the needs of their child.[14]

Insensitive caregiving

2.18 The corollary of Bowlby's secure base hypothesis was that if a caregiver's responses lacked sensitivity to the infant's initiations, over time this would also lead to a set of predictable behavioural responses by the infant. Recurrent experiences of a parent/caregiver who is insensitive to the child's overtures for comfort, soothing and proximity promotes the development of different sets of emotions and responses in the child, seemingly driven by the child's experience of the anxiety evoked through not knowing whether the caregiver will respond to their needs or not, or if their response will bring the comfort the infant needs. Insensitive caregivers lack one or more of the ABC qualities of sensitivity outlined above.

Misattunement

2.19 The caregiver is unable or only occasionally able to connect with or accept the child's heightened emotional state, coping with such encounters through ignoring or discouraging the child, or responding to the child with the caregiver's own dysregulated emotions.

2.20 *Impaired co-regulation* with repeated experience of non-contingent communication, the infant/child develops coping strategies to locate a sense of balance or connection, through disengagement (avoidant insecure pattern) or

---

[11] See footnote 10.
[12] Hughes *Facilitating developmental attachment: The road to emotional recovery and behavioural change in foster and adopted children* (Aronson, 1997).
[13] Winnicott *The family and individual development* (Tavistock, 1965).
[14] Hoghughi and Speight 'Good enough parenting for all children – a strategy for a healthier society' [1998] Arch Dis Child, 78 (4) 293–296.

an intensification of emotional displays (ambivalent-resistant pattern). In essence, their child adapts their attachment behaviour to fit the caregiver concerned.

2.21 *Lack of coherence* leading to impairments in the infant/child's development of a sense of predictability about the caregiver's intentions and responses

2.22 Because the infant's responses are generally understood as adapted ways of relating to the caregiver, the demonstrated behaviours are taken as indicative of the child failing to experience security, and the child's responses in the relationship came to be regarded categorically; the relationship was understood as being marked by an *insecure attachment*.

2.23 Various studies have examined the incidence of these relationship behaviour patterns displayed by infants in separation and reunion with their caregivers. See Table 1 – typical percentages amongst a community sample:

Table 1: Attachment in the general population

Attachment Classification	Percentage of study population at 12 months of age
Securely attached	60–70 %
Insecure avoiding	15–20 %
Insecure ambivalent-resisting	10–15 %
Insecure disorganised	5–10 %

Patterns of attachment behaviour

2.24 Researchers have asserted that these patterns of behaviour represent the best solution available to the child to maximise feelings of safety and comfort from the caregiver, and to minimise potential exposure to risk and danger. The observed attachment pattern suggests the child's template for how they might best live with the parent. This begs the question: what may have been the parent/caregiver's way of relating to their child that promotes such a pattern of responding?

2.25 With children who are assessed as being securely-attached, parents are observed as being sensitive to the needs of their child. This allows the child to develop a sense of safety and certainty; their prediction is of things being alright. Sensitive parents will imaginatively anticipate their child's physical needs (hunger, fatigue, toileting, temperature) social needs (eg not enough or too much stimulation, judging how much variety of activities to provide) and particularly emotional needs – responding to their child's emotional state with appropriate intensity and sensitivity. Further, the sensitive parent will meet these needs whilst simultaneously being aware of and responding to their child's states of activity and emotional intensity at the moment of need.

2.26 Parents/caregivers of children who display the *avoidant* pattern of responding have been observed to be unavailable and even rejecting of their child's approaches for comfort. The quality of the caregiver's interactions with the child might for example have a distant quality. Some parents have found themselves overwhelmed when their child is expressing their needs emotionally and respond by closing down such features of the caregiver-child relationship, discouraging attachment behaviour from the child. It is important to bear in mind though that the research that has aimed to investigate for a straightforward association between the insecure attachment categories with subsequent psychopathology has met with little success[15] unless considered alongside other risk factors such as poverty, domestic violence and negative life events.[16] Insecure attachment per se is not evidence of disorder, nor of prior maltreatment.

Case study 1: Janine

2.27 Janine was adopted through an international adoption agency when she was 5 years of age, having spent the first years of her life in a large baby orphanage. There were many children in the orphanage per caregiver and Janine most likely had direct contact with an adult caregiver just a few times each day. She had been nominated for adoption at age 3 years but, for reasons unknown, this did not proceed beyond initial introductions and she remained in the orphanage until shortly before her fifth birthday.

2.28 After her adoption to the UK, her adoptive parents were surprised how quickly she seemed to settle down. She showed no regrets or upset at leaving her carers at the airport and recalled other passengers on the flight back to the UK commenting on how 'good' she behaved. Janine seemed to settle very quickly into her new family and was accepting of suggestions to learn a musical instrument, and always helped around the house often without being reminded. She kept her bedroom clean and tidy. On starting school, she was a model pupil and always strove to achieve her best, even to the point of what others consider to be pedantic perfectionism.

2.29 At the same time, Janine's parents reported feeling uncomfortable as to how she seemed around the home and school. She didn't seem to need her parents to comfort her if she had hurt herself; indeed, they would only know if Janine had been hurt if they had witnessed the accident directly – otherwise Janine would not seek any help or show distress. When she was 7 years old, it was discovered almost by chance that she had sustained a broken finger in an

---

[15]　Allen 'The Use and Abuse of Attachment Theory in Clinical Practice With Maltreated Children, Part 1: Diagnosis and Assessment' [2011] *Trauma, Violence, & Abuse*, 12 (1), 3–12.

[16]　Sroufe et al *The Development of the Person. The Minnesota Study of Risk and Adaptation from Birth to Adulthood* (Guilford Press, 2005).

accident thought to have occurred several years previously. In contrast to this ultra-self-contained side, from time to time Janine seemed to deteriorate quickly into overwhelming distress or fury, seemingly following a fairly inconsequential event. Her parents gave typical examples of Janine becoming intensely angry when it transpired she was wearing an unsuitable pair of shoes for an activity during a family outing, collapsing into inconsolable tearfulness if she played a wrong note whilst playing the piano to her family in an informal 'concert'.

2.30 In a relationship characterised by an insecurely *ambivalent-resistant* attachment dynamic, the child's pattern has formed in response to the caregiver being available inconsistently. The child becomes uncertain as to how they will be responded to (or not). Caregivers in these situations have tended to show variable degrees of responding, sometimes sensitive and at other times not. This level of uncertainty evokes significant anxiety in the child which is then experienced through different kinds of behaviour, driven by affect: anxiety and fear, clinginess (an incessant and forever unsatisfied desire for comfort) and protest in the form of anger. In many children, these different emotional displays are alternated so as to provide maximum opportunities for engagement of the caregiver who is tasked to respond to increasingly intense, and lengthy, episodes of emotionality. This relationship dynamic can be extremely hard to shift once established as the parent/caregiver finds themselves unable to reassure the child; responding to the anger/anxiety display only serves to reinforce to the child that heightened emotional displays are required to obtain the best guarantee that the parents will respond.

Case study 2: Daniel

2.31 Daniel, aged 6 years, is presenting with enormous difficulties getting into school in the morning, particularly at the school gate as he says goodbye to his mum. Daniel's mother Julie had a difficult time during Daniel's early years, as Daniel's father left the family when he was around 3 months old. He had been having an affair with Julie's best friend and left Julie and the children to move in with her. Julie was devastated at these revelations and very quickly struggled to cope with the needs and demands of a young baby and his toddler elder sister Ellie, aged 2 years. Julie had little family support nearby and care and health service provision was patchy; they lived in a rural area.

2.32 On a good day, Julie felt motivated and able to start getting things sorted, she got out with the children and was able to take them to nursery and also went shopping and tidy the house. On the bad days however, which were by far in the majority, sometimes she would stay in bed for most of the day, eventually getting up to heat up a bottle for Daniel, especially after he'd been crying for a while. Sometimes she hoped he'd settle on his own, and others it's believed Ellie would try and find leftover milk for Daniel to have. On really bad days, the children might not get to nursery at all. Daniel would cry for hours and, despite Julie's best efforts to comfort him, seemed inconsolable.

2.33 Julie said that when his toddler tantrums started, Daniel's behaviour had become so much worse. The tantrums could last for hours on end and she felt there was nothing she could do to help him calm down. He was always following her around the house, which she found quite irritating, and acknowledged that she would speak to him sarcastically and a little sharply when Daniel continually asked question after question, particularly about things she thought he knew the answer to. She couldn't even go to the toilet without him calling for her from the other side of the door! Daniel talked all the time and, if he had the slightest bump, he would burst out in tears and it took ages to settle him down again. Getting Daniel into nursery had always been tricky, but school was that much harder. The teachers had to scrape him off her in the mornings. Fortunately he got on well with the teaching assistant in class and he seemed to settle with her, eventually. Julie felt exasperated: why wouldn't he be more like that with her?

2.34 In essence, the child who deals with a relationship by reducing or avoiding emotional involvement, arousal or dependency (insecure-avoidant pattern) appears to be attempting to switch off their attachment behaviour. As this becomes an ingrained response in the relationship, there is a potentiality that the strategy is used more generally, at least in the first instance, to other relationships such that the child becomes progressively self-contained. The strategy is primarily cognitively based. In contrast, the child with an insecure-ambivalent/resistance pattern of relating copes by keeping attachment behaviour switched on more or less constantly. Their strategy for dealing with caregivers and other important people is primarily an affective one.

2.35 *Disorganised attachment*: Ainsworth's system for categorising attachment security in infancy has maintained in research and clinical practice to the present day, with one important refinement initially contributed by Mary Main and colleagues.[17] There were a small number of children in the Ainsworth studies who seemed to have no consistent strategy for managing the experience of separation and reunion. They displayed a range of behaviours indicating fear, overt conflict, confusion and disorientation, but in no discernible pattern to the researchers. In the original studies, these children were described as *unclassifiable*. Main and Solomon concluded that such children's attachment behaviour followed no consistent strategy to quell their needs and these children tended to display behaviour that suggested they were confused as to whether they should approach their caregiver or avoid them. They asserted that this chaotic display that oscillated between the two attachment styles was in response to parents who were so unpredictable and frightening that the child could never be sure as to how they should try to engage the caregiver. The child

---

[17]   Main and Solomon 'Procedures for identifying infants as disorganised/disoriented during the Ainsworth Strange Situation' in Greenberg, Cicchetti and Cummings (eds) *Attachment in the preschool years: Theory, research, and intervention* (University of Chicago Press, 1990), pp 121–160.

found themselves in a double bind of what Main[18] termed 'fright without solution', 'where the caregiver simultaneously becomes the source and the solution of the infant's alarm'. Intense fear is not an emotion that can be tolerated for long before the individual begins to develop powerful psychological defence strategies to manage the overwhelming stress.[19]

2.36 With the child's attachment behavioural system thrown recurrently into chaos in this way, there is no way for the child to develop an organised, coherent strategy to respond to their caregiver. Such children develop profound difficulties in regulating their emotions, communicating with others, with managing higher-order cognitive tasks such as concentration and sustained attention which can undermine academic achievement.[20] The ongoing difficulties in achieving a sense of balance and coherence in subsequent close relationships also appears to place such individuals at the risk for interpersonal aggression later in life, including domestic violence.[21]

Case study 3: Callum

2.37 Callum, aged 8 years, was taken into an emergency foster care placement with his two younger siblings after they have been found wandering around the streets late at night, near their home. They were poorly clothed and had been throwing stones at passing cars. Their mother Tara had significant learning difficulties and the family had been given extensive support over the years. Tara had 6 children, ranging from 2–14 years. It appeared the family home had become a regular venue for parties featuring significant drug and alcohol use and at which Tara apparently often became severely intoxicated. Fights and arguments were common and there are also suspicions that the children were exposed to violent pornography and witnessed adults having sex around the house and garden.

2.38 On arrival at the foster home, Callum was described as 'a whirlwind'. He and his younger siblings fought ferociously, with seemingly little provocation. Callum challenged and opposed his carers at every turn. He would run off and hide, although his carers quickly got the sense he placed himself such that they would discover him quickly. When on his own with a carer he could be much calmer and accepting of their care. However if these times were interrupted by anyone else, and particularly by his brother or sister, Callum would become extremely angry and blamed his carers for many seemingly unrelated events. When with the carer he would sometimes reflect on 'when I was at home' and during a number of such episodes Callum had soiled himself. As the carer

---

[18]   Main 'Recent Studies in attachment. Overview with selected implications for clinical work' in Goldberg et al (eds) *Attachment Theory – Social Developmental and Clinical Perspectives* (Analytic Press Inc, 1995), 407–470.

[19]   Hopkins 'Overcoming a child's resistance to late adoption: how one new attachment can facilitate another' [2000] J Child Psychother, 26(3), 335–347.

[20]   Bombér *Inside I'm hurting: practical strategies for supporting children with attachment difficulties in schools* (Worth, 2007).

[21]   Fonagy 'Male perpetrators of violence against women: An attachment theory perspective' [1999] J Appl Psychoanal Studies, 1(1), 7–27.

helped him clean up, Callum again seemed to become extremely confused and panicky, alternating rapidly between intense anger and fear which often ended up with him trying to bang his head against furniture or trying to hit the carer.

Reactive attachment disorder

2.39 Formal diagnostic classification of attachment behaviour seems always to have been beset with controversy. Until recently, reactive attachment disorder (RAD) could be diagnosed in either of two forms, inhibited type (the child is unable or unwilling to form relationships) and disinhibited type (the child will approach any potential caregiver). These were re-conceptualised in 2013 with the publication of the 5th edition of the *Diagnostic and Statistical Manual of Mental Disorders*[22] into two distinct disorders, reactive attachment disorder and disinhibited social engagement disorder. Both require historical evidence of neglect/pathogenic care that have limited the child's opportunity to form selective attachments. However RAD seems to be regarded more as an internalising disorder, due to dampened positive affect, and disinhibited social engagement disorder seems to be conceptualised as similar in appearance to attention deficit hyperactivity disorder (ADHD). Children diagnosed with disinhibited social engagement disorder may subsequently have developed selective attachments, but their social relationship management remains indiscriminate and this reflects research findings that children who were extremely deprived in infancy, yet have subsequently formed selective attachments, can still demonstrate indiscriminate behaviour.[23]

Parental history and narrative

2.40 A significant development in attachment theory was made when Mary Main and her colleagues undertook to explore the relationship between a parent's state of mind in relation to attachment concepts, and their child's earlier behaviour in the strange situation procedure.[24] In developing the adult attachment interview (AAI) interviewees are asked for specific recollections and impressions about their childhood experiences, in particular of their recalled memories about their parents' behaviour, and of being parented. From this and subsequent studies, a highly significant correlation has been repeatedly shown between the manner and content of an interviewee's recollection and, for parents, how they subsequently relate (in attachment terms) to their child.

2.41 A particularly significant predictive characteristic of the AAI, as it relates to future parenting behaviour, is the *coherence* of the interviewee's narrative. A narrative is understood as being coherent if it is of sufficient quality, quantity,

---

[22] American Psychiatric Association *Diagnostic and statistical manual of mental disorders* (American Psychiatric Publishing, 5th edn, 2013).

[23] Bruce et al 'Disinhibited social behavior among internationally adopted children' [2009] Dev Psychopath, 21, 157–171.

[24] Main et al 'Security in infancy, childhood, and adulthood: A move to the level of representation' [1985] Mon Soc Res Child Dev.

relevance and clarity.[25] The AAI is a window on how an individual makes sense of what happened to them as a child, and how they understand the impact of these events on their subsequent development and relationships. A key feature is that the interview is analysed according to *how* the various stories are told, in addition to the content of the recalled memories and viewpoints.

2.42 Interviewees whose attachment narratives are succinct, describe relationships and events with clarity and are evidenced with appropriate examples may well be assessed as showing a coherence of their life history. Many individuals experience events involving a spectrum of emotions and challenges to their coping strategies, for example that might involve separation or loss – such as bereavement or divorce – and challenging aspects of family relationships such as neglectful or insensitive caregiving (arising from, for example, parental mental health difficulties or financial problems, also conflict within the extended family or local community). If the individual has integrated these experiences, through coming to an understanding of the factors and dynamics which may have underpinned their caregivers' motives and actions, then they are more likely to hold in mind a coherent story of their earlier experiences and this coherence demonstrates *reflective function*. Reflective functioning (also known as mentalising) is 'the mental function which organises the experience of one's own and others' behaviour in terms of mental state constructs'.[26] Adults who are classified as secure (or autonomous) include both those who have experienced childhoods where they were well supported and experienced consistent and reliable childcare (but also those individuals who may have experienced adversity of some kind) and can talk about and reflect on these experiences with appropriate insight. The latter individuals are thought of as having an earned type B attachment, whereas the former are considered 'naïve' type B's – their childhood was fortunately unencumbered by elements of threat and danger that fell outside of their zone of proximal development.[27]

2.43 When an AAI story narrative is characterised by a level of distortion, communicating confusion and what might appear to be a lack of resolution or a depth of understanding about their earlier life experiences, the story narrative is classified as *incoherent*. Dismissive narratives often describe parents or caregivers in glowing terms, but the interviewee struggles to back up this global praise, or might contradict the positive comments at another point in the interview. These individuals seem unaware of the inconsistency of what they are saying. Other dismissive narratives are highly impoverished in terms of content and detail, and interviewees often claimed that they cannot recall specific

[25]   Grice 'Logic and conversation' in Cole and Moran (eds) *Syntax and Semantics: 3. Speech Acts* (Academic Press, 1975), 41–59.

[26]   Fonagy and Target 'Attachment and reflective function: Their role in self-organisation' [1997] Dev Psychopath, 9(04), 679–700.

[27]   Thompson 'Early attachment and later development: Familiar questions, new answers' in Cassidy and Shaver (eds) *Handbook of attachment* (Guilford Press, 2nd edn, 2008), pp 348–365.

memories or details of specific childhood episodes. It has been suggested[28] that interviewees classified as dismissive greatly minimise the (emotionally-laden) attachment-related experience from their childhoods.

2.44 Adult Attachment Interview participants whose attachment-related stories are characterised by a predominantly emotional focus on the motives and actions of significant adults during their childhood are classified as *preoccupied*. For these individuals, questions related to the interviewee's childhood attachment experiences draw out 'excessive attention to attachment-related memories at the cost of loss of focus on the discourse content'[29] so the clarity and manner of the recalled experiences are compromised by what often seems to be a confused, ruminative quality.

2.45 Finally the AAI classification status of *unresolved/disorganised* refers to interviewees who seemed to experience lapses in coherence/reasoning when recounting events that may well have been experienced as traumatic (eg the interviewee experienced traumatic loss or abuse).

2.46 The descriptions of adult attachment styles as determined by the AAI can be aligned and/or compared with the groupings of the secure-insecure-disorganised attachment categories used to understand the relationship behaviour of infants and children:

Table 2: Comparison of Child and Adult Attachment Classifications

Child Pattern	Adult Pattern	Characteristics
Secure attachment	Secure (free, autonomous)	Balance of cognition & affect used in relationships; Stories of previous relationship experiences make sense: coherence
Avoidant attachment	Dismissive	Reliance on cognition; minimal recall of emotional material and of the relevance of close relationships
Ambivalent-resistant attachment	Preoccupied	Focus on emotions
Disorganised attachment	Unresolved	Highly incoherent recall of memories and relationships, dissociation, rapid shifts in mood and behaviour

---

[28] Main 'Cross-cultural studies of attachment organisation: Recent studies, changing methodologies, and the concept of conditional strategies' [1990] Hum Dev, 33(1), 48–61.

[29] Van IJzendoorn 'Adult attachment representations, parental responsiveness, and infant attachment: a meta-analysis on the predictive validity of the Adult Attachment Interview' [1995] Psychol Bull, 117(3), 387.

Attachment beyond infancy

2.47 Critiques of the Ainsworth[30] and Main & Solomon[31] ABCD model of attachment classification have noted the difficulties in translating and integrating the methods of investigating attachment status into clinical practice.[32] A further concern by some clinicians has been that the attachment classifications derived from the strange situation procedure place an over-inclusive focus on determining attachment status in terms of security/insecurity.[33] Bowlby had initially stated that child's attachment status was not itself a disorder, but constituted a risk factor in the development of clinical problems. Subsequent research has confirmed Bowlby's belief-status of attachment security on its own remains of quite limited psychopathological significance.[34] Concerns have also been expressed as to how attachment relationships are most helpfully conceptualised after infancy, given the increasing complexity of a child's network of social relationships and the differences of opinion as to how attachment should be assessed in older children.[35]

2.48 A model of attachment that explicitly references and incorporates the multiple developments in the brain and mind functioning that take place during the lifespan (eg social, moral, cognitive) is the dynamic-maturational model of attachment and adaptation (DMM) developed by Patricia Crittenden.[36] This model is expressly dimensional and illustrates how an individual (from child through to senior, ie across the lifespan) employs cognitive, emotional and behavioural strategies to adapt to, and navigate, close relationships. The model is helpful in understanding how children whose experience of more extreme parenting behaviour can develop more extreme repertoires of responding around the avoidant and ambivalent attachment patterns.[37]

2.49 The DMM model is similarly grounded in the work of Bowlby and Mary Ainsworth, and is additionally informed by understandings about child development, family systems and how humans respond to threat.[38] A central characteristic of the DMM is that the core motivation propelling attachment

[30] Ainsworth 'Infant–mother attachment' [1979] Amer Psychol, 34(10), 932.
[31] Main and Solomon 'Procedures for identifying infants as disorganised/disoriented during the Ainsworth Strange Situation. Attachment in the preschool years: Theory, research, and intervention' [1990] 1, 121–160.
[32] Spieker and Crittenden 'Comparing two attachment classification methods applied to preschool strange situations' [2010] Clin Child Psychol Psychiat, 15(1), 97–120.
[33] Rutter et al 'Emanuel Miller Lecture: Attachment insecurity, disinhibited attachment, and attachment disorders: where do research findings leave the concepts?' [2009] J Child Psychol Psychiat, 50(5), 529–543.
[34] Ibid.
[35] Thompson and Raikes 'Toward the next quarter-century: Conceptual and methodological challenges for attachment theory' [2003] Dev Psychopath, 15(03), 691–718.
[36] Crittenden *Raising parents* (Willan, 2008).
[37] Crittenden et al 'A dynamic-maturational approach to treatment of maltreated children' in Hughes et al (eds) *Handbook of Psychological Services for Children and Adolescents* (Oxford University Press, 2001), 373–398.
[38] Crittenden 'Attachment and risk for psychopathology: The early years' [1995] J Dev Beh

behaviour is an innate drive to protect the self against perceived or actual threat and danger and to later reproduce. The child's approaches to caregivers therefore constitute attempts to reduce exposure to perceived dangers in the environment. Bowlby was quite clear in his writings about attachment that the theory was ethologically-informed and, as such, the ultimate function of complex behavioural systems is to ensure survival and procreation.[39] The DMM is developmentally sensitive in that the model illustrates how the range and sophistication of self-protective behaviours and responses available to the individual are extended from infancy, through childhood and adolescence and into adulthood. The model gradually expands, incorporating the effects of maturation and expanding social contexts that allow for an increasing range of self-protective strategies over the lifespan.[40] The DMM model recognises the developmental shifts in neurological organisation that take place from infancy-toddlerhood and at puberty, and Crittenden has suggested[41] that maturation may interact with individual functioning to lead to changes in how the individual manages information and acts in order to negotiate relationships and keep the self safe and later attract a reproductive partner.

2.50 The model therefore links attachment strategies to maturation across cognitive, emotional and behavioural domains over the lifespan, offering ways of linking the presence of extreme psychopathology to earlier (attachment-based) relationship adversity. An important dimension of the DMM is that it integrates the relevance of sexual desire: attachment relationships in adolescence and adulthood involve partner selection and the navigation of intimacy, as well as more basic strategic concerns relating to how, when and with whom sexual desire might be satisfied.

Ped, 16, S12–S16; Farnfield et al 'DMM assessments of attachment and adaptation: Procedures, validity and utility' [2010] Clin Child Psychol Psychiat, 15(3), 313–328; see also footnote 36.

[39] Bretherton 'The origins of attachment theory: John Bowlby and Mary Aisnworth' [1992] Dev Psychol, 28, 759–772.

[40] Pocock 'The DMM-wow! But how to safely handle its potential strength?' [2010] Clin Child Psychol Psychiat, 15(3), 303–311.

[41] Crittenden *A dynamic-maturational approach to continuity and change in pattern of attachment. The organisation of attachment relationships: Maturation, culture, and context* (Cambridge, 2000), 343–357.

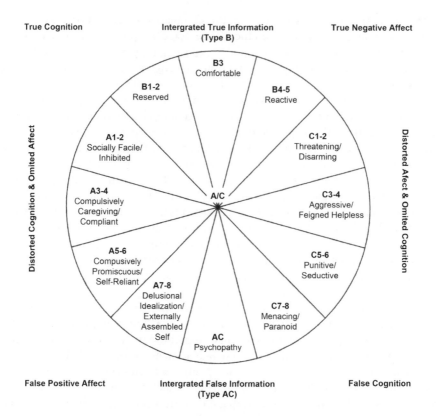

Figure 1. Dynamic-Maturational Model of self-protective strategies in adulthood

2.51 With the attachment system being activated in the presence of perceived threat or danger to the self, attachment behaviour over time becomes a process of learning how most effectively to engage others (or not) in order to minimise exposure to threat and danger, including the perceived or actual threat posed by caregiver. In this respect, the DMM views presenting patterns of interaction with caregivers, and responses to threats, as adaptations the individual makes (on the basis of their prior experiences) in order to maximise possibilities for increasing survival.

2.52 The factors that underpin danger-avoiding/safety-seeking behaviour are: (a) temporal order/cognition ('if x happens then y follows'); (b) intensity of affect (the degree of the mind/brain's emotional response to current experiences; and (c) somatic reactions (how the body responds to these percepts/ experiences). In the DMM these information-processing systems are termed *dispositional representations* and constitute a development of Bowlby's descriptions of memory systems.[42]

---

[42] Bowlby *Attachment and Loss, Vol 3. Loss: Sadness and Depression* (Hogarth Press, 1980);

2.53   Individuals who are able to access and integrate information from both their cognitive and affective systems in response to the current situation will maximise the information available to the self, and are likely to respond in the most adaptive (and flexible) way. In other words, at times of stress they are better able access data from previous experience to inform in-the-moment responding/behaviour: 'what happened previously in this sort of situation?' – and this is taken along with how the current situation evokes emotional and bodily memories ('how this makes me feel') to guide response. Integrated processing of this kind is characteristic of individuals functioning in the type B, secure category of attachment. However there is acceptance in the model that within the type B/secure category, there will be individuals whose behavioural responses overall are less emotionally-based ('reserved') as well as those who will experience and display emotion more freely ('reactive').

2.54   Although the baby's brain undergoes significant growth and change over the first two years of life, it is still an immature organ relative to the capacities that come online over the course of development. This is especially so as the individual begins to use language (both for communication with others as well as for thinking) and is required to function in increasingly complex social contexts. As a result of this immaturity in infancy, all behavioural displays are based on *true* information; that is, small babies do not attempt to deceive or hide their intentions or feelings. During the second year of life, most infants are beginning to display a capacity to leave out certain aspects of processing, such as negative emotions (type A, avoidant behaviour) or increased displays of negative emotion (type C, ambivalent-resistant behaviour).[43]

2.55   As children develop, acquisition of social-cognitive abilities bring to the individual child the possibilities of underplaying or exaggerating cognitive or affective information in order to influence how attachment figures (and other important figures, ie teachers and other adults in positions of responsibility or authority in the child's life) might respond to them.

2.56   From toddlerhood onwards, children develop the capacity to convey false information in order to achieve their goals, and this can be seen when a child displays *false positive affect*, inhibiting negative feelings whilst substituting them for ostensibly positive emotional displays. The child's true feelings are hidden and what others see appears to be someone who is apparently content and managing well. This is a characteristic of the type A pattern, where the child has experienced a negative/punishing response by caregivers to displays of negative affect. For example, as a child comes to learn that the nursery worker or teacher becomes irritated and ignores them when they cry, a fitting adaptation by the child will be to curb such behaviour. The 'secure' child will

---

Crittenden *Raising parents* (Willan, 2008); Farnfield et al 'DMM assessments of attachment and adaptation: Procedures, validity and utility' [2010] Clin Child Psychol Psychiat, 15(3), 313–328.

[43]   Crittenden *A dynamic-maturational approach to continuity and change in pattern of attachment. The organisation of attachment relationships: Maturation, culture, and context* (Cambridge, 2000, 343–357).

respond in this way if it is a better way of being 'with' this caregiver, as will a more generally inhibited child – but a type C child, being predominantly emotionally-expressive, would find this behaviour much more difficult to present. At a lower level this is seen as socially superficial or inhibited behaviour.

2.57 More extreme displays of avoidant behaviour include compulsive caregiving behaviour (a consequence of the child taking on the caregiving role on behalf of their incompetent or extremely withdrawn caregiver) or compulsive compliant behaviour, a relationship strategy that develops out of repeated experiences of caregivers who are extremely hostile or physically threatening. The child's strategy for managing this ongoing threat has been to mollify the caregiver at all costs. This has the effect of making the care-giver seem more functional than they actually are but if successful should increase protection.

2.58 Similarly, cognitive information can also be falsified, and this is more characteristic of the type C pattern beyond infancy. False cognition might be seen in the child who appears to be so overwrought with emotion – which might be anger or intense anxiety or fear – that they cannot organise themselves as to what to do next (hence requiring the caregiver's support and attention). These displays are based on the child 'splitting mixed feelings of anger, fear and desire for comfort, exaggerating some displays while inhibiting others and alternating the exaggeration and inhibition contingent upon the caregiver's behavior'.[44] This behaviour is developmentally appropriate at around the end of the second year of life ('the terrible twos') and it is maintained amongst higher-risk children who employ these behaviours to control the involvement of caregivers. Farnfield et al[45] describe these coercive behaviours as the 'push you [aggressive pattern] – pull me [feigned helplessness pattern]' strategies.

2.59 The onset of adolescence marks a further significant developmental shift in terms of cognitive and emotional functioning, notably increased capacities for metacognitive reasoning and thinking (metacognition was originally described by Flavell[46] as 'knowledge about cognition and control of cognition'). This developmental shift allows for an increased range of deceptive strategies (false cognitions and affects) to protect the self. Adolescence is a stage of major physical development that concludes with sexual maturity. There are also significantly increased psychosocial demands on an adolescent, as they embark into complex social relationships both within the family but particularly within their peer group and outside the orbit of parental supervision. This involves the adolescent in not only organising how they come across so as to be sufficiently attractive and appealing to others (including prospective romantic/sexual

---

44   Spieker and Crittenden 'Comparing two attachment classification methods applied to preschool strange situations' [2010] Clin Child Psychol Psychiat, 15(1), 97–120, p 100.

45   Farnfield et al 'DMM assessments of attachment and adaptation: Procedures, validity and utility' [2010] Clin Child Psychol Psychiat, 15(3), 313–328.

46   Flavell 'Metacognitive aspects of problem solving' in Resnick (ed) *The Nature of Intelligence* (Lawrence Erlbaum Associates, 1976).

partners) but also in deciphering what might be falsified, deceptive displays by others. Perhaps the hope for many adolescents of beginning to understand this new level of complex interpersonal behaviour underpins the content of many adolescents' conversations that seem devoted to deciphering the true and false intentions of others: 'she is so fake' or 'he can be so two-faced …'.

2.60 For those young people who arrive at puberty with continuing insecurities governing significant relationships, the potential exists for the development of more significant psychopathology, an acknowledged vulnerability of the adolescent developmental stage.[47] Compulsively promiscuous behaviour is a description for those young people who may interact widely yet strive to avoid any depth of intimacy in relationships. Those who develop a compulsive self-reliant self-protective strategy have effectively given up on relationships, and aim to live without the need to depend on others. These higher type A strategies describe the emphasis that the individual places on isolating themselves from intimate, reciprocal relationships with attachment figures. Adolescents protecting themselves using emotional strategies (type C) employ an expanded repertoire of self- and other-deceptive strategies, incorporating the young person heightening emotion and then blaming others for their intense upset.

2.61 The DMM proposes that attachment behaviours should be viewed as relationship- and situation-specific strategies for protecting the self from actual or perceived threat and danger.[48] As such, a single attachment classification to describe a child is not necessarily appropriate, even though the child may have a number of relationships that are characterised by similar dynamics. Therefore, individuals living in relationally-complex or maltreating environments may invoke both cognitive and affective strategies to adapt to specific relationships or perceived threats to security. For such individuals, who must place a necessary reliance on displays of falsified affect and cognition in order to organise against potential dangers, within the DMM their overall strategy is conceptualised as A/C. Others have considered this to be a subcategory of disorganised attachment.[49] Beyond adolescence, some individuals (usually those who have begun to use false positive emotion and false cognition as children) are at risk of developing more complex forms of attachment-related psychopathology (see Figure 1, above).

ATTACHMENT AND THE TIMESCALES OF THE CHILD

2.62 Attachment theory and assessments of a child's 'attachment functioning' are often used in the family court context and in child care proceedings. When

---

[47] Meltzer et al *Mental Health of Children and Adolescents in Great Britain* (The Stationery Office, 2000).

[48] Spieker and Crittenden 'Comparing two attachment classification methods applied to preschool strange situations' [2010] Clin Child Psychol Psychiat, 15(1), 97–120, p 99.

[49] Van Ijzendoorn et al 'Disorganised attachment in early childhood. Meta-analysis of precursors, concomitants, and sequelae' [1999] Dev Psychopath, 11, 225–249, p 228.

used clinically it is by far from a simplistic model, especially when applied beyond infancy and as a framework to understand a child's more extreme behaviour in the context of their important relationships. It has been suggested that the stages of significant neurological shifts that occur at the infancy-toddlerhood and at puberty represent an opportunity for reorganisation of attachment strategies as new information becomes available to the individual[50] and both assessments and recommendations would benefit from acknowledging the potential for change at the time of these transitions.

2.63 Further, there is some criticism around the use of the broad term 'attachment disorder' by clinicians assessing maltreated children, and especially because lists of 'symptoms' of attachment disorder also map onto other child and adolescent mental health categories including learning disability, conduct problems and post-traumatic stress disorder.[51] Attachment is often spoken of as 'belonging' to the individual child, and it is the child who 'has' attachment problems or 'shows' behaviours indicative of attachment disorder. Yet attachment is about what happens between two people in a relationship. Current classification systems are not designed to diagnose relational problems, and this is perhaps an underlying factor in the perceived inadequacy of the diagnostic criteria to classify disturbances of attachment.[52]

2.64 Bowlby believed that if a child develops a vulnerable working model of relationships, it constituted a significant risk factor to the development of subsequent psychopathology. There is ample clinical evidence that testifies to the problematic consequences of early psychosocial adversity, multiple placement transitions, as well as of ongoing exposure to caregivers' communications and behaviour that represent a threat to the child's sense of psychological and physical safety. Therapeutic approaches to address insecure and disorganised attachment behaviours are available[53] and will be highlighted in other chapters of this book. However recent discoveries of the adverse impact of insecure and disorganised attachment relationships on the developing brain[54] suggest that permanent neurological change can result, potentially creating lifelong vulnerabilities.

---

[50] Crittenden *A dynamic-maturational approach to continuity and change in pattern of attachment. The organisation of attachment relationships: Maturation, culture, and context* (Cambridge, 2000), 343–357.

[51] Allen 'The Use and Abuse of Attachment Theory in Clinical Practice With Maltreated Children, Part 1: Diagnosis and Assessment' [2011] *Trauma, Violence, & Abuse*, 12(1), 3–12.

[52] Ibid.

[53] Hughes *Facilitating developmental attachment: The road to emotional recovery and behavioural change in foster and adopted children* (Aronson, 1997); Golding *Nurturing attachments: Supporting children who are fostered or adopted* (Jessica Kingsley, 2008).

[54] Glaser 'Child abuse and neglect and the brain. A review' [2000] J Child Psychol Psychiat, 41(1), 97–116.

CHAPTER 3

IMPACT OF DELAY IN THE CHILD PROTECTION SYSTEM: CONSEQUENCES OF ABUSE AND NEGLECT ON CHILDREN AND YOUNG PEOPLE

Helen Dent

INTRODUCTION

3.1   In March 2012, Daniel Pelka died from a blow to his head having suffered horrific abuse and neglect described by Judge Laura Cox as 'unimaginable acts of cruelty and brutality'. Daniel attended school but teachers believed his mother's claims that he had an eating disorder and learning difficulties. Serious case reviews found that the professionals involved (health, police and social work) had succumbed to the 'rule of optimism' and that they had failed to communicate their separate concerns (drug misuse, domestic violence, criminal record, bruising and emaciation) despite the recommendations in Lord Laming's report[1] following the death of Victoria Climbié and his progress report[2] following the death of Baby P.

3.2   Death is the ultimate, but thankfully rare consequence of systemic delays to respond to signs of child abuse and neglect. This chapter will take a psychological perspective on the causes and consequences of delays in the child protection system and offer suggestions to overcome these.

3.3   It is well-known that disadvantage continues through generations of some families, whilst others overcome adversity to thrive. Poor physical and mental health, reliance on state funding, alcohol and drug misuse, criminal activity and maltreatment of children are all associated with disadvantage. It is therefore clearly in the interests of society as well as individual children and families to break this cycle. Research has identified factors that make a difference, but it is not always clear how best to implement these.

---

[1]   *The Victoria Climbié Inquiry Report* [2003].
[2]   *The Protection of Children in England: A Progress Report* [2009].

3.4   This chapter will address what children need, **the consequences of abuse and neglect** and the additional harm that may be caused by delays in the child protection process and the associated failure to meet children's needs in a developmentally appropriate timescale.

3.5   In addition to addressing what children need the chapter will also explore, again from a psychological perspective, what are the **reasons for delays, the barriers to resolving these and the impact on children.**

3.6   The chapter will also provide suggestions for the **questions that should be asked** by all professionals involved in child protection cases to ensure that they acquire the most relevant information and make decisions in the best interests of the child.

CONSEQUENCES OF ABUSE AND NEGLECT

What do children need?

3.7   Children need the security of responsive, gentle, loving and consistent parenting. The factors that have emerged as most significant in recent research are the parent's ability to perceive, understand and respond appropriately to the child's needs. This enables a secure attachment relationship to develop in which the child experiences safety with the confidence that his or her needs will be met. It is also important for the parent to respond contingently and empathically to the child's behaviours which enables the child to feel 'held in mind'; to envision the child's mental state and mirror the child's affect which begins the process of affect regulation and underpins the child's ability to understand others as having separate mental states from him or herself.[3]

3.8   Unfortunately, no parent is perfect. Indeed, most of us worry about whether we are doing enough for our children or, at times, whether we have caused them harm. The concept of 'good enough' care, developed by Donald Winnicott,[4] a paediatrician and psychoanalyst, is helpful and essentially maps onto the concept of secure attachment. An infant develops a secure attachment when the carer is sufficiently responsive to their needs.

3.9   Children whose needs are met are likely to develop a 'secure attachment style' (see Barnett, this volume) and consequent high self-esteem, regulated emotions and good social skills. They will have learned to trust their parents, carers and teachers to meet their needs and will be able to focus on exploration and learning to reach their potential in education. On the whole they will be confident and able to take advantage of what life has to offer.

---

[3]   Fonagy et al *Affect Regulation, Mentalisation and the Development of Self* (Other Press, 2004); Schore *Affect Regulation and the Repair of the Self* (Norton, 2003); Trevarthen 'Intrinsic motives for companionship in understanding: Their origin, development, and significance for infant mental health' [2001] Inf Ment Health J, 22, 95–131.

[4]   Winnicott *Playing and Reality* (Routledge, 1971).

Risk factors for inadequate parenting

3.10   Currently, research surveys indicate that about 60% of people in the UK have a secure attachment style.[5] What about the other 40%? Clinical experience suggests that most parents wish to do the best they can for their children and research indicates that circumstances or contextual factors have a powerful impact.

3.11   Important contextual factors are financial, social, educational status, alcohol and drug misuse and the parents' own attachment style and parenting competence. Poverty is a well-documented risk factor for physical and emotional health.[6] Children who are born into financially disadvantaged families will have poorer life chances. Since the industrial revolution in this country, social factors have been linked to financial, because families tend to live in similar socio-economic clusters. Children from disadvantaged families may not be exposed to positive models of family life to aspire to.

3.12   Cultural factors are increasingly considered to be a factor in child protection cases. Clearly they vary and are very complex. A useful guiding principle is that in this country child-rearing has to adhere to acceptable standards according to the 1989 Children Act. Research data from the USA indicate that ethnic differences in child maltreatment are mostly caused by socio-economic factors, except for children of mixed heritage who appear to have an increased risk of being abused or neglected.[7] This risk has been linked to greater social and economic disadvantage in the mothers of bi-racial children.[8] Children who are disabled also have an increased risk of being abused.[9] The reasons for this are complex and will comprise the children's vulnerability and any communication difficulty, which can hinder making an allegation and render that allegation more difficult to comprehend. An allegation from a disabled child may be met with incredulity in the context of a generally protective attitude to disabled children.

3.13   All contextual factors will have an influence on the developing child and an impact on his or her life chances. However, the greatest influence will come from the parents or main care givers. Parenting is not taught and people generally parent as they have been parented. For more detail on how different styles of parenting impact upon children's behavior and psychological health see Barnett on Attachment Theory in Chapter 2. Most research focusses on the

---

5   Cassidy and Shaver *Handbook of Attachment: Theory, research and clinical applications* (The Guilford Press, 2008).

6   Gilbert et al 'Child Maltreatment 1. Burden and consequences of child maltreatment in high-income countries' [2009a] *The Lancet*, 373, 68–81.

7   Miller et al 'Prevalence of maltreatment among youths in public sectors of care' [2011] Child Maltreat, 16, 196–204.

8   Rauktis and Fusco 'Transracial mothering and maltreatment: are black/white biracial children at higher risk?' [2012] *Child Welfare*, 91, 55–77.

9   Govindshenoy and Spencer 'Abuse of the disabled child: a systematic review of population based studies' [2007] Child Care Health Dev, 33, 552–558.

contribution of maternal behaviour, but recent research[10] has shown that fathers' disengaged and remote interactions with 3-month-old infants predicts externalising behaviour problems at 1 year. Complex models of the interaction between risk factors suggest that parental risk factors can be modified by the environment and the community[11] which means that effective interventions can be broadly based.

Prevalence of abuse and neglect

3.14   Abuse falls into three main categories: physical, sexual and psychological or emotional. Psychological abuse often co-occurs with physical and sexual abuse, but seems rarely to be reported alone, perhaps because it is harder to detect and substantiate. Indeed, children who suffer one form of abuse are at risk of other forms of abuse.[12] There is some evidence that rates of physical and sexual abuse are decreasing in the Western World and that rates of abuse and neglect vary in different parts of the world. These data provide evidence that it is possible to reduce child maltreatment.[13]

3.15   Annual prevalence rates of physical abuse have been estimated at about 9% of the child population,[14] though in common with all forms of abuse, this is probably an underestimate due to parents' reticence to admit abusive acts, professional caution in ascribing blame and children's tendencies to protect even abusive parents.[15]

3.16   Prevalence estimates for sexual abuse vary, not surprisingly, as it is difficult to disclose and equally difficult to assess veracity. London et al[16] reviewed research papers from 1990 and concluded that the majority of abused children do not reveal abuse during childhood. Recent research supporting this view was conducted by Radford et al[17] in the UK. They surveyed 1761 adults aged 18–24 years, of whom 1 in 9 (11.3%) reported contact sexual abuse as children. They also conducted a survey of 2275 children aged 11–17 years, in which only 1 in 20 (4.8%) reported contact sexual abuse.

---

[10]   Ramchandani et al 'Do early father–infant interactions predict the onset of externalising behaviours in young children? Findings from a longitudinal cohort study' [2013] J Child Psychol Psychiat, 54, 56–64.

[11]   Gilbert et al 'Child Maltreatment 1. Burden and consequences of child maltreatment in high-income countries' [2009a] *The Lancet*, 373, 68–81.

[12]   Ibid.

[13]   Gilbert et al 'Child Maltreatment 1. Burden and consequences of child maltreatment in high-income countries' [2009a] *The Lancet*, 373, 68–81.

[14]   Woodman et al 'Performance of screening tests for child physical abuse in Accident and Emergency Departments' [2008] Health Technol Assess, 12, 1–118.

[15]   Everson et al 'Concordance between adolescent reports of childhood abuse and Child Protective Service determinants in an at risk sample of young adolescents' [2008] Ch Maltreat, 13, 14–23.

[16]   London et al 'Disclosure of sexual abuse. What does the research tell us about the ways that children tell?' [2005] Psychol Pol Law, 11, 194–223.

[17]   Radford et al *Child Abuse and Neglect in the UK today* (NSPCC, 2011).

3.17 Psychological or emotional abuse is the most common form of maltreatment seen by child and adolescent mental health services.[18] It can comprise ignoring, rejecting, isolating, ridiculing, humiliating, threatening, exploiting, corrupting, verbally assaulting, terrorising or neglecting the child's physical or emotional needs. It is likely to be the most prevalent form of maltreatment as it is highly likely to be a factor in physical and sexual abuse. A growing body of evidence indicates under reporting of psychological abuse[19] possibly due to variations in professional judgment as to what comprises maltreatment.

3.18 Neglect is defined as '... the persistent failure to meet a child's basic needs which is likely to result in serious impairment of the child's health or development'[20] and can have extreme consequences both in terms of threat to life and physical and emotional damage. Brandon et al[21] in an analysis of serious case reviews, found that neglect was the most common category of concern. Although signs of neglect may be obvious, the decision about whether these reach the threshold for concern, particularly in the UK which requires a 'persistent state of omission' may be difficult to take. There is evidence of wide variation in professional judgements about what constitutes neglect, caused by reliance on subjective definitions about neglect and a focus on their relationship with the parents rather than the parents' behaviour towards the children.[22] Prevalence estimates vary between 1% and 10% of the child population.[23]

Impact of abuse and neglect

3.19 All forms of child maltreatment have an adverse effect upon self-esteem, emotional regulation, social skills and the child's ability to explore their environment and engage in learning. At the most extreme, the World Health Organisation estimated that 0.6% of all deaths and 12.7% of deaths due to injury in children under 15 years, were caused by abuse or neglect.[24] Improvements in brain imaging techniques have produced a burgeoning of research indicating that maltreatment affects the developing brain,[25] though caution should be exercised when applying such findings to individual cases.

---

[18]   Gilbert et al 'Child Maltreatment 2. Recognising and responding to child maltreatment' [2009b] *The Lancet*, 373, 167–180.

[19]   Ibid.

[20]   HM Government *Working Together to Safeguard Children: A Guide to Inter-agency Working to Safeguard and Promote the Welfare of Children* (DCSF Publications, 2010).

[21]   Brandon et al *Understanding Serious Case Reviews and their Impact. A Biennial Analysis of Serious Case Reviews 2005–07* (Department for Children, Schools and Families, 2009).

[22]   Horwath 'The missing assessment domain: personal, professional and organisational factors influencing professional judgements when identifying and referring child neglect' [2007] Brit J Soc Work, 37, 1285–1303.

[23]   Gilbert et al 'Child Maltreatment 1. Burden and consequences of child maltreatment in high-income countries' [2009a] *The Lancet* 373, 68–81.

[24]   Pinheiro *World report on violence against children* (United Nations Secretary-General's Study on Violence against Children, 2006).

[25]   Belsky and de Haan 'Annual Research Review: Parenting and children's brain development: the end of the beginning' [2011] J Child Psychol Psychiat, 52, 409–428.

There is also a growing body of research that shows an association between child maltreatment and mental health problems[26] and child maltreatment and progression to criminal activity.[27]

3.20   Many studies, including the ACE project[28] have shown serious and long term adverse consequences of child maltreatment. In a systematic review of high quality research (prospective longitudinal studies and randomised controlled trials) Gilbert and colleagues[29] identified the following consequences of maltreatment that can be supported by the literature:

- Lower educational achievement.
- Lower status employment and poorer economic achievement.
- Externalising behaviour problems (aggression, acting out).
- Criminal behaviour, particularly violence.
- Mental health problems (anxiety and depression) particularly in adolescence but continuing into adulthood.
- Post-traumatic stress disorder (PTSD).
- Personality disorder.
- Attempted suicide.
- Self-injury.
- Alcohol abuse in adolescence and adulthood, particularly in women, which brings additional risks of foetal alcohol syndrome and inadequate parenting.
- Drug misuse.
- Obesity, anorexia and bulimia.
- Prostitution or sex working.
- Teenage pregnancy and abortions.
- HIV/Aids and other STIs.

3.21   Many of the research papers reviewed found that severity of maltreatment had an impact upon the severity of outcomes, and that there was a cumulative effect such that repetitions of maltreatment created more negative consequences. An important conclusion to draw from this finding, is that intervening to prevent maltreatment can have an ameliorative impact at any stage, not just during early life.

---

[26]   Gilbert et al 'Child Maltreatment 1. Burden and consequences of child maltreatment in high-income countries' [2009a] *The Lancet*, 373, 68–81.

[27]   Browne et al *The cycles of violence: the relationship between child maltreatment and the risk of later becoming a victim or perpetrator of violence* (Policy Briefing. Copenhagen: WHO, Violence and Injury Prevention Programme, 2007).

[28]   Felitti et al 'Relationship of childhood abuse and household dysfunction to many of the leading causes of death in adults. The Adverse Childhood Experiences (ACE) Study' [1998] Am J Prev Med, 14, 245–258.

[29]   Gilbert et al 'Child Maltreatment 1. Burden and consequences of child maltreatment in high-income countries' [2009a] *The Lancet*, 373, 68–81.

Reasons for and impact of delay in the system

3.22 'The defence budget is £42.4bn. The Crossrail budget is about £40bn. The child protection budget is £113m and actually we've got a catastrophic epidemic of child maltreatment in this country'.[30]

3.23 Money is always important, and often at the root of complex and intractable difficulties. With greater financial resources, much more could be achieved. Nevertheless, some interventions have been shown to be cost effective[31] and there are improvements that should be made that would not inevitably take place if the budget were increased. We all have a responsibility to do our best to make improvements for the lives of children, families and the communities they live in, within whatever constraints we work.

Resilience

3.24 Some children appear to thrive despite living in adverse circumstances, although resilience factors (intelligence, 'sunny' temperament, pro-social personality) have been found to make a difference in low rather than high stress environments.[32]

3.25 However, some children who appear to thrive have in fact learned how to suppress expression of their needs in order to survive in a hostile environment with a carer who has an 'avoidant' attachment style. Parents with an avoidant attachment style are unable to tolerate their infants' cries or other expressions of need and retreat, thus depriving the infant of their 'secure base'. Infants quickly learn that their parent becomes more distant when they cry and so remain quiet in order to keep their parent close. This suppression of emotion may lead to a delay in detection of the child's needs, because these are unnoticed. Professionals may not know how to investigate in these situations or may be worried that their concerns are unwarranted. Haringey Local Safeguarding Children's Board has published *Key Messages for Practice*[33] in response to recent serious case reviews, which provides a helpful starting point for these situations: 'try to understand what the world looks and feels like for that child; get a narrative of the child's day-to-day experience rather than answers to yes/no questions'.

Rule of optimism

3.26 The 'rule of optimism' is a term used in child protection contexts for believing parents when the evidence does not support such a belief. Parents are

---

[30] Camilla Batmanghelidjh, Founder and Director of Kid's Company in London, UK, quoted in the Observer colour supplement, 09.02.14.

[31] Petrou et al 'Cost-effectiveness of a preventive counseling and support package for postnatal depression' [2006] Int J Technol Ass Health Care, 22, 443–453.

[32] Jaffee et al 'Individual, family and neighbourhood factors distinguish resilient from non-resilient maltreated children: a cumulative stressors model' [2007] Child Abuse Negl, 31, 231–253.

[33] Haringey LSCB *Key Messages for Practice* (2014).

the key to children's welfare and professionals rightly believe that if a parent can be helped to change this will benefit the child. Such a belief may be accompanied by an attempt to create a therapeutic bond in order to facilitate parental change. Adults often find it easier to speak with other adults than with children and so may gain more information from parents than from children. These factors can lead to a greater focus on parents than children and the 'rule of optimism', which is a perceptual bias leading to selective observation of information that fits the bias, may operate under such circumstances. Brandon et al[34] found in their analysis of serious case reviews, that 'good parental engagement sometimes masked risks of harm to the child'. Overwork and carrying a heavy case load may increase a professional's susceptibility to this bias. The maxim *'Parental Participation is Not the Same as Cooperation'*[35] is a useful antidote for all professionals working closely with parents.

3.27 The rule of optimism may both delay the initial acceptance of threshold risk and may lead to inappropriately giving the parents another chance and returning a child from care. Financial factors, always powerful within systems, may hinder more senior staff from detecting the presence of such a bias. Indeed, Brandon et al[36] noted that 'the needs and distress of the older young people were often missed or too challenging or expensive for services to meet'.

Multi-agency collaboration

3.28 A common finding in serious case reviews is the lack of effective collaboration between professionals from different agencies, social services, NHS, police force, education services and the independent sector. This deficit endures despite being a major focus of the Laming Report in 2003.

3.29 Professionals may be hindered from communicating because of concerns over confidentiality and the difficulty in deciding what constitutes a 'need to know', particularly in contexts when reports to child protection services need a high threshold of suspicion.[37] Indeed, the 'need to know' may not become apparent until information has been shared; separate concerns may seem unimportant, but together may create a disturbing pattern.

3.30 Some professionals may not value the views of other professions sufficiently or may not consider it is their responsibility to take the first step in making contact. Brandon et al[38] writing about serious case reviews, state that: 'When professionals with low levels of confidence consider a child is at risk of harm and others do not, they will struggle to challenge the decisions and behaviour of their multi-agency colleagues'. They may also wish to avoid

---

[34] Brandon et al *Understanding Serious Case Reviews and their Impact. A Biennial Analysis of Serious Case Reviews 2005–07* (Department for Children, Schools and Families, 2009).

[35] Haringey LSCB *Key Messages for Practice* (2014).

[36] See footnote 35.

[37] Gilbert et al 'Child Maltreatment 2. Recognising and responding to child maltreatment' [2009b] *The Lancet*, 373, 167–180.

[38] See footnote 35.

having to tell a parent that they have raised a concern with another agency. Serious case reviews indicate that some parents can be very plausible and adept at manipulating the beliefs and behaviours of professionals. It is not uncommon for 'splitting' behaviours to occur, whereby a parent criticises other professionals and asserts that you are the only one who really understands. Such behaviour can lead to the professionals mirroring the dysfunctional behaviour observed in the families and should be treated with caution and scepticism in the child protection context.

Lack of resources

3.31 Professionals involved in child protection related work are commonly busy or seriously overworked and governed by externally imposed targets, which shape not only their behaviours but those of managers' right up to the highest level. Brandon et al[39] state that 'The capacity to understand the ways in which children are at risk of harm is complex and requires clear thinking. Practitioners, who are overwhelmed, not just by the *volume* of work but also by its *nature*, may not be able to do even the simple things well'. The solution they suggest 'Good support, supervision and a fully staffed workforce' must come, therefore, from the highest level, ie government'. In the introduction, I argued that child protection affects everyone. From this perspective it is important for society to decide through the vote whether policies that will enable more money to be spent on child protection should be implemented.

Children's rights and parents' responsibilities

3.32 The Children Act[40] states that the welfare of the child is paramount, which implies that this trumps all other legislation. Nevertheless, the Human Rights Act[41] is sometimes quoted as inferring the right of parents to private family life, particularly when there is little direct evidence of harm to a child. A focus on parental understanding of their responsibilities towards their child would be more consistent with child welfare and may enable clearer professional perception of the parent's ability to consistently prioritise the child's needs.

The child's timescale

3.33 Another professional bias, strongly associated with the rule of optimism, is the tendency to ignore or downplay the importance of the child's timescale when trying to make a difference within the family. Children develop very quickly and the most fundamental shaping of the brain occurs during the first 3 years, when deeply held patterns of belief about the self and the world form into 'internal working models' or 'schemas'. Schemas are the foundation for a

---

[39] Brandon et al *Understanding Serious Case Reviews and their Impact. A Biennial Analysis of Serious Case Reviews 2005–07* (Department for Children, Schools and Families, 2009).
[40] Children Act 1989, s 1.
[41] Human Rights Act 1998, Art 8 of ECHR.

child's social understanding and cannot easily be modified because they are formed and encoded in the brain before verbal language develops.

3.34 Every delay increases the strength of maladaptive schemas and diminishes the power of the remedial action that can be taken. At the most fundamental level, it takes thousands of repetitions of an action to create a new skill and even more to overwrite an already established neuronal pathway. Try and change a deeply ingrained skill to experience this for yourself, such as writing with your left (or right) hand. So the earlier a change is implemented, the greater the chance of it being successful. Another important reason for minimising delay is that the most effective remedial action will be given in the same modality as the care which underpinned the original schema. Such care, physical nurturing behaviour and close supervision, is clearly far easier to give to a toddler than a teenager. Additional evidence for this position comes from recent research showing better outcomes for children who are placed in care before seven months of age.[42]

3.35 Nevertheless, it is crucial that decisions are not rushed or taken lightly and that proper in depth assessments are made. For example, although the recent Government agenda to speed up the adoption process has the important advantage of achieving permanence in a timely manner, it also carries the risk of making rushed decisions and placing children with adopters who can't meet their needs. Even prior to this agenda, hasty and ill-considered placements have been approved with devastating consequences for both children and the potential adopters.

The adversarial legal system

3.36 Children, particularly in sexual abuse cases where their allegation may be the only evidence, may be advised not to undertake therapy until the trial has taken place. Despite the publication of CPS guidance in 2001, *Provision of Therapy for Child Witnesses Prior to a Criminal Trial*, many lawyers believe that defence barristers will be able to use pre-trial therapy to discredit or cast doubt on the child's evidence. Delays between allegation and trial are commonly over a year and may be much longer, which constitutes a substantial proportion of a child's life. Untreated mental health problems can impact upon educational achievement and employment.[43]

---

[42] Tarren-Sweeney 'Retrospective and concurrent predictors of mental health of children in care' [2008] Child Youth Servi Rev, 30(1), 1–25.

[43] Gilbert et al 'Child Maltreatment 1. Burden and consequences of child maltreatment in high-income countries' [2009a] *The Lancet*, 373, 68–81.

EFFECTIVE INTERVENTIONS AND THE IMPACT OF DELAYING THEIR IMPLEMENTATION

Types of intervention

3.37 Intervention for child maltreatment can take various forms:

Contextual

- providing a new context eg placing the child in another form of care – adoption, foster, residential;
- changing the context eg removing the abusive adult from the child's home;
- modifying the context eg providing therapy or parent training for the carers; providing extra help or specialist input into the home eg support worker or health visitor; providing specialist consultations to the network around the child;

Relationship focussed

- modifying the relationship between the carer and the child eg family therapy; various forms of attachment focused interventions;

Child focussed

- modifying the child's understanding, perception or self-control eg cognitive behaviour therapy (CBT); child psychotherapy; play/art/music therapy.

Evaluating interventions

3.38 In our culture certain forms of evaluation are more highly valued than others. In particular, randomised controlled trials (RCTs) are considered to be the 'gold standard'. However, there are drawbacks to RCTs, one of which is that it relies on group data, within which there are always exceptions. This is reasonable for informing population health strategies but will not be reliable for each individual case. There is a second important drawback when using RCTs for mental health interventions. Whereas with physical diseases the reliability of diagnosis can be established and assessed against laboratory data, there is much concern over the reliability and validity of psychiatric diagnosis and there is currently little physical evidence available for corroboration. The usefulness of the RCT for mental health interventions is therefore limited both by the uncertainty of whether a client matches the mental health profile of the research participants, and indeed how homogeneous the research sample really is, and whether the main research data or the outlying results are most apt for the client.

3.39 Prospective or longitudinal studies that follow a cohort of children over a number of years are rare but can provide useful data about causal relationships.

Smaller qualitative or single case studies are useful for evaluating mental health interventions, but the likelihood of finding a study that matches a client's situation will be low. Another approach is to evaluate each intervention undertaken.

3.40 In clinical psychology, good practice requires a theoretically driven formulation for each client which will underpin a bespoke intervention strategy. At each stage the psychologist will evaluate the goodness of fit of the formulation and modify the intervention appropriately. The parents or carers of children who have been abused or neglected have failed to respond contingently to their needs. Therapists who deliver off-the-shelf packages of treatment are unlikely to have the knowledge and skill to assess need and to intervene in a manner that responds contingently to the client's needs. Clinical psychology time is expensive but the risk of using therapists who do not have this level of competence is that treatment may become yet another form of maltreatment.

Impact of contextual interventions

Providing a new context

3.41 Moving the child to a new context or home tends to be reserved for the more severe cases of child maltreatment when it is considered that the carers will not be able to make sufficient changes in a timescale suitable for the child's developing needs. The type of new context provided should depend on the child's needs but will be strongly influenced by available resources. Research suggests that once importance issues such as level of resource, health and safety have been addressed, the most important factor that will make a difference to the success of the placement is the main carer's attachment style. Kaniuk, Steele and Hodges[44] found that success in adoptive placements was related more to the attachment style of the adoptive parents than to child characteristics and needs. Research in the USA indicates that enhanced foster care placements (higher level of training, better access to resources and support) provide better outcomes than standard foster care.[45]

3.42 Although some research and outcome data have shown that children placed in care have worse outcomes than children who remain with birth parents,[46] this must be balanced against the likelihood that children who are removed are likely to have experienced more severe maltreatment and that their parents will have had greater difficulty with childrearing.[47] Some research does show that children placed in care have better outcomes, at least in the short

---

[44] Kaniuk et al 'Report on a longitudinal research project exploring the development of attachments between older, hard to place children and their adopters over the first two years of placement' [2004] Adopt Fost, 28, 61–68.

[45] Kessler et al 'Effects of enhanced foster care on the long term physical and mental health of foster care alumni' [2008] Arch Gen Psychiatry, 65, 625–633.

[46] Lawrence et al 'The impact of foster care on development' [2006] Dev Psychopathol, 18, 57–73.

[47] Zuravin and DePanfilis 'Factors affecting foster care placement of children receiving child protective services' [1997] Soc Work Res, 21, 34–42.

term, than children who remain with abusive parents.[48] The main factor associated with better outcomes appears to be being placed at an early age, specifically prior to 7 months of age, which protects the child from maltreatment and allows security of attachment to develop.[49]

Modifying the context

Therapy for the parent

3.43 Therapeutic interventions for parents can be very effective for the parents, particularly if their difficulties are mild, situation specific and have little adverse impact on the child. When difficulties are more severe and global, therapy can still help the adult and any future children. However, the downside for the currently maltreated child is that there are often long waiting lists for therapy and the therapy itself is likely to take months or years. Moreover, therapy is emotionally draining, particularly for deep rooted difficulties of the type that affect parenting. During this process, the parent's ability to care for the child is likely to decrease before any progress is seen.

3.44 Early interventions for parents aimed at promoting behaviours that underpin attachment security overcome most of these disadvantages. Some examples are the work of Murray and colleagues with mothers suffering from post-natal depression[50] which has shown that intervention can improve the bond between mother and child even when the depression does not improve; interventions developed in Sure Start programmes such as baby massage; mellow parenting[51] and the early intervention to promote attachment behaviour developed by PO Svanberg[52] which has demonstrated success with high risk parent-child dyads.

---

[48] Davidson-Arad et al 'Short term follow up of children at risk: comparison of the quality of life of children removed from the home and children remaining in at home' [2003] Child Abuse Negl, 27, 733–750.

[49] Tarren-Sweeney Retrospective and concurrent predictors of mental health of children in care [2008] Child Youth Servi Rev, 30(1), 1–25.

[50] Petrou et al 'Cost-effectiveness of a preventive counseling and support package for postnatal depression' [2006] Int J Technol Ass Health Care, 22, 443–453.

[51] Puckering et al 'Taking Control: A single case study of mellow parenting' [1996] Clin Child Psychol Psychiat, 1, 539–550.

[52] Svanberg et al 'Promoting a secure attachment: A primary care prevention model' [2010] Clin Child Psychol Psychiat, 15, 363–378.

Parent training

3.45   There are many parent training programmes available, which do have a positive impact on parenting, at least in the short term. Triple P[53] and Incredible Years[54] have been rigorously evaluated and found to decrease rates of child maltreatment.[55]

Specialist home visitation

3.46   There are very variable outcomes for interventions which provide support to families in their homes, partly due to the quality of the research but also due to the quality of provision. Universal services such as health visiting in England have not been subject to rigorous research scrutiny but nevertheless are generally considered to reduce child maltreatment. Moreover, the research of PO Svanberg[56] has shown that health visitors can be used in simple and cost effective early interventions with high risk families. Simple provision of non-specialist social support has not been found to be effective.[57] Well-designed specialist and multi component programmes such as Home Visitation,[58] Nurse-Family Partnership in the USA[59] and Early Start in New Zealand[60] have produced positive outcomes in terms of reduction in abuse and neglect. Video interaction guidance[61] is a relatively new and promising intervention which uses filming and feedback to promote positive relationships by increasing parental sensitivity and attunement. A multi-centre research trial is currently underway in the Netherlands.

Relationship focussed

3.47   Interventions aimed at modifying the relationship between the child and their parent or carer are intuitively sensible and many have been driven by attachment theory research.[62] Approaches such as *Developmental Dyadic Practice*,[63] *Mellow Parenting*,[64] *Narrative Family Therapy*, *Theraplay*[65] and

53   Sanders *Every Parent. A positive approach to children's behaviour* (Addison Wesley, 1991).

54   Webster-Stratton *The Incredible Years. A trouble shooting Guide for Parents of children aged 3–8* (Umbrella Press, 1992).

55   Hughes and Gottlieb 'The effects of the Webster Stratton parenting programme on maltreating families: fostering strengths' [2004] Child Abuse Negl, 28, 1081–1097.

56   Svanberg et al 'Promoting a secure attachment: A primary care prevention model' [2010] Clin Child Psychol Psychiat, 15, 363–378.

57   MacMillan et al 'Child Maltreatment 3. Interventions to prevent child maltreatment and associated impairment' [2009] *The Lancet* 373, 250–263.

58   Olds et al 'Effects of nurse home visiting on maternal and child functioning: age 9 follow up of a randomised trial' [2007] *Pediatrics*, 120, 832–45.

59   Krugman et al 'Update on child abuse prevention' [2007] Current Opinion Pediatr, 19, 711–718.

60   Fergusson et al *Early Start Evaluation Report* (Early Start Project Ltd, 2008).

61   Kennedy et al 'Video interaction guidance, Relationship based intervention to promote attunement, empathy and wellbeing' [2011] Ed Child Psychol, 27(3).

62   Schore *Affect Regulation and the Repair of the Self* (Norton 2003).

63   Becker-Weidman and Hughes 'Dyadic Developmental Psychotherapy: an evidence-based treatment for children with complex trauma and disorders of attachment' [2008] Ch Fam Soc Work, 13, 329–337.

bespoke interventions based on concepts such as PACE⁶⁶ are increasingly being used and a research base is being developed. Deciding upon which approach should be guided by a formulation approach such as that used by clinical psychologists.

Child focussed

3.48 Interventions aimed at helping the child should be used with caution. The primary focus on intervention, particularly with younger children should be with the context and the network surrounding the child.⁶⁷ Many of the interventions that have a good evidence base for children who have not been maltreated, such as behavioural, cognitive behavioural and systemic interventions, may not be suitable or effective for children who have been subject to maltreatment. In the UK, the child focused approaches that are commonly used or have been found to be effective for children who have been maltreated, are cognitive behaviour therapy for PTSD, art therapy and Theraplay. Interestingly, the charity Kid's Company is reportedly the biggest employer of art therapists outside the NHS.

Questions that should be asked

What information has been gathered?

3.49 Have professionals listened carefully to the child using open question to facilitate a narrative about their life? Use of closed, yes/no questions is more likely to elicit answers that the child thinks the interviewer wants to hear.

3.50 Have professionals observed the parent's caretaking activities, particularly when there may be stresses or challenges, eg getting ready for school, bedtime, mealtime?

3.51 Has the child/parent interaction been observed when the child is stressed (eg when being left at nursery or school) or distressed (eg when child has fallen over or when parent has enforced a boundary)? It is only when the child feels unsafe or distressed that attachment style can be assessed. Children with an insecure or disorganised attachment style may exhibit a positive relationship with their parent at times, for example during supervised contact when sessions are comfortable and hopefully stress free for the child. When such contact sessions are used to assess the parent child relationship, there is a high risk of overestimating the parent's competence and the quality of the parent child

---

64 Puckering et al 'Taking Control: A single case study of mellow parenting' [1996] Clin Child Psychol Psychiat, 1, 539–550.
65 Jernberg and Booth *Theraplay. Helping Parents and Children Build Better Relationships Through Attachment Based Play* (Jossey-Bass, 2nd edn, 2001).
66 Golding and Hughes *Creating Loving Attachments* (Jessica Kingsley Publications, 2012).
67 Dent and Golding 'Engaging the Network: Consultation for Looked After and Adopted Children' in Golding et al (eds) *Thinking Psychologically about Children who are Looked After and Adopted: Space for Reflection* (Wiley, 2006).

relationship. It is important to remember that attachment behaviours are shown when the child feels unsafe and so attachment style is most reliably ascertained at times when the child feels unsafe.

3.52 Has information been obtained about all the significant adults in a child's life, including father, mother's partners and friends?

3.53 Have all relevant professionals, including those that work with the adults, been consulted to ask for information about the child and their family, including teachers, doctors, nurses, the police and social workers? Research published by the NSPCC[68] indicated that one reason for under reporting by educational professionals was that UK teachers had restricted access to qualified social workers.

3.54 In private law divorce cases, has an adequate assessment of child safety been undertaken when decisions are made about contact with allegedly abusive parents?[69]

3.55 How has this information been considered?

3.56 When there is a consensus view, has anyone played 'devil's advocate' and challenged this? 'Groupthink'[70] is a known psychological phenomenon, in which people who prefer harmony are more likely to shift their opinions towards consensus by minimising the importance of conflicting information. Decisions made under these conditions are not safe. Groups in which at least one member is willing to challenge ideas may not be so pleasant, but the outcome is likely to be of a better quality.

3.57 Has a 'healthy scepticism' been operated in response to the parent's explanations about their child's emotional, behavioural or physical presentation? Gilbert and colleagues[71] suggest that 'the key issue is the preparedness of clinicians to *contemplate the possibility* that a child's presentation could, at least in part, be explained by maltreatment'. Haringey LSCB[72] recommends that professionals be prepared to 'Think the Unthinkable'.

3.58 Have the parents' past behaviours been given sufficient weight? It is possible for people to change, it is not easy to do so. Moreover, people in disadvantaged situations will struggle more than most to make deep and lasting changes. In the absence of very compelling evidence to the contrary, past behaviour is the best predictor of future behaviour for most people.

---

[68] *Baginsky Schools, social services and safeguarding children. Past practice and future challenges* (NSPCC, 2007).

[69] *Ofsted inspection of the experience of Cafcass service users in the family courts in South Yorkshire* (Ofsted, 2008).

[70] Janis *Groupthink: Psychological Studies of Policy Decisions and Fiascos* (Houghton Mifflin, 1982).

[71] Gilbert et al 'Child Maltreatment 1. Burden and consequences of child maltreatment in high-income countries' [2009a] *The Lancet*, 373, 68–81.

[72] Haringey LSCB *Key Messages for Practice* (2014).

What is the least worst decision?

3.59 Child protection is complex and multi-factorial[73] and there is frequently no simple solution and the solutions themselves may be inherently harmful. A child may have to be taken into care, but statistics suggest that the outcomes for children in care can be worse than for children who remain in dysfunctional families. Children who need special care also have a strong need for stability, but the provision of special care may involve many changes. Siblings may be very reliant on each other but too challenging to be placed together with the same carers. A cost benefit analysis needs to be made for each child when such a dilemma occurs and alternative solutions considered, eg can sufficient support be provided for long enough to the birth family to enable the child to thrive; can current carers receive training to enable them to provide specialist care; could the sibling group be placed in a customised residential unit?

Timescales for the child

3.60 What will be the impact for the child of remaining in a dysfunctional home? Both in terms of the entrenching of the difficulties caused by that environment and the loss of time for implementing positive interventions that should help the child to engage more constructively with all aspects of their life.

---

[73] Gilbert et al 'Child Maltreatment 1. Burden and consequences of child maltreatment in high-income countries' [2009a] *The Lancet*, 373, 68–81.

CHAPTER 4

CHILDREN AND YOUNG PEOPLE'S EXPERIENCE: THE VOICE OF THE CHILD IN THEIR EXPERIENCE OF TIMESCALES

Dr Roger Morgan

4.1   In my past role as Children's Rights Director for England, I had a statutory duty to secure the views and experiences about rights and social care of children in care or receiving social care services, care leavers, and children living away from home in residential education such as residential special schools, boarding schools and colleges. The approach adopted with my then team was to secure and publish the 'pure views' of children, without selection for any particular position, cause or campaign, and without adding commentary or context from sources other than children. This resulted in a series of published 'children's views' reports, affording, literally, unadulterated children's views to researchers, policy makers, politicians and practitioners. This chapter draws on that work and those publications to extract children's views and experience on the subject of timescales and their perceptions of timescales and their impact on their lives.

4.2   The methodology used in securing children's views fell midway between consultation and research. Varying by topic in both nature and scale, and often offering children a choice of means of inputting their views, the methods included large scale password accessed web surveys, with hundreds or in some cases over two thousand respondents, small scale discussion groups, combined discussion and electronic voting groups, large scale electronic voting sessions in cinemas or planetariums, children's conferences with question cards for completion at 'bases' to be found treasure-hunt style, quarterly discussion groups with government ministers, and weekly questions sent out to the membership of our own mobile text and email consultation panel.

4.3   Children in care go through experiences and events that do not impact on other children's lives; they go through processes of entering care and leaving care, separation from family and friends, including siblings, probably moving to live in different placements during their time in care, often at short notice, their lives are subject to statutory care plans, social workers and review meetings, and they have greater acquaintance than most children with inspectors, complaints procedures and court proceedings. All of these involve various intended, actual and perceived timescales for the children involved.

KEY CHILDREN'S VIEWS ON CARE

4.4   As background to discussion of children's views on timescales in care, it may be helpful to set out a synopsis of the headline views of children on care policy and practice generally, derived from consultations to ascertain children's views over the past decade. The list of ten top and frequent children's policy requests is:

- Counter bullying.

- Ensure children actually receive what the law entitles them to receive.

- Ask and take notice of children's views according to their understanding rather than their age.

- Keep information about children confidential, and only share their information on a strict need to know basis.

- Only change a child's placement in their own best interests.

- Have a choice of placements each time a child has to move in care, introduce them to new placements gradually, monitor how they settle, and have a backup placement in case it doesn't work out.

- Make decisions for each child as an individual, not according to what you believe is 'generally best for children'.

- Do not unnecessarily separate siblings.

- Keep children informed of what is happening and what is expected to happen.

- Give children an effective and accessible means to challenge or appeal decisions about them.

4.5   Overall, children in care do not see their care experience as negative – indeed, 91% of children in the national Care Monitor Survey in 2013[1] rated their care as good or very good. But concerns over timescales and experience of the major impact the passage of time can have on issues such as family contact feature frequently in the views and experiences children express about entering, being in and leaving care.

ENTERING CARE

4.6   We have regularly monitored children's views of the timescales around coming into care. According to the Care Monitor,[2] 71% of children in care thought, looking back, that coming into care was right for them at the time. Importantly, this figure does not change significantly over time, and 72% continued to think that being in care was still right for them at the time of the 2013 survey.

---

[1]   Children's Care Monitor [2014].
[2]   Ibid.

4.7   Perception of the 'rightness' of being in care does however change over time from the point of entry into care. Children who had not wanted to come into care at the time were about twice as likely afterwards to think it had been right than that it had been wrong for them.[3]

4.8   The level of knowledge of why you are in care has changed over time. Children generally want to know why they are in care. Approximately seven out of ten children in care know why they had to come into care.[4] However, those who had been in care more than 6 years were less likely to know why they were in care: this information was less likely to be given only a few years ago than it is now (it is unlikely, given the personal significance and general wish to know amongst those in care, that children who had been told had simply forgotten again over time).

4.9   The point of time at which children entering care first met the key care professional of a social worker varies widely. There is apparently no fixed sequence of social work support, then assessment by a social worker involving the child, discussion of possible plans and placements, and support over the move to a first placement. Out of 50 children surveyed on this issue,[5] 16 had met a social worker weekly or more before coming into care, while 11 said they had only met a social worker once, and another 11 that they did not meet one until they had actually come into care. Fewer than half had been told how they could contact a social worker before they came into care.

4.10   Forty-three per cent thought that more support could have stopped them needing to come into care.[6] Thirty-six per cent thought that even if they and their families had been given more support, they would still have had to come into care.

4.11   On entering care, the child experiences a time of rapid and even sudden change. For their parents, even though change in their lives or ability to parent may be the key to eventual return of their child from care, the experience is one of slowing down of social care activity for them, and parents of children in care often describe very slow, if any, work or support towards the child's return.[7]

4.12   There are particular points in time as they progress through the care system that children consider they need extra advice and information. These are generally at times of major change; when first coming into care, when they are without a social worker or during a change of social worker, when changing placements, and when leaving care.

---

3   Before Care [2010].
4   Ibid; see also Children on the Edge of Care [2011]; Getting Advice [2010].
5   Before Care [2010.
6   Children on the Edge of Care [2011].
7   Parents on Council Care [2008].

PLACEMENT IN CARE

4.13 Eighty-three per cent of children in care in 2013 thought they were in the right placement for them.[8] Children often do move to live in more than one placement during their career in care.

4.14 In the 2013 Monitor Survey, 71% thought their last placement change had been in their best interests, 69% (a rising proportion) thought that the last time they changed schools because of a change of placements, this too had been in their best interests, socially or educationally. Professionals and politicians typically count changes of placement, and any consequential changes of school, as generally negative. They can be, but children's views are more nuanced and see placement and school changes as 'changeover times' that can be either positive or negative depending on the circumstances, needs and perceptions of the individual child.

4.15 The timing of placement change is seen by very many children in care as highly sensitive and often problematic. In the 2013 Monitor Survey, 41% of children who had moved placement reported that they had been given less than a week's notice that they were going to be moved. Being given good notice of moving to live somewhere new, other than in an extreme emergency, is a key timing element for most children in care. The timescale also needs to be sufficient to allow for consultation over the move and alternative future placements, provision of information between potential placement and child, and gradual introductions and trial visits before the final move.

4.16 According to the 2013 Monitor Survey, only 57% of children thought that they had been given enough information about their present placement before moving in, and only 54% had visited their present placement before they were moved in to live there. Only 21% said there had been a choice of more than one placement when they last moved.

4.17 There are then two key timescale issues in arriving at a new placement.[9] One is that you often have no time to settle before the placement decision is finalised. Children often wish for a backup placement as well, in case they don't settle in the first, but this is usually not available. The second issue is that on arrival you have a very short timescale in which to adjust to the expectations and 'house rules' of your new placement. These are often about things like whether you are allowed to get food from the fridge if you are hungry, whether you should or shouldn't flush the toilet at night, or whether you can have a shower when you want to without asking first. These rules differ from placement to placement – but getting them wrong could have major consequences in whether for example you were seen as considerate or not. You are rarely told about these things but have to discover them (or, embarrassingly, ask about them) in very short time.

---

[8]   Children's Care Monitor [2014].
[9]   Having Corporate Parents [2011].

4.18 There is a general professional aversion to placing a child at a significant distance from their home area. This is for many well founded. For some however distance is needed – because it places a travelling time barrier between the child and risks of abuse from people back at home, or from dangers and temptations of peer pressures there.[10] For a few children, the distance and travel time are critical to prevent them from simply running away from a placement back home to a family they have just been removed from.

4.19 Children, unlike the law, opted for time rather than distance or administrative area to define whether a placement is 'distant' from home. Their definition of a distant placement is one that is more than 2 hours' travel time away (the legal definition is based on administrative areas). The use of time to define distance is found elsewhere too – indeed, it is standard in astronomy.

4.20 One major type of placement for some in care is placement for adoption, which differs dramatically from the often changing placements while continuing to be in care in that it is intended to be permanent with new parents. The speed of adoption is something that has received major government attention, including recent legislative change, and on which we have secured children's own views and recommendations to feed in to the legislative process.[11]

4.21 In short, children generally consider that adoption takes too long, *but* the solution is not simply to increase its speed, but to dramatically improve the correlation of the speed and timescale of adoption with the needs of the individual child. Adoption should take the time it needs to take for the individual child, but not have any unnecessary delays or take longer than it needs to.

4.22 Alongside the message of reducing delay children want the message of not going so fast that decisions are made to 'get adopted quick' rather than 'get adopted right'. Many children stress the vital importance of taking the time to find the right adoptive parents for them, including switching to new adoptive parents if things are not working out right before the adoption is finalised, and including taking the time to try the very difficult task of finding an adoptive placement for siblings together to avoid their separation, so that this is at least properly tried even if it fails, and not dismissed in the interests of time. Children even advocate that if adoption with siblings is preferred, and proves not to be possible, there should be a break point in the adoption process for the whole adoption plan to be reviewed – to reconsider whether the priority is for one or more to be adopted even if separated, or for the siblings to be kept together.

4.23 Legislation has recently been passed allowing children to be placed with their potential adoptive parents as foster children first, while the adoption process is being pursued (albeit with the slight risk that the adoption might not

---

10   Changing Children's Homes [2013].
11   About Adoption [2006]; Adoption with Siblings and Contact with Parents [2012]; Changing Adoption: Adopted Children's Views [2013]; Improving Adoption and Permanent Placements [2013]; Adoption Breakdowns [2014].

be approved in the end). Importantly, the children's view of this and the legislators' view of this differ in terms of timescale intention. The legislative intention is to shorten the period the child has to wait, perhaps with other foster parents, before they can move in to their new adoptive family. The children's perception when we consulted them was that this 'fostering for adoption' extended the timescale for checking that the adoptive placement was the right one – that it positively constituted a 'trial run' of the adoption before it was finally decided.

4.24 A final cautionary note from children on adoption challenges the general professional view that adoption is an end point to uncertainty in the care system and the start point of the alternative chance of stable family life. In our consultations on adoption, children have stated clearly that although it may be the end of one time phase in their lives, it is also the start of another time period which can require continuing support and assistance over a long timescale.

ISSUES WHILE IN CARE

4.25 Being kept safe from harm is probably the highest aim of being in care. Children are clear that they need to know how to keep themselves safe, but have advised a very different timescale to the one they usually experience.[12] They have advised that very young children, while still usually accompanied everywhere by a caring adult, should be told in no uncertain terms exactly what dangers are around them, including details of abuse, and how to protect themselves from them – if this scares them, that is part of the point of driving their protection. An instance of knowledge early in childhood as an inoculation against falling foul of future risks as they grow and leave the immediate protection of trusted adults.

4.26 One timescale factor that many children report in care relates to behaviour and staff or carer response to it. We frequently hear of incidents where escalating difficult behaviour of a particular child leads to escalating staff reactions that result in violence on the part of the child and use of physical restraint by staff members.[13]

4.27 Children are very clear on the timescale issues here. They do not deny either that sometimes the behaviour of some children presents sufficient risk of injury to themselves or others, or risk of serious damage to property, to justify and indeed require use of physical restraint by staff. But they are all too aware that it is often a minor challenge or incident that develops over a short timescale into risk of violence or restraint – the escalation process. Children speak of the need to intervene to calm and de-escalate early enough in this 'vicious circle' timescale to prevent both violence risk and need for physical restraint – but that as time passes, this becomes increasingly difficult for either

---

[12] Safe From Harm [2004].
[13] Children's Views on Restraint [2004]; Children's Views on Restraint [2012].

child to achieve by calming themselves down and retaining self-control, or staff to achieve by backing off or using methods of diversion.

4.28 Children also speak of the longer timescale of escalation and use of restraint. The curtailment of the immediate incident by successful restraint is not the end of the matter. It is the end of the incident, but risks also being the start of a longer-run timescale of resentment and potential future retribution and damaged relationships.

4.29 Seventy-one per cent said they were usually or always told about major changes coming in their lives before they actually happened, but 9% that they were never or not usually told. A salutary timescale sequencing issue is that many have told us they wish to be kept informed of lack of progress in important matters, such as fortnightly, rather than being kept waiting in the dark until the final outcome is known and can be communicated to them, often weeks or months down the line.

4.30 A very common complaint of children in care is that they are not allowed to stay overnight for sleepovers with their friends, as most children and teenagers do – unless their friends' parents have first been police checked. This is (thanks to repeated government messages that this is not, and never has been, a requirement) a reducing concern – but it still prevents overnight sleepovers for many children in care. The issue is twofold – one of equity and one of timescale. The equity issue is that children in care are effectively discriminated against because other children can have sleepovers without their friends' parents being police checked. The timescale one is well summarised by the teenager who said 'by the time your carers have got hold of your social worker and they have arranged a police check, the sleepover has become a distant memory'.

4.31 One feature of being in care is that your personal information is often passed between many and successive professionals – you have a file about you and over time lots of people have open access to your file. Children have expressed the concern that over time your information becomes increasingly common knowledge, and there needs to be protection from this process by countermeasures such as stricter need to know rules.[14] There also needs to be recognition that once your information is 'out there', over time it can be passed on to second and third hands without your knowledge. The main concern at this is not just a wish for protection of privacy as a principle, but that information becomes degraded over time. It can accumulate errors and become outdated if not regularly updated.

4.32 Another concern of children at the holding of information over long timescales is that of erosion of even the best security measures. As time passes, the risks of access being achieved by hacking increases (and children are very

---

[14] Passing It On [2006]; Children's Consultation on the Children's Index [2007]; Making Contact Point Work [2007].

aware that there is an illicit interest out there in securing information about themselves as vulnerable children), but more mundanely and probably, security measures such as keys and passwords get diluted as people like social workers and administrators pass them to successors, write them down in various places, or lend them to others to use on their behalf or while they are away.

4.33 Bullying is an issue for children in many settings, not only in care. Consulting children in care or living away from home,[15] we defined bullying more by frequency than content, but then asked what comprised the bullying.

4.34 Nine per cent of children reported being bullied often or always, 29% that they were being bullied sometimes, often or always, and 52% that they were never bullied. The most common form of bullying was teasing or name-calling, followed by being left out of things, rumours being spread about you, being threatened, being treated unfairly, being hit or physically hurt, being bullied through a mobile or computer, and having property taken or damaged. Sixteen per cent of those in care said they were bullied for being in care.

4.35 Timescale however came in to the children's accounts of bullying. Children themselves defined bullying not only in terms of severity or nature, but also in terms of frequency over time. Something that is an extra-ordinary incident, although severe, may not be seen as bullying – but something, even less severe, that is persistent over time is much more likely to be seen as bullying. Similarly, time comes in to protecting oneself against bullying too. One is vulnerable to bullying when one is new and so has not been any time with a group, but then one is less vulnerable if one (a) blends in and (b) secures membership of a protective peer group in sufficient time to terminate or pre-empt initial vulnerability.

4.36 A further issue involving key timescales is that of running away from care. In two consultations with children, many of whom had themselves run from care and returned or been returned,[16] we heard that there are four main categories of running away: running off simply to have fun somewhere with the intention of returning later; running *from* problems or relationships one cannot stand where one is living; running *to* be somewhere or with someone one wants to be (often home to a birth parent); and being classified as running away when one is 'absent without leave' such as staying out later than allowed. Timescales are critical here. The first and last of these categories involve an intended, closed and short timescale, with the intention always of returning at a particular time to end the running episode. The third also involves an intended, short and closed timescale although differs in that the time 'on the run' is interpreted very differently by the child and by staff. For the child, the time ends when they arrive with the person or in the place they were going to. For the staff member, the time 'on the run' continues until they are returned to where they are supposed to be.

---

[15] Children on Bullying [2008].
[16] Running Away [2006]; Running Away [2012].

4.37   The second category of running away however is the most dangerous, because it often involves a timescale that has no intended end. The child is just running, and often has no intended timescale for returning. They may simply be putting time and distance between them and where they are running from, often at a point of crisis, often without any plan of time or place, and thus incurring great risks of exploitation or falling into crime or homelessness.

REVIEWS AND SOCIAL WORKER CONTACT

4.38   The social worker is the key decision-maker and support figure for a child in care. A major concern of children is that their social workers however are not constant over time, and do not always fit their timescales as a child.[17] Social workers often change as one leaves and another arrives, breaking the trust and relationships that have built up over time and often losing the understanding and information that have built up too.

4.39   Social workers are also often able to reach a reasonable way ahead for a child which does not last for the time it takes to implement, because they are overruled, either by general policies (for example, limiting placements out of the authority's area) or by more senior staff in control of the necessary finances (but often without any personal knowledge or contact with the child).

4.40   Even a good social worker is often difficult to get hold of to the timescale of a child. Often a child will wish to talk something through with their social worker when it first arises, but find their social worker is preoccupied with serious cases and crises, or that messages are not returned. Time and escalation into a crisis are the factors that eventually command immediate attention by a social worker. Children are very understanding of the pressures on social workers, but they wish they could have discussion and advice early in the timescale of an escalating problem or concern.

4.41   Sixty-one per cent of those in care reported that their social worker or other caseworker visited them at least once every 6 weeks. When consulted on proposed government changes to the minimum statutory frequency of social worker visiting, children advised that the proposed 6-monthly frequency was insufficient and that the maximum time lapse between visits should be reduced.[18]

4.42   Sixty-six per cent of children in care knew they had a care plan, and of those 75% knew what was in it, 72% agreed with it, and 63% had a say in what it said. Eighty-three per cent said their care plan was being kept to. Sixty-eight per cent thought their current placement would be permanent until they left care.

---

[17]   About Social Workers [2006].
[18]   Planning, Placement and Review [2010].

4.43 A key point raised by children on statutory care reviews is that the timing of any change of placement should be linked to a review, so that other than in genuine emergency no placement could be changed without first being agreed at a review meeting.[19] Children then went further and proposed that the timing of reviews should be improved so that in addition to regular reviews at a legal frequency, children in care themselves should have the right to require a review to be convened at any time during their care to discuss and if needs be amend their plans and any intended change of placement.[20] Both these proposals from children have now been incorporated into law.

KEEPING AND LOSING CONTACT WITH FAMILY AND FRIENDS

4.44 Children consulted over children's rights wished to add a new right to the United Nations Convention on the Rights of the Child. At priority number nine in their top ten rights, they wanted to add a right 'to keep in touch with my parents, grandparents, brothers and sisters if I want to and they want to, wherever we all live'.[21]

4.45 Seventy-one per cent of children in care who also had a brother or sister in care said they had been separated from one or more of those brothers or sisters by being put in different placements.[22]

4.46 Contact with family (both parents and siblings) and friends is often lost as time passes.[23] Loss of contact appears to be a function of time since last being together, and children frequently attribute loss of contact to passage of time alone. There are other points in time that can sever or further erode contacts, principally a move to a new placement, the adoption of a brother or sister, or the arrival of a new partner with a parent where the child and their parent's new partner do not get on.

4.47 On loss of contact with time, we found half the children in care we consulted had at least monthly contact with their birth mother, but 18% had lost all contact with her. Twenty-three per cent had at least monthly contact with their birth father, while 46% had lost all contact with him. Fifty-six per cent had contact with a brother or sister at least once a month, and 36% had at least monthly contact with a relative other than a parent, brother or sister.

---

[19] Planning, Placement and Review [2010].
[20] Changing Children's Homes [2013].
[21] The United Nations Convention on the Rights of the Child: How Children Say the UK is Doing [2014].
[22] Children's Care Monitor [2014].
[23] Keeping in Touch [2009]; Adoption with Siblings and Contact with Parents [2012].

4.48 Thirty-five per cent had lost all contact with friends they had before coming into care, while 14% had at least monthly contact with a friend they had made in an earlier placement.

4.49 Few kept in regular contact with previous carers: 16% (mainly foster children) had at least monthly contact with a previous carer.

4.50 Contact can be of many sorts – including visits, telephone, email, networking sites, keeping up to date with major family news, and exchange of photographs.

4.51 Renewal of contact after it has been lost becomes increasingly difficult with the passage of time since last contact, and meeting people after losing contact can be awkward and needs to be gradual over time. Keeping at least some contact kept open the option of more contact again when the young person was older. Contact with parents keeps you in touch with your own culture and family history and can be a route to information and contact with brothers and sisters.[24] The children asked wished contact to depend on whether both the child and the parents want to stay in touch – but even if they don't, the option of renewing contact in the future should be kept open, to counter the impact of passage of time.

4.52 A significant conclusion is that effort is needed to maintain appropriate contact simply to counter the erosion of contact as time passes.

COMPLAINTS PROCESSES

4.53 Twenty-three per cent of children told us they had made a complaint at some time. Sixty-one per cent thought the last complaint they had made had been sorted out fairly (this percentage is rising), but 16% had not been told the outcome of their last complaint.[25] So for the child, making a complaint can have no end-point in time. Once a complaint has been made, the person deciding on any action in response should always go back to the child after any complaint or suggestion, to tell them the results, what had been decided, and why.

4.54 The children's view was that complaints should be sorted out as quickly as possible, but it is not right to set standard timescales for all complaints. Some need longer than others to sort out properly.

4.55 Children wish to be kept informed of progress (or lack of it) regularly during the time a complaint is being considered. Talking with children, there is almost a rule that during the time something is being considered or a process is under way, the standard interval for information updates should be fortnightly.

---

[24] Adoption with Siblings and Contact with Parents [2012].
[25] Getting the Best from Complaints [2005]; Young People's Views on Complaints and Advocacy [2012].

4.56 At the end of the process, it is then important to check up on what has changed. An additional point on complaints timings is that many children do not wish to progress straight into using a complaints process, but wish to have the chance to talk things over with an adult they trust before deciding whether or not to make a complaint.

4.57 Children generally opposed the idea of complaints procedures including a deadline within which a complaint has to be made about an event. Children might not have been able to make a complaint at the time, if they did not feel confident enough, or if they were still with the same carers so felt unable to complain about them. A complaint becomes easier to make after time and immediate care arrangements have moved on.

4.58 Most children agreed that a decision should be stopped if the child made a complaint, as long as this would not leave the child in a worse or dangerous situation. It was especially important that if a child complained about being moved from their placement, they should not be moved until that complaint had been sorted out, as long as they were safe where they were.

4.59 Some children were concerned that once you had made a complaint, the process and timing took on a life of their own – you lost control of what happened next, and the results could be very different from what you expected. Sometimes nothing happens with a complaint until it has been moved on up the procedure, and it is usually best to try to get things sorted out informally if you can without making a formal complaint. We heard that sometimes you have to make a problem get worse before a complaint about it will be taken seriously. And some children will do something drastic – like running away – if a complaint doesn't sort a problem out for them.

4.60 Although it is easy to consider the outcome of a complaints process as its end, there are subsequent consequences. Just over a third of the children we consulted said that their last complaint had made things either a bit better or much better for them. But over a quarter said that it had made things either a bit worse or much worse for them. Making a complaint was likely to make a difference, but was only slightly more likely to make things better than worse.

LEAVING CARE

4.61 Children become adults at the age of 18. For those in care, this also means the ending of their status as children in care, and consequentially the ending of their life in a children's home or foster home and the abrupt start of independent adult life – far earlier and more abruptly than happens for the majority of those not in care, and without the facility most of their peers outside care have to leave and return once or more times as they adjust to living independently from home.

4.62 For children in care, life plans can exist formally, extending over a considerable time ahead. In our consultations we found children to have very clear perceptions of what they expected to happen in their future, when, and dependent on what. Just over three quarters of the children knew what their care plan said about whether or not they would be returning to their family.[26] One in three did not know when they would be likely to leave care again, but most expected to be staying in care for at least 2 years. One in three thought they would be in care for less than 6 months. The top two determinants of the timing of leaving care were seen as being when things had been sorted out at home, and when the young person became 18.

4.63 Nine out of 10 children had a clear view on what the long-term goal for them should be. Thirty-four per cent thought the best thing for them was to stay in care, and in the placement they were in. Another 14% thought they should stay in care, but move to a different placement. Forty per cent thought they should now leave care, but fewer than half of these thought they should go back to their birth parents. Nineteen per cent of the children thought they should leave care and go back to live with their birth parents now. Another 5% thought it would be right to go back to their birth family some time in the next year. Another 19% thought they would one day be able to go back to live with their birth family, but only after things had been sorted out at home. Fifteen per cent thought they might be able to return to their birth family when they were much older.[27]

4.64 Going back home should not be sudden but gradual, done cautiously and with support to children in getting to know their parents again. Going back home will always bring back underlying issues for both children and parents, and these need to be thought about and dealt with.[28]

4.65 One of the main concerns of foster children is of what will happen when they leave their foster home, which they understand they have to do at 18.[29] Many supported the recent change in the law to allow foster children to remain (and be financially supported) with their foster carers as adults up to the age of 21, if they and their former carers wish. For many, this removes the endpoint of foster care placement from the end of legal childhood.

4.66 For those living in secure units, for either welfare reasons or following offending, the timescales of leaving the unit have a special significance.[30] Those in security often speak in terms of 'time left to serve' and of looking forward to returning to family, freedoms and friends. But they also talk of their time in security as 'time out' from the dangers and threats of peer pressures and risks of reoffending or risks to their own safety or welfare. Leaving security is seen by many as the ending of safer protected time, albeit at the expense of losses of

---

[26] Before Care [2010].
[27] Young People's Views on Leaving Care [2006]; After Care [2012].
[28] Children on the Edge of Care [2011].
[29] Being Fostered [2005]; Children's Views on Fostering [2012].
[30] Life in Secure Care [2009].

freedom and contacts with family and friends, and the restarting of a time of reintroduction of risks to oneself from others and of risking 'getting back to my old ways'.

4.67 Out of those asked, four out of 10 had wanted to leave care at the time they did leave – and another four out of 10 had not wanted to leave when they did. Only a quarter thought that, looking back, they had left care at the right time. Forty-six per cent thought they had left care too early, and only 17% that they should have left care earlier.

4.68 The time of leaving a care or residential education environment is a life watershed. Young people have had a great deal done for them. Their main needs are met: items they need are provided, they are kept safe, and there are things to do with friends around. When they leave, they lose all this support and structure, and have to cope for themselves and deal with basic things that they had always been able to take for granted before. For those leaving care, boarding or residential college, future independent adult life is a daunting unknown.[31]

HEALTH CARE

4.69 Children advising us on health matters made three related timescale points.[32] First, that in their experience, when there was no emergency, they had had to wait too long to get a doctor's or hospital appointment. Secondly, when they went for a doctor's or hospital appointment, they usually experienced long delays before actually being seen, regardless of the stated time of their appointment. But thirdly, when they were eventually seen, the time actually in the appointment was too short, and did not allow sufficient time to ask everything they had wanted to ask, or sometimes to understand what had been said to them. They wanted shorter waits to get an appointment, shorter time in waiting rooms, and longer appointments.

4.70 An interesting timescale view from children in care is that routine health checkups while in care are too widely spaced apart at once a year, and should be more frequent.[33]

INSPECTION

4.71 Settings in which children in care are placed, such as children's homes and residential special schools, are subject to regular statutory inspection, previously by a series of welfare inspectorates, currently by Ofsted. Formally, inspection is an assessment of welfare provision at a point in time – the time of inspection, which is based on records and evidence of past practice and events,

---

[31] Learning Independence [2012].
[32] Children's Views on Guidance for Doctors [2012].
[33] Planning, Placement and Reviews [2010].

observation of the present, and is intended to have predictive value in assessing future risk and assuring future welfare. Children have some very specific takes on the timescales of inspection.

4.72 These come from a series of consultations and children's audits of the inspection process carried out by the Office of the Children's Rights Director.[34]

4.73 Children generally advocated unannounced (or 'surprise') inspections, to ensure that the timescale of the inspection does not include preparation time that may present a picture of the establishment to the inspectors that is not how things usually are. Twenty-six per cent of children we surveyed in 2011 said they had been told to prepare things for the inspectors, mainly by tidying things up.

4.74 Children's perception was that during the inspection time itself, inspectors tended to listen more to staff interpretations of events than to children's, and to spend more time looking at records than observing current experience of children. Children wanted a sequence of inspectors first asking children for their observations and experiences, then corroborating those against observation, with staff interviews and study of records, and finally re-checking conclusions with children as the consumers of the welfare provision of the establishment.

4.75 While inspectors may wish to focus on the long term performance of an establishment, children often saw inspectors visiting as opportunity to raise current personal concerns. Children were also often less sure of the long term purpose of an inspection, and sometimes saw the event as a short term need to help their home or school 'pass' its inspection, akin to helping their team to win a competitive event.

4.76 On timing of inspections, children were against the trend towards 'proportionate' inspection, where frequency is reduced if all has previously been found well, and increased if problems have been identified by inspectors. They wanted minimum frequencies of inspection maintained, with the timing unrelated to previous findings, though agreeing that additional inspection work should be carried out where problems had been found or were reported.

4.77 For establishments themselves, and the readers of inspection reports (though not necessarily for inspectors or inspectorates themselves), the inspection report is the culmination of an inspection and the ending of an inspection round. For children the timescale runs beyond the inspection report and focuses on whether needed change is triggered and actually occurs following the inspection and reporting time. They focus more strongly than inspectorates on the importance of the post inspection period, and consistently advocate routine follow up inspections.

---

[34]   The Children's View of Inspection [2005]; Does Inspection Make a Difference? [2005]; Sorting Out Inspection [2005]; A Pilot for a Children's Audit of Inspection [2008]; Social Care Inspection: the Children's Audit [2011].

APPEARANCE IN COURT

4.78 We consulted children to input their views to a government review of the family justice system.[35]

4.79 Children wanted courts to hear and take account of their views, but time and situational pressures often militated against this. Most who had been involved in a court said they hadn't been able to get their views over to the court as they had wanted to. Some hadn't been given the chance, others had been too nervous to say what they wanted. Time in court was too short and daunting for many to feel able to get their views over. The time before the attendance usually included anxiety that they would not be able to make good use of their 'one shot chance' to convey their views. The time after a court appearance was often characterised by regret and frustration that they had not done so competently, and anxiety that this one point in time event would now determine their long-term futures.

4.80 Children also had a clear view on the timescale and time limits for completion of family court cases. Half thought that the then proposed time limit of 6 months for completing a case was too long.

4.81 Children we consulted were concerned that not only had they experienced a one time chance to get their views over, but that the involvement of decision makers in courts ended once the case had finished. They never got feedback on how their decisions had turned out for the child whose lives they had decided. Children in our consultation proposed to the Family Justice Review that the justice system should always check up on what had happened to each child after a court had decided their future. This was a proposal taken up by the Review, and later accepted by the government for a pilot trial. Again, the post event time has a higher significance for children than the event itself in which professionals have invested their time.

4.82 Finally in relation to family justice, children consulted thought that when parents split up, a lasting decision should be made by each parent on whether or not they were continuing to be part of their child's life for the long term, taking the child's wishes and interests into account. In this, parents should have to decide whether or not they want to stay firmly part of the child's life, and should not be allowed to drift in and out of the child's life when they feel like it.

CONCLUSION AND LAST WORD

4.83 From our consultations, children have a clear view of how long things should take, and in what sequence they should happen. They also have a clear and long term view of plans for their future. But they can be frustrated by a number of timescale factors: often, major life changes are imposed with far less notice and preparation than they want; sometimes support or information are

---

[35] Children on Family Justice [2011]; Family Justice Review: the Children's Verdict [2011].

not available in advance of changes happening; often professional help comes late in a sequence and only when a crisis has developed; time can exert its own negative influences – in the short term through the escalation of behaviour into violence and restraint, and in the longer term in the erosion of family contact with the passage of time; and sometimes professionals perceive issues as ending in resolution when children perceive them as changes of time phase in life rather than resolutions or endings, as with completion of a complaint, or the passage of an adoption order.

4.84 The last word in this chapter goes to a young person looking to his past and his future from his perspective in care:

> 'I want to be free of my past, better than my present, and always ambitious for my future. The only thing that can help me get there is funding and my own willpower.'

CHAPTER 5

PARENTS' CAPACITY TO CHANGE AND THE IMPACT UPON THE CHILD IN SCHOOL

Louise Michelle Bombér

INTRODUCTION

5.1   It's all too easy to overlook the issues arising concerning education when thinking about the capacity of a parent to change, in the timescales of the child. To best do this we need to become travelling companions, willing to consider what these particular children may have experienced; to regard the impact of this upon his/her well-being, development, functioning, and learning capacities; and to reflect upon what is actually needed in order for them to make the most out of education.

5.2   The children we are considering in the court arena have usually experienced extraordinary stress in their lives. As children are not designed to tolerate this high level of stress in their hearts, minds, and bodies we now see many of them compromised in many areas developmentally in school. (The trauma tree included in this chapter will support us to assess the possible vulnerabilities around for these children in the school context.) I will be focussing mainly on their executive functioning, affect regulation, and psychological development, as well as thinking about how developmental vulnerabilities in these areas can disrupt their learning capacities and the possibility of being able to make the most of all that education can offer in its fullest sense.

5.3   Many of these children will have experienced intense internal and external pain, vulnerability, humiliation, and intimacy betrayal at the hands of their parent. These children are then wired for stress with a faulty alarm system that can become activated by numerous internal and external stress triggers as a result of these traumatic experiences. This is the inherent legacy for those children who have lived through a parent's own vulnerabilities, inadequacies, misuse of power, authority, and control. Sometimes these affects are for life, especially where education is concerned. Decisions made during these formative school years can either lead to breakdown or breakthrough for the child.

Important questions need to be asked. Discernment and wisdom are needed in order for us, the grown-ups, to make the right choices, particularly around timings.

5.4   I will consider the power relationships have in a child's life during his or her formative school years and think about the necessity of the exploratory system being switched on for learning. I will also reflect on the concept of time, necessary developmental milestones, the ordinary transitions in school life, and the significance of permanency. I will also consider how the child's concept of self can seriously impede his/her education and how being able to self-regulate can play such a significant part in managing the low-level stressors inherent in 'learning' and in navigating their way through the school context.

5.5   Relational traumas and losses significantly compromise a child's well-being, development, functioning, and learning capacities in the educational context. These issues need to be carefully considered before making choices that will affect a child or young person's educational journey.

THE DEMANDS OF SCHOOL

The big ask ...

5.6   There are extensive demands in the school environment. We tend to overlook this as most children seem to manage them relatively well, leaving school with a sense of purpose and destiny concerning their futures. These children have usually experienced consistent good enough care before and during their school years which has helped form a healthy attachment system necessary to be able to optimise their exploratory system – the system in each one of us concerned with curiosity, exploration, and taking risks necessary in learning. (We will explore this more later.) Having this kind of start means that they will usually have a robust sense of self, with enough self-confidence and self-worth about who they are and their capabilities, together with well-developed internal controls, to be aware of and to be able to manage differing states, sensations, and feelings – both significant within the school context.

5.7   There are 12 descriptors that I consider key for children in order for them to make the most of all the opportunities afforded them within education. From my descriptors you will find some examples to illustrate what they would have needed to have experienced together with their parent first, their primary attachment figure, to be able to step up to the demands of the school context.

5.8   These children need to be able to:

- Separate from their parent, and join together and connect with teaching staff. They therefore need to have experienced a relatively secure attachment together with their parent in order to be able to do this.

- Relinquish control to the teaching staff as they engage the child in the process of learning. They therefore need to have experienced sufficient safety, security and stability around their parent so that they can trust the adults' motives and intentions in the school context. Children have a template for how to relate to adults based on their experiences with their parents, because humans are evidence-seeking creatures.

- Take the risks required in learning. There are many opportunities to venture into the unfamiliar and unknown, as well as many opportunities to make mistakes. They therefore need to have experienced their parent supporting them to feel confident about themselves through many connecting experiences.

- Manage stress, as there are many low-level stressors in school. For example, making a mistake, taking a risk by learning, falling over, forgetting equipment, not understanding something, conflict, misattunement, losing a friend, coping with another's upset. They therefore need to have experienced low-level stressors at home that have been co-regulated by their parent. They also need to have experienced their parent managing their own stress through co-modelling in order to have learned how to manage stress.

- Have a concept of where they are in time and space so that they can make sense of the school system. The child needs to have experienced their parent being predictable and providing structure in the form of established, consistent routines.

- Be flexible in their thinking so that they can manage the unexpected or unplanned changes that are inevitable in everyday school life. For example the supply teacher due to the teacher being off sick; having to stay inside at play as it is raining outside; or discovering that a lesson has had to be moved because the hall is not free. They therefore need to have opportunities to experience their parent adapting and being flexible themselves through co-modelling. They need to have learned how to manage disappointment by their parent providing comfort and understanding at these times.

- Manage expected and planned changes, for example moving from part-time to full-time school, reception to Year One, infants to juniors, juniors to secondary, secondary to college; from teacher to teacher, room to room, teaching style to teaching style. They therefore need to have experienced relative stability and security at home, and a parent making sense of and processing everyday changes together with them so that they are not phased when change inevitably comes.

- Be organised as school is busy and fast paced. There is much National Curriculum content to be covered between the hours of 9am and 3pm every day during term time from age 4 onwards. There is equipment to remember and coursework to be completed, as well as homework to be delivered on time. They therefore need to have experienced lots of structure and supervision at home to support and teach them this and to have watched a parent modelling organisation to them.

- Have the capacity for short-term/working memory as there is much to remember during an ordinary school day. The short-term memory is needed for both storage and retrieval. They therefore need to have experienced safety, security and stability at home with their parent in order to be freed up enough to use this well. If they are experiencing calm and happiness during their childhood their minds are capable of focussing on the present, not being preoccupied with other matters.

- Inhibit their impulses and behaviours as there will be social expectations in school for the benefit of everyone's learning. They therefore need to have experienced lots of connection, structure and supervision back at home with their parent so that they have a healthy self-awareness and can use self-control. Again this is learned through countless experiences with their parent – their primary attachment figure.

- Relate well – making and maintaining friendships and relationships as school is very much a relational community. Children won't be able to optimise their time at school being or feeling isolated. They therefore need to have been encouraged and supported with social skills by their parent through experiences with them, their siblings, and peers, and by observing their parents getting on with others. They will also need to have experienced enough stability in a familiar context in order for relationships to be enabled to mature and deepen.

- Have hope in order to aspire, dream, and have a sense of future. They therefore need to have experienced fun, playfulness, laughter, and safety together with their parent so that they are freed up enough to be able to do this. A happy childhood means that children are able to anticipate and imagine their futures in a positive way.

5.9   When we start to consider the links between home and school in this way we start to realise the significance of our decisions made in court arenas during the formative school years. We sometimes forget how much is required for a child to be in a position to be able to settle to learn in the school context. The impact on education is often overlooked. Education has the capacity to offer new opportunities and possibilities to all, regardless of background, but sensitivities and vulnerabilities could mean these opportunities and possibilities could be easily sabotaged by what is going on in the home context.

A RELATIONAL APPROACH

Every relationship has the power to confirm or challenge all that's gone on before ...

5.10   Children and young people being considered in the court arena have usually experienced significant relational poverty and relational wounds in their short lives to date – usually at the hands of family members. Because they have been wounded within relationship it makes sense that healthy, appropriate and sustained relationships are the vehicle towards adaption and recovery. For many of these children and young people school provides the opportunity for this second chance learning that they need. For some this will be the only opportunity to come into contact with those who have the capacity to provide this. This means that **all** relationships, including those with midday supervisors, teaching assistants, mentors, form tutors, teachers, heads of year, are going to need to be considered as significant for these children. We need to consider that these possible significant others may be in the process of providing this type of relationship for a child. This may involve becoming an additional attachment figure. Children and young people are in education for a big percentage of their lives between the ages of 4 and 18, so these relationships have the capacity to be influential, in some cases even life-changing. There is the possibility of being in relationship with a member of staff for 6 years during the primary phase and again for 6 years during the secondary phase. Classroom observations by those who have been therapeutically trained are key, as are discussions with the child and familiar staff because it is important that we protect and honour special relationships for this child or young person. For sound mental health we need to have experienced at least one person getting alongside us, rooting for us, believing in us. These individual members of staff could contribute much to the life of a child.

5.11   Their early experiences have led to distrust, especially of adults, and yet in the school context a pupil is expected to relinquish control and follow the lead of grown-ups! In secondary this can include 12–15 members of staff. What a big ask! We need to give them opportunity to get attached to those who are significant at school. For many children and young people living in troubled contexts school and in particular school staff become their secure base. It is there, through their relational experiences with key staff, that they experience (sometimes for the first time) safety, security, and stability. Permanency within healthy and appropriate contexts such as foster care, adoption, and school allows the child or young person to start practising relative dependency in a healthy way – something that is usually quite alien to their experience. Building trust takes time, as I'm sure you can appreciate.

5.12   It has been my experience that those who have experienced extraordinary stress in early relationships with family members need at least 18 months of experiencing the permanency of at least one attachment figure in order to start relaxing into their contexts and making the most of the opportunities afforded them. We have observed how these pupils can suddenly make significant progress in both their overall development and learning after this period of time. If permanency continues to be experienced for up to 36 months we see sustained developmental movement and the beginnings of safety, security and stability being internalised. This experience of permanency is therefore seen as pivotal in the life of a child or young person in the school context.

5.13   So with this in mind we cannot afford to think only about the possibility of a home placement changing but also about the implications if the school placement was to change too. Are significant relationships present there? What purpose do they serve? Is there any way that the school placement could be enabled to continue? How can we honour and protect the significant relationships made there? If both home and school placements must change what preparation work needs to happen in order to help strengthen the child's resilience? How can follow up work be instigated? How can relationships be honoured and relational capacities strengthened? How can the child's grieving be supported?

5.14 Let's now consider some of the different areas that are likely to be compromised due to the impact of relational traumas and losses upon a child's safety, security, and stability. I will reflect upon how this impacts their exploratory system and children's concept of time and permanency, and think through how the necessary developmental milestones areas are adversely affected and how transitions become stress-inducing for these children. The development of their concept of self and their regulatory capacity will then be considered, and finally, their social development and behaviour.

THE EXPLORATORY SYSTEM

Emotional growth and well-being has a direct correlation to learning

5.15 We can give a parent countless opportunities to 'get it right' whilst at the same time denying a child or young person the security, stability, and safety that they need in order to settle to learn. There is a human cost to waiting. Unless a child or young person's attachment system is attended to sufficiently, their exploratory system cannot be optimised. The attachment system is a primal system in each one of us that is concerned with safety, security, and stability. The exploratory system in each of us allows curiosity, exploration, and the risk-taking necessary in learning. The attachment system is a primal system always overriding the exploratory system if it goes unnoticed or if it is not attended to sufficiently. If the attachment system is attended to well then watch the pupil thrive by their exploratory system coming online fully! If this system isn't attended to adequately then these pupils can remain stuck developmentally, taking over the caregiving role of their attachment system themselves. Those of us who work in schools are sadly too familiar with the phrase 'not reaching their potential yet ... emotional factors seem to be getting in the way' on their school reports. This reflects their preoccupation with matters to do with safety, security, and stability.

5.16 As school staff we tend to observe pseudo-independent behaviours as these children attempt to meet their own needs in whatever way seems to give some type of relief, even if it is interpreted as inappropriate or unhealthy to onlookers. What other option do they have? They learn quickly not to depend upon grown-ups, and yet their minds, bodies, hearts and souls are not designed to manage this type of responsibility.

5.17 If we don't pay attention to the attachment system of a child or young person there can be more extreme implications for school life. Hypervigilance, over-reactive responses, and an inability to read the motives and intentions of others can leave them so preoccupied that there is no capacity left to focus on a learning task, lesson content, the national curriculum. Soon these pupils are often so stressed that internal alarms can go off at any time in response to usual low-level stressors, often in a very exaggerated way. This is due to having a faulty alarm system created by living with extraordinary stress back at home. Fight, flight, or freeze responses are commonplace when experiencing extraordinary stress. What other option does a human being have, especially a young one? This is an adaptive response in a traumatic context, but obviously a maladaptive response in the healthy secure context of school. It takes a long, long time for the body, mind, heart, and soul to catch up with the reality of the 'here and now' after experiencing extraordinary stress as a result of relational trauma or loss.

5.18   These pupils are unable to manage stress on their own and so often much staff input is required – wondering aloud, commentating, and soothing strategies such as sensory breaks to relieve the pressure of anxiety, shame, and stress is commonplace. Recovery time can take hours, days, or weeks as many school staff will be aware. Most senior managers spend a lot of time in school at present dealing with the aftermath of this build-up of tension and stress upon the child. These pupils therefore get left behind in terms of their work and experiences together with their peers. This exacerbates an already poor view of themselves and others. Many lose hope and sink into despair. When this happens education becomes more and more out of reach and can then start to be viewed by the pupil as a pointless activity. We are at risk of losing many along the way through exclusion, school refusal, criminal activity, drugs, alcohol, self-harm, knife crime, mental distress, and even suicide. The cost of this is severe on both individuals and the community at large.

THE CHILD'S CONCEPT OF TIME

The never ending story ...

Permanency

5.19   Weeks and months, even 1 or 2 years can go by as courts consider the best decisions for families. Many children are left in limbo, not understanding what is going on or what could happen. A day in the life of a child can be experienced by a child or young person as an eternity. Consider your own childhood where days went on and on, and you could never imagine growing old! Do you remember your summer holidays as a child? Time stretched on and on and on during lazy days. You could pack so much in. Now, older, time speeds by so, so fast. We often catch ourselves saying 'I can't believe it's already December'. Not so in the life of a child. Their perception is so different to ours. Our timescales are considerably different. Being in limbo for such a long time can really unsettle children. They can become so preoccupied that their education becomes severely disrupted. Who could therefore get alongside them to support them to tolerate this uncertainty? Who is skilled up to pass on strategies for managing the 'not knowing'. From experience education staff are too aware that many professionals shy away from these difficult conversations with children as they become uncomfortable and distressed themselves. These children are not stupid, they do have an idea of what is going on as they have been experiencing life with mum or dad, so they know the score. Who is going to be their travelling companion, opening up what these children already know and filling in the gaps? Yes, these children will hurt but what could they do to manage this hurt whilst this process continues on as the pain experienced now will not last forever.

5.20 It is hard to put ourselves into the shoes of children and young people, especially when it comes to perception. We tend to rush about, overlooking detail, but a child notices every detail. They watch – they are always watching. They notice far more than we ever do. They are designed that way. There is so much for them to take in and process, and they do: colours, textures, shapes, designs, faces, body language, atmospheres, social meanings. Every second they are laying down new memories, new learning. Young brains are adapting constantly in order to be able to live in whatever home context they have been born into. The brain wires up on a 'use it or lose it' basis. Neural pathways are experience dependent. Children develop strong neural pathways that are relevant and necessary for their own context. This is why in our schools that despite the same stimuli children respond in such different ways. Those with rich, healthy relational experiences have more dense networks in their brains. Flexibility comes with complexity, which means they are able to be more flexible in their thinking. Children are born open to learning and with this great gift comes great vulnerability, in the wrong hands.

5.21 We can add to this an understanding of time that is already compromised by the relational wounds children have experienced. For example so many find it hard to understand where they are within time and space during the course of a day, never mind a week or a month. With this in mind many children and young people are left confused and disorientated by decisions made in 'adult time'. By the time we reach our verdict so much has happened in a child's week or month. Who will take the time to explain in a way that the child will understand? Who will be brave enough to stay connected to the child despite difficult, painful feelings when choices are made that the child doesn't understand or want to hear? These children need our time. We, as grown-ups, have taken the time we have needed in order to consider the best choice for this child. Now it is our responsibility to give the child the time they need in order to make sense of that choice. If done well troubled children have the opportunity to move forwards. If done badly these troubled children can fragment and break down.

PROCESSING TRANSITION

What's happening next?

5.22 The nervous system is activated when we experience any kind of transition. For children who have experienced instability in their lives every change unsettles and alarms them, even those changes we might consider minor. If we consider what children have lived to date we quickly realise that many have experienced powerlessness at the hands of adults. It is possible that parents have manipulated and controlled them for their own purposes. It is possible that adults have made decisions on their behalf. It is possible that they don't understand or want what is happening to them, even if we say it is in 'their best interests'.

5.23 As a result, these children can experience being 'out of control' during transitions. This is because they already feel that they have had no choice over what has happened to them – they were completely dependent on the adults around them as they were only children. As children, their only possible exit plan is to fight, flee, or freeze. Most young children choose the freeze option around their parent as this seems the safest choice, and an adaptive response to extraordinary stress. However, in another context, say school, when together with another adult any kind of transition can often trigger an over-reactive response from the child's stress system.

5.24 For children, powerlessness is very real. Surely this explains why as they get older they start to exert control themselves in whatever ways they can. Maybe by not writing. Maybe by refusing to co-operate. Maybe by choosing to run and not walk. Maybe by eating now not later. In schools we call this controlling behaviour. Yet many of us are far too aware that these children may now feel the desperate need to control whatever they can due to their experiences of powerlessness. This controlling behaviour disrupts their learning process and others' learning too: another legacy of the consequences of experiencing relational trauma and loss.

5.25 All of us know every transition has pros and cons. There is usually a mixture of feelings around with an intensity usually correlated to the significance of the transition. For a child with executive functioning difficulties who needs considerably more time than his/her peers to process change, transitions can be very difficult to manage. If moved too fast or not given enough support processing change these children are vulnerable to presenting with behavioural difficulties as they attempt to communicate their distress in the only way they know how – through their bodies.

THE IMPACT OF TRAUMA UPON DEVELOPMENT

5.26 So much seems to happen and be experienced in short bursts during childhood. From being in the womb the brain is growing at a rapid rate in the first early years and neural pathways are being laid down in response to experience. Childhood and adolescence is the time for negotiating developmental stages. Every stage has developmental milestones. These milestones are like building blocks and there are optimal times for particular developmental tasks to be optimised. For example think about all that should usually happen for a pupil at 5, 11 and 16. Home or school disruption can interfere with the necessary developmental tasks being negotiated at each stage and consolidated. However, if the child's basic needs for safety, security, and stability are not being met then this will significantly compromise development. This must all be weighed up to determine the best context for the child.

5.27 It is widely known now that children who are experiencing relational traumas and losses can become very stuck developmentally. It is as if the body, mind, heart, and spirit just shut down. Many of us are familiar with the term 'failure to thrive', but though this term is usually referred to in relation to the child's physical presentation it is also true in other areas of well-being too. I will never forget working with Danny who was 10 and yet seemed more like a 5- or 6-year old emotionally and socially. When I reflected upon this with his mum wondering aloud about what might have happened around the age of 6 she quickly became very distressed and described extraordinary stress in the family home that had left Danny physically shaking. Those of us working in education are too aware of the huge costs upon a child being left in these contexts. The Dannys can so easily be misinterpreted within the education context as once the stuckness sets in it is then hard to decipher whether what is being observed is just a learning difficulty, or a developmental vulnerability caused by trauma, or both.

5.28 Let's explore the trauma tree on the next page. It illustrates all the different developmental vulnerabilities possible caused by prolonged neglect, deprivation, loss, abuse, violence, upheaval, or any combination of these, that the child has experienced in his or her early childhood – fundamentally affecting the development of brain, body, and the relationship between them. As you can see, many areas can be affected. All of these developmental vulnerabilities can seriously impede a child's capacity to learn and to make the most of all the opportunities afforded to them in school.

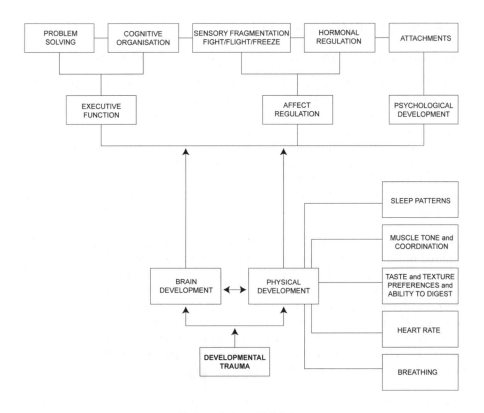

The Trauma Tree's 'roots' are in the
prolonged neglect, deprivation, loss, abuse, violence, upheaval
or any combination of these that the child has experienced in his or her early
childhood, fundamentally affecting the development of the brain, body and the
relationship between them

© *Family Futures 2011*

5.29 For a long while now an organisation called the Nurture Group Network has been heralding nurture groups in schools across the UK. Schools are becoming increasingly innovative and skilled in their practices in order to accommodate troubled children. Attachment aware schools, SafeBase teams, Key adults; resources including Safe Spaces, sensory breaks; school counselling and therapy are attempting to support the children we are considering in this book. For some children this is the only way they can access some education as they are so developmentally behind, desperately needing over-compensatory experiences of safety, security, and stability. I sometimes wonder whether by providing children with what they need in the school context that maybe their right to safety, security, and stability at home could be overlooked and maybe even toxic contexts colluded with? Surely the child should be entitled to the same level of safety, security and stability in every context, whether at home or school? We did sign the UN agreement for the rights of the child after all. However, how do we balance the rights of the child with the rights of the parent? Too often they are in conflict.

THE DEVELOPMENT OF SELF

'We learn who we are through the eyes and mind of another'

5.30 A child or young person often has a very fragmented sense of themselves. We know that even with the best therapist in the world there are many adults still struggling with feeling flawed as a result of experiencing relational wounds and poverty at the hands of their families during childhood. Many believe that it must have been something about them that made Mummy do this, or Daddy do that. It is very hard for a child to believe that Mummy or Daddy had any kind of vulnerability or that they shouldn't have done what they did as children look up to their parents and have a strong sense of loyalty, whatever the personal cost. Loyalty runs deep.

5.31 In school a robust sense of self is necessary in order to engage in the risks required in learning and in order to manage the many relationships inherent in the school community. If the child or young person has a fragile sense of self, which is so often the case, then they are at risk on many different levels. In order to defend against this vulnerability/fragility they can use masks as defences. These masks can interfere with the task of learning hard to recover from ordinary everyday interactions that others would manage well. These pupils can collapse so easily and take a long time to recover. Whilst this is in process they miss out on their learning.

5.32 They split off parts of themselves in order to cope. Some parts of themselves work very well in the school context. Others don't. Some parts are kept hidden (especially the more vulnerable parts). We, as teachers, end up having a very confused picture of who they are and what they are actually capable of as it all depends on which part turns up for which lesson. Assessments undertaken are therefore not always a true picture of the whole child/young person's strengths or vulnerabilities.

5.33 Toxic levels of shame play a big part in this fragility. Usually these children and young people have had countless experiences of being shamed – often for very ordinary things like needing the toilet, feeling hungry, needing some affirmation or being scared by nightmares. They have often experienced adults manipulating, grooming, abusing, neglecting, controlling, and using them to meet their own needs. These types of experiences can leave the child or young person with an overdose of shame. These children and young people view themselves, others and the contexts they are in through their insecure attachment lens. They expect the worse. Why wouldn't they? Rather than seeing themselves as a combination of parts and having the luxury of flexible thinking in order to adapt to situations, they view themselves as all good or all bad and their rigidity in this can serve to cause relational difficulties with staff and peers, as well as strengthening their already faulty sense of self. Rather than understanding that teachers use small doses of shame in order to teach socialisation they experience exposure and often unravel – in class. This unravelling further alienates the child or young person from their peer group.

5.34 Does the child/young person have a coherent sense of what they have experienced at home so that when topics are raised about their identity, family, and home contexts both in lessons and out in the corridors, they will know how to respond? Usually for a child to make sense of who they are and what makes them tick they will have countless experiences of connection together with their parent. There will have been plenty of time for reflections on their strengths, their gifts and capacities. They will have experienced memory-making whilst past events were reflected upon together. However, the children being considered in the court arena will not necessarily have had positive feedback or indeed any feedback. We have many children in school right now who have no real sense of who they are or where they have come from. They often have very muddled, complex narratives that even adults find hard to make sense of – never mind children. They have often been left with a very distorted sense of their self – often fuelled by lies and disturbing experiences that have further confused them. So in school these children can often unravel or melt down in front of us regularly due to this fragility. This again interferes with their ability to access education. They can also struggle with so many of the topics covered within the national curriculum. Many topics are emotive for them: another legacy of relational trauma and loss.

THE CHILD'S DEVELOPMENT OF REGULATION

'Dance me through the panic until I'm safely gathered in ...'
Leonard Cohen, 'Dance Me to the End of Love'

5.35 Most children and young people in our classes spend the majority of the school day in either a calm or alert state. Current school interventions assume this calm/alert state which is the best state to be in for learning and so the majority are served well in the school context. However, children and young people who have experienced significant relational traumas and losses spend most of their time in the classroom and out and about in the school context in a state of alarm, often escalating into fear and even terror states very quickly when their anxieties are not understood or worked with. There are so many possible stress triggers for them in the school context due to the extraordinary stress they have lived that going to school can feel like running a marathon. For children like these the physical cost is immense as it is exhausting being so hyper alert and sensitive all the time. When in these states learning is compromised significantly as the preoccupation for the child/young person is primarily defence. The socio-engagement system in the brain is switched off at this time.

5.35 Children or young people who have experienced extraordinary stress at the hands of their family haven't experienced the soothing, the safe holding, the meaning making of how to manage different states, sensations, and feelings. For children who spend a lot of time in a state of alarm or terror there is only the capacity to focus on the second or minute in hand. However those who spend most of their time is a state of calm or alert are able to focus for longer periods of time and to have a sense of future. In education this is significant. Pupils need to be able to aspire to something in order to direct their strengths, gifts and abilities. Many pupils who have remained in alarm or terror states for too long become stuck, under-achieving and disillusioned when there was once so much possibility.

5.36 In school pupils are expected to have appropriate internal controls to manage themselves. However, these children and young people are at risk as they are out of synch, not even aware of what is going on in their bodies, minds, hearts, and souls – never mind being able to control them. These children and young people can therefore move into overwhelm very quickly. Their states need to be monitored on a continual basis. Staff are needed to become their external stress regulators as these children are not able to manage themselves yet. This involves the use of regular sensory breaks throughout the school day. However, if the frequency and duration of these sensory breaks is not assessed appropriately then we have pupils in school who not only disrupt their own learning but the learning of others: another legacy of relational trauma and loss.

FINAL WORDS

5.37 During this chapter I have outlined the cost involved of not getting it right for the children in our care – their education suffers. Yet we also know that access to education has the capacity to offer second chance learning by providing the opportunity for development, influencing the future outcomes for a child.

5.38 I have also outlined what can happen if we do consider the significance and permanency of additional attachment figures in school itself. Relationships in school do need to be honoured and protected for those most troubled children so let's only move them from their school if absolutely necessary. School and the relationships there can be a lifeline. To take that away could be detrimental. Remember relationships are the vehicle towards adaption and recovery, so let's do all we can to protect these relationships – walking a mile in these childrens' shoes – not just our own.

5.39 I'm sure many more questions have probably been raised as a result of reading this chapter. This was my intention. The more we explore this area the more we become aware that the rights of a parent are often in conflict with the rights of a child. We are therefore dealing with a complex paradox. I'm hoping that we will continue being reflective about the impact upon a child, especially as I wonder whether it is now time to redress the balance? Wisdom and discernment are needed. Let's not forget the significant role that education plays in the life and timescales of a child.

5.40 Finally let's remember that children coming out of traumatic situations do not have the internal structures necessary in order to integrate stress, so we have an ethical responsibility to ensure they do not become traumatised or further traumatised at the hands of their parent, and that they have access to those who can help them with regulation. The impact upon a child's access to education can be severely compromised otherwise. And education matters.

Further reading

K Golding & D Hughes *Creating Loving Attachments: Parenting with PACE to nurture confidence and security in the troubled child* (Jessica Kingsley Publishers, London & Philadelphia, 2012)

H Geddes *Attachment in the Classroom: the links between childrens' early experience, emotional well being and performance in school* (Worth Publishing: London, 2006)

L M Bombér *Inside I'm Hurting: Practical strategies to support pupils with attachment difficulties in school* (Worth Publishing: London, 2007)

L M Bombér *What About Me? Inclusive strategies to support pupils with attachment difficulties make it through the school day* (Worth publishing, London, 2011)

L M Bombér & D Hughes *Settling to Learn: settling troubled pupils to learn: Why relationships matter in school* (Worth Publishing, London & New York, 2013)

M Boxall *Nurture Groups in School: Principles & Practice* (Paul Chapman Publishing: London, 2006)

L Cozolino *The neuroscience of human relationships: attachment and the developing social brain* (W.W.W Norton: New York, 2009)

H T Forbes & B B Post *Beyond Consequences, Logic & Control: A love based approach to helping children with severe behaviours* (Beyond Consequences Institute, LLC, Orlando, FL, 2006)

S Gott *Teach to inspire better behaviour* (Speechmark Publishing, Bicester, Oxon, 2011)

P Greenhalgh *Emotional growth & learning* (Routledge, London & New York, 1994)

B Harris *Befriending the two headed monster: personal, social & emotional development in schools in challenging times* [2008] British Journal of Guidance & Counselling 36 94, 367–383

D Hughes *Attachment Focussed Parenting* (W.W.W Norton, New York, 2009)

P Levine *Waking the tiger: Healing trauma* (North Atlantic Books, California)

B Perry & M Szalavitz *Born for love: Why empathy is essential – and endangered.* Harper (Collins Publishers, New York, 2010)

C Taylor *Caring for children and teenagers with attachment difficulties* (Jessica Kingsley Publishers, London, 2010)

B Van der kolk *Traumatic stress: The effects of overwhelming experience on mind, body and society* (Guildford Press, New York, 1996)

Young Minds *Improving the mental health of looked after young people: an exploration of mental health stigma* (2012)

CHAPTER 6

THE IMPACT OF NEURODEVELOPMENTAL DISORDERS AND DISABILITY IN ASSESSING TIMESCALES AND THE CAPACITY TO CHANGE

Judy Eaton

6.1   The first part of this chapter will outline the clinical features of autism spectrum conditions and will address the challenges which face families who are trying to parent children with neurodevelopmental difficulties, the potential problems in and timescales for accessing either a diagnosis or ongoing mental health support.

6.2   This chapter also aims to discuss the range of difficulties which can occur in individuals diagnosed with an autism spectrum condition and the potential impact that this can have for these individuals when they come in contact with the family courts.

6.3   Of particular relevance in care proceedings is the assessment of parenting and the capacity to change. The issue of parenting ability and autism spectrum conditions is currently under-researched. This chapter, therefore, draws upon the available evidence and discusses the potential impact of the known neurocognitive deficits that are associated with autism and highlights how this may impact upon parenting.

IDENTIFICATION, ASSESSMENT AND DIAGNOSIS

6.4   Autism is a neurodevelopmental disorder which produces difficulties in the areas of communication, social interaction and flexibility of thought and behaviour. It is described as a 'spectrum' condition as it can produce difficulties which can be relatively minor and hard to identify through to difficulties which render it impossible for an individual to live an independent life (these individuals usually have an associated or co-morbid learning difficulty). It is often cited that up to 70% of young people on the autistic spectrum will have a significant degree of cognitive impairment. Many children with moderate to severe learning difficulties will have features of autism and are often identified quite early in life. However, clinical experience has shown that, in addition to these children who are often described as 'severely autistic', there exists a large cohort of young people who have average or above average intelligence who present with significant levels of challenging or 'difficult' behaviour. Asperger's syndrome is the diagnostic term currently used to describe those individuals on the autistic spectrum whose intellectual ability is within the average or above average range. However, in the recently published DSM V (*Diagnostic and Statistical Manual – V*), the term Asperger's syndrome as a separate diagnostic entity is no longer included. In future individuals will be diagnosed as having low or high functioning autism. Guidelines for the assessment and diagnosis of autism spectrum conditions are laid out in detail in the NICE (National Institute for Clinical Excellence) *Guidelines for the Assessment and Diagnosis of Autism in Adults* (published December 2011) and the NICE *Guidelines for the Assessment and Diagnosis of Autism in Children and Young People* (published September 2011).[1]

6.5   These documents contain guidance produced for clinicians who are responsible for providing assessment and diagnosis. Most clinicians will use these guidelines alongside either the *DSM IV/V* (*Diagnostic Statistical Manual*)[2] or the ICD10 (*International Classification of Diseases*)[3] descriptors of mental health or developmental conditions to guide their diagnostic decisions. It is, however, important to appreciate that there is no one clinical assessment protocol or set of assessment tools that are either recommended or followed by most clinicians in the assessment of either adults or children with autism and it is widely accepted that informed clinical judgement is the most accurate and reliable means of establishing and defining a diagnosis.

Diagnosis in children and adolescents

6.6   In children and adolescents, the accepted signs and symptoms which might raise concerns about possible autism (as cited in the NICE Guidelines 2011) are outlined below:

Social interaction and reciprocal communication behaviours

- Spoken language.
  Spoken language may be unusual in several ways:
    — very limited use;
    — monotonous tone;
    — repetitive speech, frequent use of stereotyped (learnt) phrases, content dominated by excessive information on topics of own interest;
    — talking 'at' others rather than sharing a two-way conversation;
    — responses to others that can seem rude or inappropriate.
- Interacting with others.

---

[1]   National Institute for Health and Clinical Excellence – Autism in Adults and Children http://guidance.nice.org.uk.
[2]   *Diagnostic and Statistical Manual of Mental Disorders (DSM-IV)* (American Psychiatric Association, 4th edn, 1994).
[3]   *World Health Organisation International Classification of Diseases (ICD-10)* (WHO, 1992).

- Reduced or absent awareness of personal space, or unusually intolerant of people entering their personal space.
- Long-standing difficulties in reciprocal social communication and interaction: few close friends or reciprocal relationships.
- Reduced or absent understanding of friendship; often an unsuccessful desire to have friends (although may find it easier with adults or younger children).
- Social isolation and apparent preference for aloneness.
- Reduced or absent greeting and farewell behaviours.
- Lack of awareness and understanding of socially expected behaviour.
- Problems losing at games, turn-taking and understanding 'changing the rules'.
- May appear unaware or uninterested in what other young people his or her age are interested in.
- Unable to adapt style of communication to social situations, for example may be overly formal or inappropriately familiar.
- Subtle difficulties in understanding other's intentions; may take things literally and misunderstand sarcasm or metaphor.
- Making comments without awareness of social niceties or hierarchies.
- Unusually negative response to the requests of others (demand avoidant behaviour).

Eye contact, pointing and other gestures

- Poorly integrated gestures, facial expressions, body orientation, eye contact (looking at people's eyes when speaking) assuming adequate vision, and spoken language used in social communication.

Ideas and imagination

- History of a lack of flexible social imaginative play and creativity, although scenes seen on visual media (for example, television) may be re-enacted.

Unusual or restricted interests and/or rigid and repetitive behaviours

- Repetitive 'stereotypical' movements such as hand flapping, body rocking while standing, spinning, finger flicking.
- Preference for highly specific interests or hobbies.
- A strong adherence to rules or fairness that leads to argument.
- Highly repetitive behaviours or rituals that negatively affect the young person's daily activities.
- Excessive emotional distress at what seems trivial to others, for example change in routine.

- Dislike of change, which often leads to anxiety or other forms of distress including aggression.

- Over or under reaction to sensory stimuli, for example textures, sounds, smells.

- Excessive reaction to taste, smell, texture or appearance of food and/or extreme food fads.

Other factors that may support a concern about autism

- The child may have an unusual profile of skills and deficits (for example, social or motor coordination skills may be poorly developed, while particular areas of knowledge, reading or vocabulary skills are advanced for chronological or mental age).

- Social and emotional development are significantly more immature than other areas of development, excessive trusting (naivety), lack of common sense, less independent than peers.

6.7 When considering the possibility of autism clinicians need to be aware that:

- Any signs and symptoms should be seen in the context of the child's or young person's overall development. It is important to consider the child's family history and attachment to parents.

- The signs and symptoms will not always have been recognised by parents or carers, the young people themselves or by other professionals. Unrealistic expectations may be placed upon both the young person to behave in an appropriate way and upon parents to impose boundaries and parent appropriately. Many parents find themselves unfairly judged by professionals as they struggle to deal with a child who simply will not co-operate with them.

- When older children or young people present for the first time with possible autism, signs or symptoms may have previously been masked by the child or young person's coping mechanisms and/or a supportive environment.

- It is necessary to be sensitive to and take account of to take account of cultural variations, but it cannot be assumed that language delay is accounted for because English is not the family's first language or by early hearing difficulties.

- Autism may be missed in children or young people with an intellectual disability.

- Autism may be missed in children or young people who are verbally able.

- Autism may be under-diagnosed in girls.

- Vital information about early development may not be readily available for some children and young people, for example looked-after children and those in the criminal justice system.

- The signs and symptoms of autism are frequently mistakenly accounted for by disruptive home experiences or parent/carer mental or physical illness.

Atypical Asperger's syndrome

6.8 Clinical experience and research[4] has shown that there also appears to a sub-type of Asperger's syndrome where the key impairment is in the area of non-verbal interpretation. This leads to a lack of ability to empathise with the perspective of another person and an inability to see the potential consequences and impact upon others of certain actions. This can lead to social and behavioural difficulties and social vulnerability. Atypical Asperger's syndrome appears most likely to co-exist with attention deficit hyperactivity disorder (ADHD) or attention deficit disorder (ADD) or with dysexecutive syndrome. Individuals with this difficulty are also likely to have some specific expressive language impairment.

6.9 These individuals will often fail at school, with many being excluded or becoming effectively marginalised from the education system by the age of 14.

6.10 They often manage to form a number of superficial friendships but will struggle to maintain these and consequently suffer from low self-esteem and poor identity. This tends to encourage the young person to either become the class joker (in an attempt to 'fit in') or behave in an increasingly outrageous or anti-social manner. At this point, there is often an increase in aggressive behaviour, towards people and objects, with the young person frequently refusing to obey rules of any kind. This then leads them into socialising with other marginalised groups and engaging in anti-social behaviour. However, there continues to be a social naivety about this group with them frequently getting caught or scapegoated.

6.11 As this group of young people move into adulthood, they become increasingly isolated and powerless, often feeling that they have nothing to lose. There can be an increasing detachment about violent and aggressive outbursts. Frequent home and job moves (often precipitated by parents being unable to cope and poor ability to maintain focus) are common as are 'fresh starts' and repeated attempts to 'find' an identity.

6.12 Those who receive a custodial sentence may well be diagnosed with anti-social, or schizo-affective personality disorder and consequently continue to be overlooked in terms of appropriate developmental assessment and diagnosis.

---

[4]   Tantam *Autism Spectrum Disorders through the Lifespan* (Jessica Kingsley Publishers, 2012).

Clinical presentation of Atypical Asperger's syndrome

6.13 The overriding clinical feature of this population is likely to be anxiety (social and generalised). Although obsessive special interests tend to be less common in this sub-group (often due to co-morbid ADHD), cognitive rigidity is still present and can manifest itself in the inability to see anyone else's point of view or admit that they may be wrong. In addition, very literal thinking and a lack of ability to understand and process ambiguous language and metaphors leads to frequent misunderstanding and this is often coupled with an inability to 'move on' from perceived injustice.

6.14 Many individuals will have experienced (often from a very young age) sudden explosive anger which appears to have come 'out of the blue'. This is often linked to high levels of anxiety.

6.15 Some young people begin to 'self-medicate' with alcohol and cannabis.

Pathological demand avoidance

6.16 Pathological demand avoidance (PDA) is another sub-type of autism. The concept of PDA as a distinct diagnostic category was first proposed by Elizabeth Newson some 20 years ago and since then a large number of children have been assessed and found to fit the clinical picture she described.

6.17 Children with PDA have an inability to tolerate demands imposed upon them and an overwhelming need to control their environment. This need for control is fueled by huge levels of anxiety, leading to the child engaging in increasingly challenging and often outrageous behaviour in order to avoid demands.

6.18 These children may exhibit superficial sociability but tend to lack responsibility and awareness of acceptable boundaries (social or otherwise). They can be extremely impulsive and demonstrate lability of mood with frequent temper tantrums and 'meltdowns'. These difficulties often become more apparent when the child begins to attend school when demands on them tend to become greater. Behaviour can deteriorate quickly and the child may resort to manipulation or even violence to avoid demands. More often the child will resort to this type of behaviour across all settings, causing huge disruption within the classroom and within the family home. However, it is not uncommon for children to 'hold it together' and remain compliant whilst they are at school and display challenging and distressed behaviour when out of school.

6.19 Avoidance tactics can include repetitive questioning, ignoring, changing the subject, talking over people, extreme behaviour such as removing clothing and their behaviour can be humiliating and distressing to parents. They can find it difficult to negotiate with peers and can become bossy and domineering during play.

Diagnosis and support for parents

6.20 Obtaining a diagnosis of any type of autism from an appropriately qualified and experienced team of professionals can be a long and time-consuming process. Many parents report having a significant struggle to access a diagnosis, with many waiting up to 2 years before their child is assessed. Even after a diagnosis, it can be difficult to access support both in terms of the child's educational needs and in terms of obtaining support for the family as a whole. Parenting a child with autism can be a very significant challenge, with oppositional and difficult behaviour, including high levels of aggression towards parents, teachers and peers, being present in a number of cases. Difficulties within the family tend to wax and wane, with problems becoming more apparent at times of stress or transition (often from primary to secondary school). The challenges of adolescence for parents of children on the autistic spectrum, including those without a significant learning difficulty can be overwhelming and their psychological needs, and those of their parents and carers, are often not adequately met.

Diagnosis in adults

6.21 For adults (or parents or carers of adults) needing assessment and diagnosis of possible autism, the challenge of finding an appropriate service can be even greater. The NICE guidelines suggest investigation of identified core features (namely social interaction, communication and flexibility of thought/stereotypical behaviour) in any adult suspected of having an autism spectrum condition (including Asperger's syndrome). Factors which have been found to present frequently in adults suspected of having an autism spectrum condition include:

- Problems obtaining/sustaining education and/or employment.
- Difficulty in initiating/sustaining personal and occupational relationships.
- Previous contact with Child and Adolescent Mental Health Services/ Learning Disability Services.
- History of neurodevelopmental difficulties (including dyslexia, dyspraxia and ADHD).

6.22 The NICE guidelines therefore suggest that diagnostic investigation of autism spectrum conditions should include the following features:

- A developmental history spanning childhood and adult life.
- The impact of any identified difficulties upon current functioning (personal/social, educational attainment and employment).
- Past and current history of mental and physical health problems.
- History of other neurodevelopmental difficulties (dyslexia, dyspraxia, ADHD).

• Sensory hypo- or hyper-sensitivities (many individuals on the autistic spectrum have difficulties with self-regulation and can be easily overwhelmed by noise or crowds).

6.23 The Autism Act passed by parliament in 2009 outlined the need for local health and social care providers to make provision for adults requiring assessment and diagnosis. However, the number of teams actually established and providing a comprehensive and timely service across the country is still relatively small. The NHS Commissioning Board have also identified the scarcity of appropriately experienced professionals who can provide assessment and diagnosis in extremely complex presentations, which in some cases, require inpatient assessment due to the mental health difficulties which often exist alongside social communication difficulties. For many adults the challenge of transitioning from child to adult health services has been described as 'falling off a cliff'. For individuals with autism without a learning disability, the struggle of obtaining appropriate support can be almost insurmountable with young adults being unable to access either learning disability services or adult mental health services (unless they are in crisis).

6.24 A study by Hare et al[5] have also outlined the numbers of individuals within the three high secure hospitals (Broadmoor, Ashworth and Rampton) and other secure hospital settings who have a diagnosis of autism. It is also apparent that a number of individuals within HM Prison services may have undiagnosed autism. Prison mental health in-reach services are often stretched to capacity and prisoners will only be seen if they are presenting with active symptoms of mental illness. Assessment and diagnosis is not routinely carried out and prison psychologists are not always trained to recognise the presenting features of autism.

Prevalence rates for autism spectrum conditions

6.25 The number of young people who are diagnosed as being on the autistic spectrum has grown dramatically in the last 10 to 15 years. One specialist team based in the West Midlands, saw referral rates for assessment rise from between 40–60 per year in 2002 to around 360 per year in 2011. Some 60% of those referred were found to be on the autistic spectrum and a further twenty percent had some form of social communication or neurodevelopmental difficulty. This pattern of increased referral rate has been seen across the developed world. It has been estimated that prevalence rates in young boys could be as high as 1:58. In the most recent large-scale population study, Terry Brugha[6] estimated an adult population prevalence rate for autism spectrum conditions of 1% (1.8%

5 Hare et al *A preliminary study of individuals with autistic spectrum disorders in three special hospitals in England* (National Autistic Society, 1999).
6 Brugha et al Autism *Spectrum Disorders in Adults Living in Households throughout England. Report from the Adult Psychiatric Morbidity Survey 2007* (Survey carried out for the NHS Information Centre for health and Social Care by the National Centre for Social research, the Department of Health Sciences, University of Leicester and the Autism Research Centre, The University of Cambridge, 2009).

of males, 0.2% of females). However, there is significant evidence to suggest that females with autism are likely to be under- or misdiagnosed. The Somerset Asperger's Team in a small scale study reported on 40 diagnoses of adults carried out from 2008–2010, of which 33% were female. Autism can be particularly difficult to identify in women as women on the autistic spectrum typically tend to display less of the rigid and inflexible behaviour observed in men with autism. Women with autism are frequently diagnosed with borderline or emotionally unstable personality disorder as they often struggle to cope with relationships with others and frequently develop maladaptive ways of coping and demonstrate features of emotional dysregulation.

AUTISM AND MENTAL HEALTH

6.26 In addition to social communication difficulties, many individuals on the autistic spectrum will have additional mental health challenges. Ghazzudin et al[7] suggested that as many as 40% of males with a diagnosis of autism show evidence of psychiatric co-morbidity (depression, anxiety, OCD, episodes of psychosis) and when considering females with autism, analysis of referrals to the Lorna Wing centre revealed that the co-morbidity of autism for psychiatric conditions in women was even higher with diagnoses of eating disorders, personality disorder and selective mutism being common. The prevalence of autistic features in both adolescents and adult women in secure mental health hospitals is very high, with many adolescent girls on the Spectrum finding it almost impossible to cope with the combined pressures of peer relationships and school demands during adolescence.

6.27 In June 2011 a report entitled 'I think I must have been born bad' the Children's Commissioner pressed for improvements in services designed to meet the mental health needs of young people in the secure estate.

6.28 During the investigation, the possibility was raised that considerable numbers of young people in custody may have undiagnosed neurodevelopmen-tal disabilities (including autism spectrum conditions) which had contributed to the behaviours that led them to offend. The Children's Commissioner was subsequently sufficiently concerned by these findings to commission a literature search seeking to establish a more accurate picture of the prevalence of such disorders in this group of young people.

6.29 Young people who may have features of the complex conditions highlighted in the subsequent report, 'No-one made a connection: the prevalence of neurodisability in young people who offend', are likely to experience significant difficulties in managing their feelings of anger, frustration, confusion or distress, often leading to offending behaviour and/or mental health problems. Conditions explored in this report frequently also involve language or comprehension delay or difficulties.

---

[7]   Ghaziuddin et al 'Depression in Persons with Autism: Implications for Research and Clinical Care' [2002] J Aut Dev Dis, 32(4).

6.30　Consequently, a significant number of young people presenting with complex, challenging presentations may not have the language to understand, or accurately describe, their feelings, symptoms, or the difficulties they face in dealing with both.

6.31　The report states that childhood neurodisability occurs when there is a 'compromise of the central or peripheral nervous system due to genetic, pre-birth or birth trauma, and/or injury or illness in childhood'. This can include the impact of drugs upon the developing foetus and syndromes such as foetal alcohol syndrome and incorporates a wide range of specific neurodevelopmental disorders, with common symptoms including: muscle weakness; communication difficulties; cognitive delays; specific learning difficulties; emotional dysregulation, behavioural problems; and a lack of awareness of inappropriate behaviour.

6.32　The study by Ghaziuddin et al[8] indicated that depression is the most common comorbid condition for individuals with autism. In higher functioning people with autism, depression rates as high as between 30–37% have been reported in comparison with a non-autistic annual prevalence rate of 10% and lifetime prevalence rate of 17%.

6.33　The same study also reported that adolescence is the most likely time for features of depression to emerge in young people with autism.

6.34　It would appear that the underlying triggers for depressive episodes in young people with autism were very similar to those which apply to the general population, namely negative life events such as bereavement and parental discord. It was also noted that, as in the general population, genetic predisposition towards depression also plays an important role. However, for individuals with autism, there is an additional factor. Poor social skills coupled with a desire to 'fit in' with a peer group appear to add to the risk factors for depression.

Autism and parenting

6.35　With regard to the potential impact of autism upon parenting ability, studies indicate that parents with autism can present with significant problems in terms of their parenting. Problems experienced by parents who meet most or all of the diagnostic criteria for autism can be difficult to identify and are frequently masked by other social or environmental factors.

6.36　In care proceedings cases, the crucial question will often centre upon the parent's capacity to change and whether they can reasonably be expected to access and benefit from parenting support within a timescale which does not prove detrimental to the child's development. The impact of poor or inadequate

---

8　　Ghaziuddin et al 'Depression in Persons with Autism: Implications for research and clinical care' [2002] J Aut Dev Dis, 32(4).

parenting upon the child's development is well documented within other chapters in this book. When a parent with autism or other neurodevelopmental difficulty is involved, the research into the ability to parent is very scarce. This chapter will, therefore, focus upon the known cognitive and perceptual difficulties associated with autism spectrum conditions and will endeavour to link these to parenting behaviours.

6.37 Potential problems which may arise in the parenting capacity of both mothers and fathers with autism spectrum conditions can be linked directly to the core neurocognitive clinical features of autism, namely weak central coherence, poor cognitive shifting and poor theory of mind. The question of to what extent are these deficits likely to impact upon an individual's capacity to parent will be dependent upon the relative impact of their autism-related deficits. The presence of neurocognitive features of autism may not be as problematic in other spheres of the parent's life but do have the potential to impact significantly on parenting capacity in a quite unique manner. It is quite possible that a parent with a diagnosis of high functioning autism or Asperger's syndrome may be relatively high functioning in other areas of their life. They may be very intelligent and be capable of holding down a well-paid and responsible job. However, this is not always an indicator that they will have the capacity to be a good parent. There are many aspects that contribute to optimal parenting. These include elements of nurturing, care taking, relating to, understanding, teaching, short and long term planning and the provision of support to the youngster (emotional, relational and financial). Good parenting by definition involves an intense and consistent interplay between parent and child.

6.38 A number of parents with high functioning autism or Asperger's syndrome, despite superficially appearing to be adequate parents, in fact have very little insight into their autism and the potential impact of their condition on their role as a parent.

6.39 There are several neurological aspects of autism that and potentially impact on the ability to parent and which would need investigation as part of a parenting assessment. These are as follows.

POOR COGNITIVE SHIFTING

6.40 Studies in the area of cognition have noted that those on the autistic spectrum may have significant difficulty shifting the scope and focus of their attention.[9] It has been suggested that this particular difficulty may stem from an innate inability to reorient attention rapidly.[10] This particular deficit is of particular significance when a parent has care and control of a young child.

---

[9]   Berger et al 'Central coherence and cognitive shifting in relation to social improvement in high functioning young adults with autism' [2003] J Clin Exp Neuropsychol, 25, 502–511.

[10]   See footnote 6.

6.41   Parents need to be able to reorient their attention frequently and often under pressure. They have to be able to deal with a variety of conflicting and concurrent demands upon their attention.

6.42   Individuals with autism have a tendency to cope with this type of pressure by a number of means; they may walk away from the situation, emotionally shut down or experience sudden explosive anger outbursts.

6.43   This could clearly present significant problems for a parent on the autistic spectrum and, as autism is a neurocognitive difficulty, associated with differences in the way the brain makes connections, the capacity to improve upon this ability may be limited.

THEORY OF MIND

6.44   Individuals on the autistic spectrum may also have impairments in their theory of mind. Theory of mind is the ability to infer the thoughts, feelings or emotions of another person.

6.45   The potential impact of this potential deficit upon a parent with autism could be that they may consistently struggle to correctly discern the thoughts, wishes, knowledge or intentions of their child.

6.46   Clearly, autism is a spectrum condition and not every individual affected has difficulties to the same extent. However, the degree to which a parent lacks this ability (especially if that parent is the primary attachment figure) could have a major impact upon the infant's ability to have his or her needs met appropriately. Research also shows that the major factor leading to a secure attachment is the caregiver's ability to respond sensitively to their child's needs and signals. The author's clinical experience of working with mothers with autism spectrum conditions supports this research. Observing a mother with autism interact with her child often results in a mildly uncomfortable feeling where it is often apparent that the timing of her responses to her baby is 'out of synch'. However, the desire to meet her baby's needs is often present, as is the wish to be a good parent.

6.47   Determining a child's intentions also requires a theory of mind (see Francesca Happe[11]). As the child grows up, therefore, potential problems could arise in terms of boundary setting, child discipline and behaviour management.

6.48   Agnosia a neurological inability to recognise and read faces. Individuals with a variety of neurological conditions can suffer from agnosia, including some individuals with autism and those with foetal alcohol syndrome.

---

[11]   Happe 'The autobiographical writings of three Asperger syndrome adults. Problems of interpretation and implications for theory' in Frith (ed) *Autism and Aspergers Syndrome* (Cambridge University Press, 1991), 207–242.

6.49 Difficulty reading and interpreting facial expressions is a problem that could make it more difficult for parents with autism to 'read' their children. Digby Tantam's work[12] addresses some of the problems that those on the spectrum experience with their inability to read facial expressions. On a day-to-day basis, it may mean that a parent with autism might struggle more than a non-autistic parent to interpret their child's behaviour. Individuals with autism also struggle to interpret tone of voice. This combined with poor impulse control (another key deficit for many individuals with autism) could lead to an unnecessarily punitive discipline style.

WEAK CENTRAL COHERENCE

6.50 Central coherence is the ability we have to focus on both details as well as the whole of a situation and to follow through on plans in a variety of areas. It is also the ability to focus on what takes priority and what is important.

6.51 Many individuals with autism have a tendency to focus on the details rather than the whole picture. This could have an impact upon the ability to parent.

6.52 It also could have child safety implications. Lack of focus of attention could prove lethal (in a car, at the sea side, at the cliff's edge).

6.53 Any one of the above three neurocognitive difficulties described above could impact an individual's capacity to parent. Together they are significant and could potentially place children at risk both in terms of physical safety and emotional well-being.

6.54 These underlying neurocognitive deficits can potentially be further compounded by the mother or father's early experience of being parented which, if poor, could have failed to provide him or her with an internal model which can be used to guide their interactions with their own child.

6.55 In addition, the mother or father's underlying social difficulties may also predispose them to having been being bullied and socially rejected whilst at school. This in turn can lead to a propensity to become involved in abusive relationships as they reach adulthood.

6.56 Social communication difficulties are also likely to contribute to an unwillingness to engage or a tendency to disengage from services or support networks. The mother or father may misunderstand or misinterpret what has been said to him or her and consequently either withdraw and disengage, become emotionally dysregulated and react with anger and frustration.

---

12   Tantam *Autism Spectrum Disorders through the Lifespan* (Jessica Kingsley Publishers, 2012).

6.57 Of particular relevance to mothers on the autistic spectrum, particularly given the known prevalence of anxiety and depression amongst individuals with autism, is the possible impact of depression upon the mother's ability to parent her child. There is a significant body of evidence which points to the long-term impact on children of maternal depression (more specifically post-natal depression). These include intellectual deficits reported by Coghill et al[13] in children of mothers who suffered from significant post-natal depression in the first year of the child's life and poorer maternal attachment and more behavioural difficulties reported in children of mothers with post-natal depression.[14] The combination of depression and the known neurocognitive deficits associated with autism, alongside the tendency to misinterpret offers of support and poor social skills could potentially lead to a poor outcome for the child.

SUMMARY AND CONCLUSIONS

6.58 This chapter has explored both the features of autism and the difficulties in accessing appropriate diagnosis and support faced by both adults and parents of children who are suspected of being on the autistic spectrum. The difficulties of parenting a child with autism should not be under-estimated and parents often find it almost impossible to access psychological therapy and advice for either their child or for themselves as parents.

6.59 The increased prevalence of autism and the significant co-morbidity of autism with other mental health difficulties were also discussed. The psychological difficulties caused by low self-esteem and bullying by peers coupled with high levels of depression and anxiety may explain the higher than expected concentration of individuals on the spectrum in both mental health services and the secure estate (including prison). It may also highlight the potential consequence of failing to support both parents and young people with autism.

6.60 Finally the issue of parenting capacity in both mothers and fathers with autism was discussed. There are no reliable statistics available for the number of adults on the spectrum who have children. However, given the population prevalence rate of approximately 1%, there is likely to be a significant number. The majority of these individuals will parent their children perfectly adequately. It is likely though that a number of young parents who are on the spectrum may well have presented with challenging behaviour as children and have been difficult to parent. Consequently they may have developed attachment issues and struggle to parent their own children. The core neurocognitive deficits associated with autism may add further potential difficulties. Capacity to change in this population is difficult to quantify. Access to appropriately

---

13   Coghill et al 'Impact of maternal post-natal depression on cognitive development of young children' [1986] Brit Med J, 292.

14   Murray 'The impact of post-natal depression on infant development' [1992] J Child Psychol Psychiat, 33(3), 543–561.

modified treatment for anxiety (eg CBT) or specific parenting courses for individuals with autism are limited and the focus has to remain upon the timescales for the child and the likelihood of potential physical or psychological harm.

CHAPTER 7

FACTORS THAT DEMONSTRATE CHANGE OR POTENTIAL CHANGE IN PARENTING CAPACITY

Sarah Birch

'It is the nightly custom of every good mother after her children are asleep to rummage in their minds and put things straight for the next morning, repacking into their proper places the many articles that have wandered during the day.'
Peter Pan[1]

WHAT IS PARENTING CAPACITY?

7.1   The term 'parenting capacity' comes from the Children Act,[2] and refers to the ability of a parent to meet their child's needs. The Department for Education has recently advocated the alternative term 'parenting capability'.[3] The main task of a parent is to facilitate and encourage the development of their child, within a safe, emotionally responsive environment. In order to do this, a parent needs to understand what their child needs at any given time and at each stage in their development. A child's basic care needs for safety, food and shelter will remain to a relative degree, alongside the need for stimulation, guidance and boundaries, and stability (Department of Health, 2000). Other needs will be more responsive to a child's developmental stage. The document entitled *Working Together to Safeguard Children*,[4] lists seven areas of need identified by children themselves which include the vigilance of their caretakers, being shown respect and being given information. A child's needs will also change according to wider family and social factors, and a parent needs to respond appropriately to these changes.

7.2   Parents also need to understand the emotional needs of their child, and to understand that emotional security and responsiveness is essential for psychological development, including the development of intellectual as well as emotional functioning. They need to understand how to provide for their

---

1   Barrie *Peter and Wendy* (Hodder and Stoughton, 1911).
2   Children Act 1989, s 1.
3   *Statutory Guidance on Court Orders and Pre-proceedings for Local Authorities* (Department for Education, 2014).
4   HM Government *Working together to safeguard children: A guide to inter-agency working to safeguard and promote the safety of children* (Department for Education, 2013).

child's emotional needs, and when or how seek help and support from others when they cannot. Parents also need to understand their own psychological and physical needs, and how these differ from their child's. They need to be able to meet their own needs, so that they can continue to meet the needs of another. Ward et al[5] summarise these tasks of parenting as the ability to 'act as beneficial attachment figures'.

AREAS OF PARENTAL DIFFICULTY KNOWN TO COMPROMISE PARENTING CAPACITY

7.3   Cleaver et al[6] in their updated publication on parenting capacity identify four main areas of parental difficulty that are known to impact on the ability to care for a child. These are mental illness, substance misuse, domestic violence, and learning disability. While it is not inevitable that all parents who suffer from such problems will be unable to parent effectively, what is clear is that children growing up with such parents are at greater risk of maltreatment, and the existence of more than one of these problem areas significantly increases the likelihood that a child will be harmed.[7] It is also known that these problem areas commonly overlap: for example poor mental health affects up to forty percent of people with learning disabilities, and almost half of people attending mental health services report problems with alcohol or drugs.[8]

7.4   These problem areas have been shown to affect parenting in a number of specific ways.[9] For example, parents with mental health problems can, variously, loose contact with reality, can experience difficulties in daily functioning, can have difficulties thinking clearly, can feel worthless and hopeless about their life, can become agitated and restless, or can become socially isolated. Mental health problems can make parents irritable and angry with their children, or emotionally unavailable.[10] Parents who abuse substances can become physically unwell, can suffer from symptoms of withdrawal, and can exhibit a range of unusual and/or risky behaviours depending on the specific substance used. Initial assessments in children's social care found that parents who abuse substances were failing to ensure the safety of their children 93% of the time.[11] Parents who are the victim of domestic violence can be

---

[5]   Ward et al *Assessing Parental Capacity to Change when Children are on the Edge of Care: an overview of current research evidence* (Department for Education, 2014), p 55).

[6]   Cleaver et al *Children's needs – parenting capacity. Child abuse: parental mental illness, learning disability, substance misuse and domestic violence* (The Stationary Office, 2nd edn, 2011).

[7]   Woodcock and Sheppard 'Double trouble: maternal depression and alcohol dependence as combined factors in child and family social work' [2002] Child Soc, 16, 232–245.

[8]   Cleaver et al *Children's needs – parenting capacity. Child abuse: parental mental illness, learning disability, substance misuse and domestic violence* (The Stationary Office, 2nd edn, 2011).

[9]   Ibid.

[10] Martins and Gaffan 'Effects of early maternal depression on patterns of mother-infant attachment: a meta-analytic investigation' [2000] J Child Psychol Psychiat, 41, 6, 737–746.

[11] Cleaver and Nicholson *Parental Learning Disability and Children's Needs: Family Experiences and Effective Practice* (Jessica Kingsley Publishers, 2007).

impaired in their capacity to parent through their physical injury, and through the psychological impact of living with the threat of and actual violence. Jones[12] found that previously competent parenting significantly deteriorated in mothers with the arrival of a violent partner. Parents with learning disabilities can struggle to understand the needs of their children, such as the need for structure, guidance, boundaries and stimulation. Assessment of children referred to child services found that over 50% of the children with parents with a learning disability were understimulated.[13]

7.5   All four problem areas have been found to be associated with the neglect of children's physical needs, with separation from parents, and with social consequences such as financial hardship, long-term unemployment, criminal activity and loss of friends and family.[14] These parental problems affect the ability to organise life and adhere to routines. The ability to control emotions and refrain from angry and frightening outbursts will be compromised, and all these areas will reduce the potential for secure attachments to develop between parents and their child.

7.6   Hobson et al[15] write that individuals with borderline personality disorder have potentially disturbing ways of relating to other people, such as hostility, and intense, idealising or denigrating exchanges. There is evidence that women with the diagnosis are prone to confused, fearful and overwhelmed states of mind, as well as having unresolved trauma issues, and these attachment-related characteristics may influence mothers' relations with their children.[16] Unresolved trauma can produce 'frightened/frightening' behaviour that can promote disorganised attachments.[17] Newman et al[18] found that mothers with borderline personality disorder tend to be less sensitive to their children.

7.7   Parents with a history of childhood abuse have also been found to have difficulty with adequate parenting, and one study found that parents who were abused as children were 17 times more likely to abuse their own child when compared to parents who had not had these experiences.[19] Brown and Ward[20] set out a number of factors associated with future harm, adapted from several systematic reviews. Factors in the parents themselves, apart from those already

---

[12]   Jones 'Assessment of Parenting' in Horwath (ed) *The Child's World: The Comprehensive Guide to Assessing Children in Need* (Jessica Kingsley Publishers, 2009).

[13]   See footnote 11.

[14]   See footnote 11.

[15]   Hobson et al 'How mothers with borderline personality disorder relate to their year-old infants' [2009] Brit J Psychiat, 195, 325–330.

[16]   Ibid.

[17]   Lyons-Ruth et al 'A controlled study of Hostile-Helpless states of mind among borderline and dysthymic women' [2007] Attach Hum Dev, 9, 1–16.

[18]   Newman et al 'Borderline personality disorder, mother-infant interaction and parenting perceptions: preliminary findings' [2007] Austral NZ J Psychiat, 41, 598–605.

[19]   Dixon et al 'Risk factors of parents abused as children: a meditational analysis of the intergenerational continuity of child maltreatment (Part 1)' [2005] J Psychol Psychiat, 46(1), 47–57.

[20]   Brown and Ward *Decision-making within a child's timeframe* (Childhood Wellbeing Research Centre, 2012).

listed, include personality disorder, lack of compliance, denial of a problem, parental stress, a history of assaultative behaviour, disordered attachment, a lack of empathy for their child, putting their own needs before their child's and impaired positive interaction between the parent and the child. Familial factors included a poor ability to negotiate between family members, a lack of autonomy, lack of ability to express feelings, poor home conditions and housing instability. Social isolation, lone parenthood, and poor neighbourhoods were also important factors, many of which are more prevalent for people with mental health or substance misuse problems.

REFLECTIVE PARENTING CAPACITY

7.8   All of the risk factors outlined so far reduce parenting capacity by compromising the ability to focus, understand and act upon on the needs of a child. The term 'reflective parental functioning' which derives from the theory of mentalisation, refers to being able to make sense of one's child as a separate being with their own thoughts and feelings. Soderstrom & Skarderud[21] also use the term 'minding the baby' to describe the way that a parent holds the baby's mind in mind, and they outline the way that a good enough parent will respond to and help to regulate their child's feelings, and in doing so help the child to develop their own reflective functioning. Bion[22] called this 'reverie'. The adult's capacity to respond to the emotional cues of their child, and to help their child to make sense of their social context, is part of the development of attachment, and in turn the development of the personality. There is clear research evidence that the attachment histories of a parent will affect their ability to form an attachment with their child,[23] and the vehicle for this causal link may be through a person's ability to mentalise their own and other people's emotional states.[24] Asen & Fonagy[25] in their paper on mentalisation-based therapeutic interventions for families define mentalisation as 'seeing ourselves from the outside and seeing others from the inside'.

7.9   So in demonstrating change, a parent needs to show above all that there have been changes in their ability to think reflectively about their child. From this will come other changes, such as their ability to respond to their child and to their own needs, and their ability to make other behavioural changes associated with their own areas of difficulty. This reflective ability is dynamic rather than static, for all parents, and will depend on situational and individual factors at any one time. There will always be strengths and weaknesses in

---

[21]   Soderstrom and Skarderud 'Minding the baby. Mentalisation-based treatment in families with parental substance use disorder: theoretical framework' [2009] Nordic Psychol, 61(3), 47–65.

[22]   Bion *Learning from experience* (Heinemann, 1962).

[23]   Fonagy et al 'The capacity for understanding mental states: the reflective self in parent and child and its significance for security of attachment' [1991] Inf Mental Hlth J, 12(3), 201.

[24]   Bateman and Fonagy 'Mentalisation-based treatment of BPD' [2004] J Pers Dis, 18(1), 36–51.

[25]   Asen and Fonagy 'Mentalisation-based therapeutic interventions for families' [2011] J Fam Ther, 34, 347–370.

reflective parenting capacity: these need to be identified in order to provide a full and meaningful picture of how a parent is functioning, and psychometric testing can be helpful in this regard.

CAN PARENTING CAPACITY CHANGE?

7.10   Research evidence tells us that children who remain with abusive and/or neglectful parents will suffer harm, and the longer a child remains in this situation, the more harm they will suffer, and the less effective interventions will be.[26] We also know that once abuse has occurred, there is a high probability that it will occur again.[27] However, a study by Ward et al[28] on decision-making in childcare proceedings found that the timescales that decisions took were too long, and were at odds with research indicating the impact of abuse and neglect in the first few years of a child's life. Therefore a clear understanding is needed of the harm that can come to children when change in parenting capacity is not possible, and what factors could suggest that change can occur within the child's timescales.

7.11   It is beyond the scope of this chapter to review the research evidence on the effectiveness of interventions designed to improve parenting capacity. However social work interventions in families where abusive parenting has occurred have been shown to be effective,[29] and there are some evidence-based interventions, that have been piloted in the UK, that have shown some promising results.[30] When capacity cannot improve, placement in Local Authority care has been show to be more beneficial to a child than remaining at or returning home.[31]

WHAT MIGHT DEMONSTRATE POTENTIAL FOR CHANGE?

7.12   It is helpful to consider what might demonstrate potential for change before considering actual change. A factor frequently cited as predictive of change is the extent of a parent's engagement with services. However, serious case reviews, after the death of a child, have highlighted the fact that some parents, particularly those with more complex needs, can present as engaged with services, when in reality their engagement may be superficial, without

---

[26]   Brown and Ward *Decision-making within a child's timeframe* (Childhood Wellbeing Research Centre, 2012).
[27]   Fluke et al 'Recurrence of maltreatment: an application of the National Child Abuse and Neglect Data System' [1999] Ch Ab Neg, 23, 633–650.
[28]   Ward et al *Safeguarding Babies and Very Young Children from Abuse and Neglect* (Jessica Kingsley Publishers, 2012).
[29]   Wade et al *Caring for abused and neglected children: making the right decisions for reunification or long-term care* (Jessica Kingsley Publishers, 2011).
[30]   Davies and Ward *Safeguarding Children across Services: Messages from Research* (Jessica Kingsley Publishers, 2012).
[31]   See footnote 29.

genuine intention to change. Behaviour that appears to be compliant with professionals is in fact 'false compliance'.[32] While conscious and deliberate attempts to cover up abuse are rare,[33] this does happen, and partial denial, for example of the full extent of harm is a frequent factor in childcare proceedings, for a number of reasons. Platt[34] identifies two types of engagement with services in childcare proceedings: behavioural indicators, such as keeping appointments, and interactional indicators such as the bond between the parent and the professional, and the parent's ability to work constructively on goal-planning. Perhaps the latter can be given precedence in identifying genuine engagement.

7.13 Even when engagement is established, there have been found to be factors that will nevertheless reduce a parent's potential ability to make changes. These include a lack of understanding of why behaviours can have an impact on children,[35] which is why a clear understanding of a parent's level of cognitive functioning is important. Social isolation, shame, and stigma can prevent people from admitting to themselves and others that there is a problem with their parenting that they need to address. Many parents in childcare proceedings have been the subject of proceedings as a child, and have learnt to distrust professionals. Experiences of neglect and abuse contribute to helplessness and passivity, as can mental health problems, or a history of disempowering relationships with institutions or authority. Ward et al[36] highlight factors associated with sustained change, such as good family support, ongoing, individually-tailored treatment, or the establishment of a 'virtuous circle' whereby an increase in self-esteem stemming from making changes enhances the ability to make further changes.

7.14 Freyer et al[37] have shown that there is a difference between a readiness to seek treatment, and a readiness to make changes. Clinical experience tells us that the desire to change, without changing, is common. Factors that might suggest a genuine desire to make changes include an internal locus of control (taking personal responsibility), identifying areas for change that are realistic and within the parent's control, a level of understanding about the extent of the problem and the impact of this on the parent's and their child's life, an understanding of the process of change and potential obstacles, and intrinsic

---

[32]   Brandon et al *Understanding serious case reviews and their impact: a biennial analysis of serious case reviews 2005–7. Research report* (Department for Children, Schools and Families, 2008).

[33]   Forrester et al 'Parental resistance and social worker skills: towards a theory of motivational social work' [2012] Ch Fam Soc Work, 17(2), 118–129.

[34]   Platt 'Understanding parental engagement with child welfare services: an integrated model' [2012] Ch Fam Soc Work, 17(2), 138–148.

[35]   Booth and Booth 'A family at risk: multiple perspectives on parenting and child protection' [2004] Brit J Learn Dis, 32(1), 9–15.

[36]   Ward et al 'Assessing Parental Capacity to Change when Children are on the Edge of Care: an overview of current research evidence' (Department for Education, 2014).

[37]   Freyer et al 'Readiness for change and readiness for help-seeking: a composite assessment of client motivation' [2005] *Alcohol Alcoholism*, 40(6), 540–547.

motivation[38] rather than external motivators. Further, consistent evidence of engagement over time, with different professionals, is also a positive prognostic indicator, as are areas of parental functioning that are already working well. Harnett[39] has suggested a procedure to assessing a parent's ability to change, which takes place over a period of 4 to 6 months, whereby specific goals are established and then the attainment of these goals assessed. It is important that the goals are individually meaningful to the parent and set conjointly with professionals.

7.15 From research into engagement and change in psychotherapy, we know that the ability to withstand the stress of change, and the intensity of the therapeutic relationship, is important. Social support, and established ways of dealing with stress, can boost this ability. Parents need to show that they are getting ready to think and feel differently, and that they have the strength and support necessary to do so. Psychometric tools can help in assessing this such as the *Butcher Treatment Planning Inventory*[40] which is a self-report personality assessment inventory that was developed empirically to aid in treatment planning. It includes validity scales, and treatment issues scales that relate to attitudes or behaviours that could interfere with treatment, with the aim of preventing premature termination of treatment.

FACTORS THAT INDICATE THAT CHANGE HAS OCCURRED

7.16 So what might indicate that a parent's ability to think reflectively about their child has increased? The most observable and concrete factors that suggest change is occurring are behavioural, and connected to the problem areas that were reducing parenting capacity. According to the specifics of a parent's difficulties, these changes could include a reduction in their substance use, the level of domestic violence in the home, or number of hospital admissions. They could also include number of contact sessions attended, number of their children's medical appointments attended, number of therapy sessions attended, and so on. These factors would not necessarily suggest psychological change, but they are necessary adjustments that need to be made to increase safety and the ability of the parent to make changes at a deeper level. They are objective measures of change, which is one of the four elements suggested by Harnett[41] in the procedure for assessing capacity to change.

---

[38] Stanley et al 'Fathers and domestic violence: building motivation for change through perpetrator programmes' [2012] Ch Ab Rev, 21(4), 264–277.

[39] Harnett 'A procedure for assessing parents' capacity for change in child protection cases' [2007] Child Youth Serv Rev, 29(9), 1179–1188.

[40] Butcher *Butcher Treatment Planning Inventory (BTPI™): Technical manual* (Multi-Health Systems Inc, 2004).

[41] Harnett 'A procedure for assessing parents' capacity for change in child protection cases' [2007] Child Youth Serv Rev, 29(9), 1179–1188.

7.17 Such changes may not be permanent: research into alcohol use, for example, suggests that even after 15 years of abstinence one in four people start using alcohol again.[42] Many parents who present a risk to their child through domestic violence, mental illness or substance abuse have grown up in an environment where similar factors were present. We know that this means that their ability to cope with daily life or with stress, their ability to understand and express their emotions, their ability to form secure attachments to others, and their ability to problem-solve, to name only a few areas, will be compromised,[43] and this will further hinder their ability to successfully make behavioural changes in their lives. A parent's ability to adapt to their own experiences of childhood abuse is known to be a protective factor in mitigating the impact of their ongoing difficulties in their parenting.[44]

7.18 However, behavioural changes, which can be very hard to make, show that change is possible for a parent, and that they have the ability to make positive decisions about their lives for the benefit of their children. We know from clinical experience and from research into behavioural change that what may seem to the outsider like an easy choice, can to the person in the situation feel overwhelming and beset with fear. Women in domestic violence situations may have come to feel that they have no choices, that leaving will put themselves or their children at risk of greater harm, or there may be significant practical barriers to ending a relationship. Motz[45] writes that in such a scenario the notion of 'choice' may not even be applicable. In describing their work with mothers who abuse substances, Soderstrom and Skarderud[46] describe a 'malign relationship with drugs' whereby drugs become 'best friend and comfort'.

7.19 A number of psychological models aid the understanding of the process of change, most notably and widely used perhaps being Prochaska and DiClemente's Trans-Theoretical Model of change which was originally developed to understand the process of smoking cessation.[47] It has been applied in childcare proceedings, as a framework for helping to understand where parents are situated on continuum of readiness for change (Morrison, 2010). Prochaska & DiClemente describe five elements of an intentional change process: contemplation, decision, action, maintenance and lapse, as well as two barriers to change: pre-contemplation and relapse. Motivating people to change therefore involves creating or increasing supports for change, whilst removing or decreasing the barriers. Effective work to bring about change cannot occur unless workers understand which stage parents are at, and are able to tailor any

[42] Hser et al (2001) 'A 33-year follow-up of narcotics addicts' [2001] Arch Gen Psychiat, 58(5), 503–508.

[43] Brown and Ward *Decision-making within a child's timeframe* (Childhood Wellbeing Research Centre, 2012).

[44] Jones et al 'Making plans: assessment, intervention and evaluating outcomes' in Aldgate et al (eds) *The Developing World of the Child* (Jessica Kingsley Publishers, 2006).

[45] Motz *Toxic Couples: The Psychology of Domestic Violence* (Routledge, 2014).

[46] Soderstrom and Skarderud 'Minding the baby. Mentalisation-based treatment in families with parental substance use disorder: theoretical framework' [2009] Nordic Psychol, 61(3), 47–65.

[47] Prochaska and DiClemente 'Stages and processes of self-change of smoking: toward an integrative model of change' [1983] J Consult Clin Psychol, 51(3), 390–395.

interventions accordingly. The stage of pre-contemplation describes a situation in which parents may not be willing, ready or able to consider change. Contemplation, on the other hand, involves thinking about and preparing for change on a range of levels, including consideration of the pros and cons of the issue; whether, if change occurs, things will be better or worse; for whom any changes will be better or worse; levels of confidence about making the change; and whether any changes can be sustained. Following the stage of contemplation, action can be taken, and this needs to be planned, and maintained to prevent relapse.

7.20 The second area of change would be within the parent's relationship with themselves. Apart from the behavioural changes already mentioned, how is the parent able to look after their own needs? Do they spend time with other people, or time on activities that strengthen their mental and physical health? How do they present themselves to professionals? Do they take pride in their appearance and their living environment? What are their sleeping and eating patterns? How do they talk about their own needs and their emotional health? Do they have greater insight into their areas of vulnerability and their need for support? Are they better able to recognise how they feel, and how this impacts on their own lives and those around them? Have they made progress in valuing themselves as a person and potentially as a parent? Do they identify themselves as a parent first and foremost, or in another role? How do they cope with daily and more unusual stressors in their lives? Can they think flexibly and constructively about their problems and how to solve them?

7.21 Psychological tests can play a role here in assessing the current psychological strengths and weaknesses of a parent, and whether these have changed. Some measures, such as the Minnesota Multiphasic Personality Inventory Version 2[48] provide a broad understanding of psychological and personality functioning, while other measures assess areas of functioning that are specific to parenting. The Parenting Stress Index[49] measures the level of stress in the parent/child system and is designed to detect those who are at risk of developing dysfunctional parenting behaviours. There is a series of questions about the child and a series of questions about the parent and a total score representing the overall level of stress. The Child Abuse Potential Inventory[50] assesses six factors known to be associated with abuse. These are distress, rigidity, unhappiness, problems with child and self, problems with family and problems from others.

7.22 The third area of observable change would be within the parent's relationship with their child, or to put it another way, their attachment with their child, how they position themselves in relation to their child, and how they think about their child. The Adult Attachment Interview (AAI) provides a

---

[48] Butcher et al *MMPI-2 Minnesota Multiphasic Personality Inventory-2™ Manual for administration and scoring* (University of Minnesota Press, 2001).

[49] Abidin *Parenting Stress Index Professional Manual* (Psychological Assessment Resources Inc, 4th edn, 2012).

[50] Milner *The Child Abuse Potential Inventory Manual Second edition* (Psytec Inc, 1986).

structured way of understanding a parent's attachment history. Alternatively, in observing the quality of a parent's interaction with their child, various writers have put forward important dimensions to look for. Maccoby[51] for example, working from the findings of Ainsworth who was an early researcher in attachment styles, identified four dimensions of caretaking. These are sensitivity/insensitivity, acceptance/rejection, cooperation/interference and accessibility/ignoring. Rohner[52] used the term 'warmth dimension' which integrates these areas, providing a conceptual framework for assessing the overall level of parental acceptance as opposed to rejection of their child, in terms of both physical and verbal responses.

7.23   An improvement in the secure quality of the attachment, the level of emotional understanding and responsiveness to their child, and their understanding of what their child needs and does not need are all influenced by a parent's attitudes and perceptions of their child. For example, it has been found that parents who are more likely to abuse their child have distorted and unrealistically high expectations of their children's ability and developmental level, and attribute more to the characteristics of their child than to their own behaviour. Parents also were more likely to have negative perceptions of their child's behaviour.[53] It therefore follows that parents who have more positive perceptions of their child's value, more realistic perceptions of their child's abilities, and greater insight into their own vulnerabilities and areas of difficulty will find the task of parenting less stressful and more rewarding.

7.24   Therapeutic approaches with parents and families using mentalisation, on which the idea of reflective parenting capacity is based, have identified 11 goals for change, which have relevance here. These are as follows: openness to discovery of other family member's thoughts and feelings; understanding that the mental states of other family members are opaque; being able to reflectively contemplate, in an open and relaxed way, the thoughts and feelings of others; understanding that other people in the family can perceive situations differently; being able to forgive angry and hurtful behaviours; understanding how their thoughts, feelings and behaviours affect others; trusting each other rather than feeling fearful; being able to learn from each other; being able to be playful and adopt other people's perspectives; encouraging optimism about change; and assuming responsibility and accepting accountability.[54]

Case example: a breakdown in the reflective parental function

7.25   Natalie was a young mother whose son had been removed from her care after he was found to have a number of injuries that were assessed as likely to

---

[51]   Maccoby *Social Development: Psychology Growth and the Parent-Child Relationship* (Harcourt Brace Jovanovich, 1980).

[52]   Rohner *The Warmth Dimension: Foundations of Parental Acceptance – Rejection Theory* (Sage, 1986).

[53]   Richman et al *Pre-school to school: a behavioural study* (Academic Press, 1983).

[54]   Asen and Fonagy 'Mentalisation-based therapeutic interventions for families' [2011] J Fam Ther, 34, 347–370.

be non-accidental. Natalie lived with her partner, who was not the father of her child, and was known to be a substance abuser. He had older children who had previously been removed from his care due to domestic violence towards his ex-partner. Natalie appeared to be immature, and emotionally dependent on her partner, despite the relationship being in some ways superficial and catered towards her partner's needs rather than hers. At the beginning of care proceedings, she reported being unaware of how her child could have been injured, but as assessment progressed, she gave concerning examples of witnessing her partner shaking her baby and feeling 'annoyed' by this. She seemed genuinely distressed by the removal of her child, but assumed a passive position in relation to the injuries her child had received, finding it hard to identify with the distress this must have caused her child, and to fully understand the risk that her partner's behaviour presented to her child.

7.26 Psychological assessment found that Natalie's experiences of being in care herself on a number of occasions from early childhood into adolescence had a profound impact on her emotional development. She came from a large complicated family, with several half-siblings and changes in who provided parenting within her wider family and as a result of the breakdowns in her mother's relationships. She had a critical and argumentative relationship with her mother, whom she deferred to, while feeling resentful of the childlike status she continued to hold, even after becoming a mother herself. She witnessed her mother being physically assaulted by a boyfriend, and spoke movingly of wanting to protect her mother, but not knowing how.

7.27 Over the years she had coped with these difficult experiences by becoming an avoidant person, who hoped for support from others but did not complain or act when she did not receive it. She tended to bury her own thoughts and feelings, and found the needs of her child, when she could not bear her own needs, impossible to understand and respond to, particularly at times that had a connection to her own experiences of witnessing violence. However she expressed an increasing determination to make changes, in order to be able to resume the care of her child. She ended her relationship with her partner, with some help from domestic violence services, making disclosures for the first time about the level of threat and intimidation in the relationship. She agreed to recommendations to attend a parenting programme, a psycho-educational course on domestic violence, and to engage in psychological therapy which would focus on her emotional needs and her relationship functioning. She continued to attend supervised contact with her child three times a week, and appeared motivated to engage with her child at these times, although concern was raised about her ability to be responsive and confident enough in her ability as a mother.

7.28 A follow-up psychological assessment 4 months after beginning her treatment showed that Natalie had made some changes in her understanding of: (a) her previous situation; and (b) her difficulties asserting herself in relationships. She had attended all the sessions of the parenting and domestic violence courses, and had continued to attend weekly sessions with a psychotherapist with a background in working with women who present a risk to themselves and/or others. She acknowledged that this work was challenging, but appeared to have formed an attachment to her therapist, and was positive about continuing regardless of the outcome of the proceedings. She had begun to lose some weight, and began to take pride in her appearance, demonstrating the start of an understanding and a valuing of herself. She had asked for time to take her son out of the contact centre to a local park. During these times her confidence seemed to increase, and a more relaxed and flexible attitude to her child began to emerge. However she continued to report to professionals that she frequently felt low in mood after contact, and that at times her thoughts about her life were hopeless. She was clearly struggling with loneliness, and had yet to form close relationships with peers who might be a support for her.

7.29 At a child protection review conference, it was recommended that as Natalie had shown clear motivation and insight into her difficulties, and as she had managed to separate herself from the ongoing risk of domestic violence, she should be given the chance to work towards reunification with her child, in a gradual and supervised process. This decision alone appeared to be a catalyst for further change for Natalie, who found a local children's centre to attend, and managed to identify a pre-school nursery for her child in the longer-term.

CONCLUSIONS

7.30 'Change is a complex process, and although it can be supported and promoted through effective interagency interventions, it cannot be imposed'.[55]

7.31 Winnicott[56] wrote 'I doubt whether any mother really and fully believes in her child at the beginning'. He described the process whereby a parent learns to believe in and understand their child, through a desire to know and understand, and through the enjoyment of responding to their child's needs. When a child is at risk, the task of the parent could be seen as going back to the beginning of this process: beginning to believe in the whole and separate existence of their child and their ability to respond.

---

[55] Ward et al *Assessing Parental Capacity to Change when Children are on the Edge of Care: an overview of current research evidence* (Department for Education, 2014).

[56] Winnicott *The Child, the Family and the Outside World* (Penguin, 1964, p 24).

CHAPTER 8

ASSESSING A PARENT'S CAPACITY TO CHANGE IN PSYCHOTHERAPY: THE USE OF THE RORSCHACH AND THE MMPI-2

Kari S Carstairs and Sarah Birch

8.1   Psychologists are often asked to assess the capacity of a parent to change when that parent has been thought to present a risk of significant harm to the children. This necessitates a full assessment of the parent's developmental history and current psychological functioning. For parents with problems in emotional functioning, psychotherapy is one of the most likely interventions. Clinical psychologists carry out assessments using a review of the background documents, a clinical interview, observation and psychometric testing. Tests provide additional, systematic data to allow inferences to be made about the nature of a parent's difficulties, what needs to change in order for parenting to improve, how change might be promoted, and the likelihood of that change. Tests can also be used to assess whether change has occurred after a period of psychotherapy. The tests of emotional functioning that have the most robust base of research literature to support their use in parenting evaluations are the Rorschach and the MMPI-2. These tests are described, and case examples are given to illustrate how the information they provide can be useful in determining a parent's capacity for change.

INTRODUCTION

8.2   Frequently, psychologists are requested to assess a parent's capacity to improve their parenting, within a timescale that would fit in with the developing needs of their child. The Children Act 1989[1] is based on the core philosophy that children are best looked after within their own family. In child protection cases, the court will need to know if and when this will be possible, or if the quality of parenting within the child's home is such that it is likely to cause significant harm and positive change cannot be expected to take place within a reasonable timeframe.

8.3   Children who are deemed to be at risk of significant harm will be placed on the Child Protection Register under the categories of emotional, physical or

---

[1]   Children Act 1989, s 1.

sexual abuse, or neglect (or a combination thereof). The parenting these children have received will have failed in a number of ways, and for many reasons. Cases referred for psychological assessment often include concerns about domestic violence, alcohol and drug misuse, sexual or physical abuse, and failure to meet a child's basic needs by providing them with sufficient food, adequate housing and clothing, and attending to their emotional needs. The myriad of different reasons why these concerns have arisen means that assessing capacity for change is complex. The specific nature of the parenting difficulty has to be established, along with an understanding of how and why this has occurred, what psychological changes would result in improvements in parenting, and whether such changes are possible in psychotherapy or other interventions. The answer to all these questions must be considered based on an understanding of the parent's own developmental history and current psychological functioning, to provide an explanatory framework, a rationale for treatment planning, and a point of comparison for considering whether change has occurred.

WHAT FACTORS MIGHT CONSTITUTE GOOD PARENTING?

8.4   Reder and Lucey[2] write that the essence of the parental role is to: 'facilitate the child's developmental lines within a safe environment'. When assessing parents within, or as a prelude to, childcare proceedings, certain factors will usually be included in order to address the question of whether parenting is adequate, and if not, what needs to change. The first area to consider is whether the parents provide adequate basic care, ie whether they are able to consistently provide their child with food, adequate housing, and an environment that is warm, safe and clean. The quality of their physical contact with their child is considered, such as the level of physical affection, and whether physical discipline is used. The parents' emotional attunement and attachment to their child are considered: can they have empathy with their child's feelings and perceptions? Can they provide emotional comfort? Can they adapt their responses to meet their child's changing emotional needs? The parents' level of cognitive ability is also considered: can they gain an intellectual understanding of their child's needs and how these change over time? Can they accept responsibility for their parenting? Their ability to deal with problems is also relevant, along with their attitude to discipline, and to receiving help and support from others within and outside the family.

PSYCHOMETRIC TESTING

8.5   Psychologists are in a unique position among other health care professionals when it comes to assessing capacity for change in relation to

---

2   Reder and Lucey 'Significant issues in the assessment of parenting' in Reder and Lucey (eds) *Assessment of parenting. Psychiatric and psychological contributions* (Brunner-Routledge, 1995, p 6).

psychological functioning because, alongside the clinical interview, background review and any other observational data gathered, they make use of psychometric techniques. These techniques provide a standardised and objective methodology for the measurement of psychological attributes. They include self report questionnaires, structured interview schedules, and tasks or problems to complete. The attributes that can be measured include cognitive functioning, personality, emotional functioning, current mental health issues (such as depression, anxiety, or trauma-related symptoms), attitudes (for example to parenting, or to the use of drugs or alcohol), relationship functioning and areas of risk.

8.6   The use of psychometric techniques is advantageous because these techniques provide a different type of information; a psychological test is a systematic way of gathering data and making comparisons between the behaviour of two or more people. The psychologist presents a test to the parent in a standardised way, so that what is presented is held constant each time the test is administered. This means that when the results of a test differ it is more likely to be the result of differences between the parent being testing and other adults rather than being a function of some idiosyncratic aspect of the psychologist who is doing the assessment. The tests are scored in standardised ways, often using a computerised scoring system which reduces administrator error. The results of the test will then be compared to a normative sample, which is a body of data collected by administrating the test to large samples of people, so that the most common ways of responding to the test can be established. This means that the results of one parent can be compared to the results of a large number of adults with similar characteristics (such as age range) to determine whether the results of the parent being assessed are unusual or remarkable in any way.

8.7   The systematic nature of psychometric techniques means that when an opinion is reached by a psychologist, that opinion is based not just on clinical expertise and experience, but on objective data which can be compared to a normative sample, and therefore to what we might consider to be within the realms of normality. Furthermore, the systematic nature of the tests themselves means that they can be used to establish links with previous, current and future aspects of psychological functioning. Tests are not considered scientific or useful unless they have a proven reliability and validity. Reliability refers to the extent that a test can be shown to measure the same variable, to the same extent and in the same way, each time it is used. There are different types of validity, but overall this refers to the extent that a test can be shown to be measuring the variable it purports to measure. The way in which the variable being tested correlates with other factors such as history of abuse, forensic history, symptomatology or future offending, provides support for such validity, and makes it possible for the psychologist to make inferences from test results about future behaviour, such as capacity to change. Research on how test scores relate to behaviour can be consulted so that the results for the parent are linked to a scientific body of knowledge.

THE RORSCHACH AND THE MMPI-2

8.8 Two of the most well researched psychological tests for assessing personality functioning, both generically and within parenting evaluations, are the Rorschach and the Minnesota Multiphasic Personality Inventory Version 2 (MMPI-2). These two tests provide a broad assessment of personality functioning which, when put into the context of the concerns for the children, can then indicate potential pathways for positive interventions with the parents aimed at improving their parenting or indicate why change is unlikely.

8.9 The Rorschach is a test that involves an information-processing, problem solving task in which the respondent is presented with ink blots and asked what they look like. Responses are scored and the scores are combined into indices. The indices relate to areas of psychological functioning, such as coping resources, perception of oneself and others, dealing with feelings, perceptual accuracy and illogical thinking. The Rorschach is particularly good at capturing information about a person as an individual,[3] while at the same time making comparisons against a normative sample. This is because while the test materials are standardised, their intentionally ambiguous nature means that each person's response to them is unique, and rich in descriptive data. As Exner[4] writes, many psychological characteristics are utilised when an individual is presented with the Rorschach inkblots, and their responses generate an understanding of their psychological organisation, as well as the products of such an organisation such as behaviour or symptoms. Responses to this test can also tell us something about an individual's attitudes and concerns that the person may not fully recognise in themselves, or would be reluctant or unable to convey more directly.[5]

8.10 The Rorschach can be administered and scored using the Rorschach Comprehensive System.[6] It is a widely used test internationally. The scoring and interpretation procedures are founded upon a large amount of normative data. The original norms were based on data from North America, and international normative studies have been conducted in 16 different countries including Australia, Asia, Europe, the Middle East and North and South America. These studies involved nearly 9,000 participants. The participants were all non-patients and results were collated to form the International Reference Sample.[7]

---

[3] Exner *The Rorschach: A Comprehensive system. Volume 1: Basic Foundations and Principles of Interpretation* (John Wiley & Sons, 2003).

[4] See footnote 3.

[5] Weiner 'Rorschach assessment in child custody cases' [2005] J Child Custody, (2) 99–119.

[6] Exner *The Rorschach: A Comprehensive system. Volume 1: Basic Foundations and Principles of Interpretation* (John Wiley & Sons, 2003).

[7] Meyer et al 'Toward International Normative Reference Data for the Comprehensive System' [2007] J Person Asst (89(1)) S201–S216.

8.11   Calloway[8] writes that the Rorschach is: 'uniquely suited for use in child custody evaluations', although it does not assess parenting per se, and of course there is no specific psychological profile that captures the essence of adequate parenting. Weiner[9] describes factors likely to positively influence parenting as being a lack of incapacitating psychological disorders, good judgement, careful decision-making, flexibility, self-control, and being able to manage stressful situations without becoming unduly upset. All of these factors can be measured by the Rorschach.

8.12   Erard[10] and Barton Evans and Schutz[11] discuss how several Rorschach variables have implications for parenting, such as the variables that measure level of adjustment, frustration tolerance, and impulsivity, sensitivity to other people's feelings, being realistic about expectations of oneself and others, and characteristic defences used when encountering intense emotional demands. Weiner[12] outlines ways in which the test can usefully identify personality characteristics that could foster or impede adequate parenting, as well as identifying childhood experiences of trauma and sexual abuse. Carstairs[13] reported on 52 parents in cases where there was evidence of child neglect, and showed that it is common for these individuals to have a high Lambda (an avoidant, defensive style of functioning) and a positive Coping Deficit Index (they are likely to be struggling to cope psychologically with demands placed on them).

8.13   The MMPI-2 is a self-report measure consisting of a list of 567 statements to which the respondent must reply true or false to indicate whether the statement applies to him or her or not. It is designed to assess personality and psychopathology. There are ten main clinical scales, supplementary scales that assess a range of specific issues, content scales and critical items. The pattern of an individual's responses across the clinical scales can be analysed by computer. The MMPI-2 is the most widely used personality inventory in research and in clinical practice in the world,[14] and it is the test most commonly used in psychological evaluations for the courts.[15] It has been researched

8   Calloway 'The Rorschach: Its use in child custody evaluations' [2005] J Child Custody, 2(1–2) p 143.
9   Weiner 'Rorschach assessment in child custody cases' [2005] J Child Custody, (2) 99–119.
10   Erard 'What the Rorschach can contribute to child custody and parenting time evaluations' [2005] J Child Custody, (2) 119–142.
11   Barton Evans and Schutz 'The Rorschach in child custody and parenting plan evaluations: A new conceptualisation' in Gacono and Barton Evans (eds) *The Handbook of Forensic Rorschach Assessment* (Lawrence Erlbaum, 2008), pp 233–254.
12   Weiner 'Rorschach assessment in child custody cases' [2005] J Child Custody, (2) 99–119.
13   Carstairs 'Rorschach assessment of parenting capacity: A case study' [2011] *Rorschachiana*, (32) 91–116.
14   Greene *The MMPI-2: An interpretive manual* (Allyn & Bacon, 2nd edn, 2000); Cox et al 'The MMPI-2: History, Interpretation and Clinical Issues' in Butcher (ed) *Oxford Handbook of Personality Assessment* (Oxford University Press, 2009), pp 250–276.
15   Pope et al *The MMPI, MMPI-2 and MMPI – A in Court A practice guide for expert witnesses and attorneys* (American Psychological Association, 3rd edn, 2006).

extensively, in many different countries[16] and is now available in 24 languages. In addition, the MMPI-2 also contains scales which assess response style, including random responding, exaggeration of symptoms and defensiveness and/or denial of shortcomings. These scales have been found to be reliable in detecting defensiveness and malingering.[17]

8.14 The MMPI-2 is routinely used in child custody evaluations of parenting in the USA where it has found to be effective in the detection of defensive responding,[18] and preliminary research has shown that it can be used reliably in the UK with reference to American norms for parental competency evaluations.[19] Although there is no one profile that is consistently associated with negative parenting characteristics,[20] parents who come before the family courts tend to approach the test defensively and attempt to make a favourable impression.[21] There are particular scale elevations which raise the possibility for parenting difficulties, and the MMPI-2 has been found to be helpful in considering aspects of functioning pertaining to adequate parenting, and in considering aspects that need to improve. For example, Caldwell[22] writes that MMPI-2 results can be used to generate expectations regarding five basic issues in relation to parenting: quality of attachment, potential for antisocial behaviour, temper control, alienation of affection, and chemical abuse and dependence. He also lists a number of variables from the MMPI-2 that are relevant to parenting such as adult role modelling factors, personal styles of interacting, and control issues.

8.15 Used together, the two tests are complementary, as the Rorschach can sometimes detect areas of pathology that the MMPI-2 can miss and the MMPI-2 can highlight concerns about defensiveness and about specific symptomatology.[23] Since the Rorschach is a performance-based method, it provides a useful counter-point to self report measures.[24] The incremental validity that is gained by using both tests together further strengthens the

---

[16] Butcher et al 'Cross-cultural applications of the MMPI-2' in Butcher (ed) *MMPI-2: A practitioner's guide* (American Psychological Association, 2006), pp 505–537.

[17] Greene 'Malingering and defensiveness on the MMPI-2' in Rogers (ed) *Clinical assessment of malingering and deception* (Guilford Press, 3rd edn, 2008), pp 159–181.

[18] Gready 'Use of the MMPI-2 in child custody evaluations and child protection evaluations: An examination of defensive responding and psychopathology' [2006] Dissert Ab Int: Section B. The Sciences and Engineering (66 (11–B)) 6272.

[19] Carstairs et al 'Comparison of MMPI-2 trends in UK and USA parental competency examinees' [2012] J Child Custody, (9) 195–200.

[20] Otto and Collins 'Use of the MMPI-2/MMPI-A in child custody evaluations' in Ben-Porath et al (eds) *Forensic Applications of the MMPI-2* (Sage, 1995), pp 222–252; Gould *Conducting Scientifically Crafted Child Custody Evaluations* (Professional Resource Press, 2nd edn, 2006).

[21] Bagby et al 'Defensive responding on the MMPI-2 in family custody and access evaluations' [1999] Psychol Asst, (11) 24–28.

[22] Caldwell 'How can the MMPI-2 help child custody examiners?' [2005] J Child Custody, 2(1–2) 83–117.

[23] Ganellen *Integration of the MMPI-2 and Rorschach in Personality Assessment* (Lawrence Erlbaum, 1996).

[24] Weiner and Meyer 'Personality Assessment with the Rorschach Inkblot Method' in Butcher (ed) *Oxford Handbook of Personality Assessment* (Oxford University Press, 2009), pp 277–298.

scientific basis of any conclusions that are drawn from the results. In addition, as the results from the two tests can sometimes suggest different interpretations, a comparison can shed further light on the meaning of the results. For example, what the MMPI-2 might suggest was a personality trait, could be revealed as more likely to be a product of the context of testing when the Rorschach results are taken into account.[25]

USING THE RORSCHACH AND THE MMPI-2 TO EVALUATE CAPACITY FOR CHANGE

8.16   Weiner[26] outlined characteristics from the Rorschach that can present obstacles to effective treatment. These are rigid attitudes, self-satisfaction, a lack of introspection and interpersonal distancing. Nygren[27] details research linking various Rorschach variables to suitability for therapy. Variables indicating currently available psychological resources and the capacity to implement deliberate coping strategies, (which is seen as akin to ego strength) are a good prognostic sign, as are those indicating the ability to deal with complicated emotions, the capacity for imagination, fantasy and introspection, assertiveness, and the expectation of co-operative relationships.

8.17   The MMPI-2 is often used to plan treatment.[28] The validity scales are in themselves helpful in this regard, as they provide information about an individual's willingness to co-operate, psychological sophistication, the level of current distress (which may be linked to motivation for treatment), and the extent to which resources to cope with difficulties may be employed.[29] Scores on the clinical scales have also been associated with treatment outcome. A high score on scale 1 for example suggests a focus on vague physical health issues, and pessimism about improvement in psychotherapy as the person tends to express psychological distress in the development of physical symptoms instead of being able to talk about thoughts and feelings. A high score on scale 6 indicates suspicion and hostility, with the potential to develop difficult relationships with others including therapists. The combination of scores overall can help to predict overall prognosis, and the nature of and length of treatment that are most likely to be helpful.[30]

---

[25]   Erard 'What the Rorschach can contribute to child custody and parenting time evaluations' [2005] J Child Custody, *(2)* 119–142.

[26]   Weiner 'Rorschach inkblot method' in Maruish (ed) *The use of psychological testing for treatment planning and outcomes assessment* (Lawrence Erlbaum, 2004), pp 553–588.

[27]   Nygren 'Differences in Comprehensive System Rorschach variables between groups differing in therapy suitability' [2004] Rorschachiana, (26) 110–146.

[28]   Butcher *The MMPI-2 in psychological treatment* (Oxford University Press, 1990).

[29]   Greene and Clopton 'Minnesota Multiphasic Personality Inventory – 2' in Maruish (ed) *The use of psychological testing for treatment planning and outcome assessment Volume 3: Instruments for Adults* (Lawrence Erlbaum, 3rd edn, 2004), pp 449–478.

[30]   Butcher et al 'The MMPI-2' in Harwood et al (eds) *Integrative Assessment of Adult Personality* (Guilford Press, 3rd edn, 2011), pp 152–189.

USING THE RORSCHACH AND THE MMPI-2 TO EVALUATE TREATMENT OUTCOME

8.18 In some cases, parents are referred for reassessment following a period of psychotherapy and the psychologist is asked to determine whether significant change has occurred. Test data provide a useful source of information that is separate and distinct from the interview data with the parent and the report that is obtained from the psychotherapist about progress in treatment. A comparison of the test results before and after therapy will indicate whether or not there has been significant change.

8.19 Murray[31] discusses the variables on the Rorschach that are associated with positive change in psychotherapy. These variables fall under the subheadings of the ability to deal effectively with experience, problems with experiences of the self, comfort in interpersonal situations, problems in modulating affect, and ideational difficulties. Conklin, Malone and Fowler[32] discuss how the Rorschach can evaluate and explore change in the capacity for mentalisation. Mentalisation refers to the ability to reflect on one's own and other's mental states and it is thought to be influential in the development of psychopathology and in its effective treatment. It includes empathy, social understanding, the capacity to form attachments, and boundary formation. Such variables have clear implications for effective parenting.

8.20 The MMPI-2 is sensitive to change in psychotherapy, whether that is more short term or longer-term psychoanalytic psychotherapy.[33] Some MMPI-2 variables are more closely associated with symptom reduction in treatment than others.[34] Overall, since the MMPI-2 taps into areas of psychopathology, the psychologist is looking for a reduction in the clinical scales to determine whether significant change has occurred.

8.21 We now turn to some clinical cases that demonstrate how the test results can be integrated into the whole picture to assist the court with decision-making.

---

[31] Murray 'The Rorschach search for the borderline holy grail: An examination of personality structure, personality style, and situation' in Meloy et al (eds) *Contemporary Rorschach Interpretation* (Lawrence Erlbaum, 1997), pp 123–138.

[32] Conklin et al 'Mentalisation and the Rorschach' [2012] *Rorschachiana*, (33) 189–28.

[33] Gordon 'MMPI/MMPI-2 changes in long-term psychoanalytic psychotherapy' [2001] Issues Psychoanal Psychol, (3) 59–79.

[34] Michael et al 'Using the MMPI-2 to predict symptom reduction during psychotherapy in a sample of community outpatients' [2009] J Contemp Psychother, (39) 157–163.

WHAT PSYCHOMETRIC INFORMATION MIGHT INDICATE A POSITIVE PROGNOSIS FOR CHANGE?

Case 1

8.22 A father aged 25 years with two children who had separated from the mother after some incidents in which the couple argued and he ended up hitting her in frustration. He had been drinking at the time and he sought help from his local drug and alcohol service to cut down. Medical tests confirmed that he was no longer drinking. The psychological evaluation was requested to determine his risk to the children. He was putting himself forward to parent them with support from his mother with whom he had a somewhat ambivalent but largely positive relationship.

8.23 The Rorschach and the MMPI-2 were administered among other measures, an extensive clinical interview and a review of his GP records. The MMPI-2 indicated that he responded openly, without being defensive. The only clinical scale that was significantly elevated was the one that taps symptoms of depression. This was consistent with the interview where he expressed remorse for having been aggressive to the mother in the presence of his children and sadness about the break-up of the family.

8.24 The Rorschach indicated that he had the following personality liabilities: (1) a hyper-vigilant personality style in which he was on the alert for signs of danger in the environment; (2) a tendency to jump to conclusions based on insufficient data; (3) a marked difficulty in maintaining good reality testing when his angry feelings were aroused; and (4) a pessimistic streak which put him at risk for bouts of low mood, which was consistent with the MMPI-2 results. The hyper-vigilance linked with an early childhood experience of sexual abuse from a babysitter. The other traits were consistent with his angry outbursts with the mother.

8.25 The Rorschach also indicated the following personality strengths: (1) an openness to thinking flexibly; (2) high ambition and striving for achievement; and (3) a capacity to be introspective and insightful. All of these traits are positive prognostic signs for psychotherapy. In the interview, he requested this help and stated that he had been to his GP for a referral which was confirmed by the review of his GP records. The recommendation was for him to engage in psychotherapy which was highly likely to be beneficial to him and to enable him to overcome the personal issues which had led to the risk to the children.

Case 2

8.26 A mother, aged 25, who had four children, and was expecting her fifth child. Her older three children had been removed from her care after concern was raised about domestic violence and drug use. She openly acknowledged using cannabis on a regular basis, but denied that there was violence in her relationship with her ex-partner, who was also the father of her children. She engaged well with the psychological assessment, and presented herself in a rational, thoughtful way.

8.27 The Rorschach indicated that she was currently troubled by intrusive thoughts about other people making decisions about her future, which was clearly linked to her position in the childcare proceedings. However she appeared to have adequate resources to cope with stress and the demands of daily living, and this is a good sign for both parenting and the ability to tolerate and use psychotherapy. While being interested in others, she appeared to have current emotional needs for intimacy and closeness that were unmet, and she had little expectation of co-operative and supportive relationships with others. This latter point may have negative implications for engagement in psychotherapy and a straightforward development of trust in a therapist. She showed evidence of a preoccupation with herself, possibly due to a tendency to see herself in a negative light compared to others, but this lack of self-satisfaction may be a motivation for therapy, and during the assessment she stated a wish to seek help in feeling more positive about herself and her abilities. Other positive indications were good reality testing, openness to new experiences and the ability to be flexible in her thinking: these assets were described by Weiner[35] as contributing to good parenting and by Nygren[36] as being good indicators for change in psychotherapy.

8.28 The MMPI-2 also showed feelings of personal inadequacy, pessimism and uncertainty about the future. This mother appeared to be very sensitive to criticism, and to be distressed at the current time about a recent difficult event. She was shy and inhibited in relationships, and may have difficulty expressing her feelings towards others. She had a number of personality characteristics that are associated with substance misuse, and this required further evaluation. She appeared motivated to seek and respond to psychotherapy. Recommendations were made for her to have the opportunity to engage in treatment for substance misuse and in psychotherapy.

WHAT PSYCHOMETRIC INFORMATION MIGHT RAISE CONCERNS ABOUT PARENTING ABILITY AND CAPACITY TO CHANGE?

Case 3

8.29 A mother aged 33 years who faced criminal charges of child neglect in relation to an incident in which she locked her four children aged from 3 to 11 years in their home and went out with a new boyfriend. The oldest child managed to summon help and reported that her mother often did this when the

---

35   Weiner 'Rorschach assessment in child custody cases' [2005] J of Child Custody, (2) 99–119.
36   Nygren 'Differences in Comprehensive System Rorschach variables between groups differing in therapy suitability' [2004] *Rorschachiana*, (26) 110–146.

police arrived. When questioned about this in the interview, the mother expressed irritation, saying that the children did not come to harm so what was all the fuss?

8.30 The Rorschach and the MMPI-2 were administered among other measures, an extensive clinical interview and a review of her GP and police records.

8.31 The Rorschach results were marked by defensiveness and during the administration of this test, she was noted to be resistant and irritated with the task, telling the psychologist that it was stupid and it had no bearing on her parenting. However, with strong encouragement to continue, she eventually gave enough responses for reliable and valid interpretation. The results indicated that there were several liabilities: (1) very limited coping skills; (2) a simplistic, disengaged approach to life where she viewed situations in a 'black and white' manner, with little room for feelings such that she is often likely to be insensitive and lacking in empathy; (3) impaired reality testing; and (4) narcissistic preoccupation with her own needs.

8.32 The MMPI-2 indicated that she responded openly, without being defensive. The only clinical scale that was significantly elevated was the one which was originally called 'psychopathic deviate' because it relates to anti-social traits. This scale has a wealth of research that indicates that those who score highly on it are irresponsible, impulsive and reckless and lack empathy for others, tending to place their need for gratification above other concerns. They are poor candidates for psychotherapy because they do not see themselves as having a problem – instead, they locate any problems in external circumstances. The psychologist argued that this result provided the court with a research base upon which to reach the decision that the incident when the children were abandoned represented behaviour that was likely to be repeated, that the on-going risk to the children was too high to consider reunification, and that the mother would be unlikely to engage in psychotherapy or if she did attend, would be unlikely to benefit from it.

Case 4

8.33 A mother who had recently given birth to her sixth child: her previous five children had all been permanently removed from her care due to neglect and emotional abuse. She had been in two mother and baby placements in the past, and while in one of these placements the foster carers described her as one of the 'least capable parents' they had worked with. She was said to be emotionally detached and unresponsive. She did not accept responsibility for her previous difficulties caring for her children. During previous childcare proceedings she had been assessed as needing therapy, but she had not accessed this, despite being given the opportunity to attend a specialist psychotherapy service.

8.34 This mother was assessed using the MMPI-2, the Rorschach and an assessment of the potential for child abuse. Her response style on the MMPI-2 showed the possibility of exaggeration. Her profile showed that she was experiencing psychological problems at the time of testing, but that her difficulties were likely to be due to long-standing personality traits: her profile matched particular scale elevations which are known to be associated with parenting difficulties (on scale 4 and 8). She appeared to be unconventional, alienated from others, unpredictable and impulsive, irritable, and having a tendency to use other people for her own gratification. Some of these features match Caldwell's (2005) five basic issues in relation to parenting. Her attitudes and difficulties were consistent with a personality disorder diagnosis, and her history included the experience of multiple forms of abuse during childhood which is commonly seen in people with this diagnosis.

8.35 The Rorschach showed a tendency to overvalue her personal worth, and to be preoccupied with her own needs at the expense of others' needs. She had a strong sense of entitlement, and a tendency to externalise blame and responsibility; this tendency was often noted in the background documentation. However, alongside her self-aggrandisement, there were indications that she experienced moments of uncertainty about her self-worth. This would be likely to lead to adjustment difficulties, and fluctuations in her mood, as she tried to manage her conflicting beliefs about herself. She showed limited capacity to form close attachments to others, and her relationships are likely to be distant and detached. This was consistent with the background documentation that contained many examples of how she was emotionally distant from her children and their feelings. She appeared to have few psychological resources, and when confronted with stress she was at risk for distress, limited frustration tolerance and poor impulse control. She was unlikely to seek psychotherapy voluntarily. The psychologist concluded that this mother would have significant difficulties empathising with her children, and understanding and providing for their emotional needs. There was a lack of positive indicators that change was possible, and it was very doubtful that this mother would give herself the opportunity to change.

WHAT PSYCHOMETRIC INFORMATION WOULD WE LOOK FOR TO ESTABLISH THAT CHANGE HAS OCCURRED?

Case 5

8.36 A mother who was first assessed at the age of 28. The reason for the referral was child protection concerns for her daughter who was aged 4 years old and who was neglected and possibly exposed to sexual behaviour. The mother worked as a prostitute and had a history of drug abuse. The child was removed.

8.37   The mother was assessed again 2 years after the first evaluation. She had given birth to a son who was aged 3 months. She had been attending a residential mother and baby rehabilitation centre with him, for mothers with a history of substance abuse. She had had some group therapy at the centre but no individual therapy. The main question for the second evaluation was to determine whether there were any changes in her psychological profile.

8.38   On both occasions, mother completed the Rorschach and the MMPI-2. In the first testing, the Rorschach indicated: (1) an unpredictable and inconsistent coping style; (2) marked stress with a risk of becoming overwhelmed and behaving impulsively; (3) rigid, inflexible views that would impede change in psychotherapy and a lack of insight; and (4) oppositional tendencies. The MMPI-2 indicated: (1) openness and no sign of defensiveness; (2) poor impulse control and a tendency to be uninhibited and self-indulgent; (3) a need for constant stimulation and attention from others, along with the capacity to present a charming façade; and (4) her relationships are usually quite superficial and manipulative.

8.39   On the second occasion, the mother approached both of the tests in a guarded and defensive stance. She presented herself in an unrealistically positive light on the MMPI-2, denying problems and maintaining an impression of self control. There was some evidence for a mild tendency towards rebellious behaviour, thrill seeking, impulsivity and self gratification but this was not as marked as it had been. She appeared to be outgoing and sociable, with a strong need for social recognition.

8.40   On the Rorschach, she responded reluctantly and gave fewer responses than in the first administration. Her reality testing was good and she took care to give socially conventional responses. Her thought processes were somewhat scattered and disjointed, suggesting some distractibility. Her main coping style appeared to be one of avoidance and suppression. On the positive side, she presented with reasonably good social skills but she appeared to be withdrawn at the time of testing.

8.41   Test results suggested that she was anxious in the second evaluation about creating a good impression. She was less overwhelmed than she had been in the first evaluation but she was achieving this increased stability by screening out many thoughts and feelings. The general trend towards thrill-seeking, problems with impulse control and a need for attention from others was still in evidence. Overall, the test results suggested that the changes she had made were fragile and somewhat superficial and that further individual therapy would be advisable if she were to provide a stable base for her son through-out his childhood.

Case 6

8.42   The mother was first seen at the age of 38. She had two sons, one of whom was 12 years old and had been diagnosed with autism and the other of whom was 8 years old and did not have any special needs. Father had left the family many years ago but maintained contact. There was an older daughter aged 20 by a different father who had been removed from mother's care at the age of 8 due to mother's use of physical punishment. Social Services were involved when the 8 year old boy went to school with a red mark on his face and reported that his mother had hit him that morning when he was slow to get dressed. Mother admitted to this. In the interview, she reported having struggled on her own with the two boys for many years without adequate social support and she said that she had been reluctant to ask for help in case this was held against her.

8.43 She presented in the first evaluation with low mood and she expressed distress at what had happened. The Rorschach indicated an emotionally withdrawn state in which she tended to back away from social interactions and a defensive position of turning negative feelings into something positive, even when this is unrealistic. Unappealing, discouraging or even threatening situations may be denied and instead she may attribute attractive qualities to such situations. This pattern of denial is usually a defensive attempt to keep oneself in good spirits by refusing to acknowledge the existence of potentially upsetting or depressing concerns. This defense is often fragile and it can crumble easily, leaving her vulnerable to bouts of low mood. The Rorschach also indicated low self esteem and good reality testing, with the capacity to think logically and coherently and come to reasonable conclusions about the relationships between events.

8.44 The MMPI-2 indicated an open and co-operative stance, with a willingness to admit to problems. The only clinical scale that was elevated was the one that taps symptoms of depression. The outcome of this first evaluation was that individual psychotherapy for depression was recommended. The older boy was placed in a special residential unit for adolescents and the younger boy was placed in foster care. Mother was given the opportunity to seek treatment and apply to the court again after she had completed this.

8.45 The second evaluation took place 14 months later. She found that her older boy was doing very well in the residential unit and she considered that it was in his best interests to stay there. She was applying to the court to have her younger son returned to her care. She had had 9 months of weekly individual psychotherapy. She reported that she benefitted from being able to talk about her feelings in therapy and the therapist provided a report to confirm that this process was helpful to her.

8.46 The Rorschach showed that she was under stress due to the situation of having to go back to court but she had developed a better capacity to be open and expressive of her feelings. Once again, she was not defensive on the MMPI-2 and her depressive symptoms had reduced markedly. Test results confirmed the reports of progress in therapy and the recommendation was for her younger son to be returned to her care with the provision of support from a parenting group.

CONCLUSIONS

8.47 Psychometric tests provide psychologists with additional, systematic data when assessing the nature of a parent's difficulties and whether change is possible. The MMPI-2 and the Rorschach are two of the most well researched tests for the assessment of emotional functioning. They are used both generically and specifically within parenting evaluations in many different countries to provide a broad assessment of facets of personality functioning. We have given six case examples to show how these tests can be used in parenting evaluations. The results from these tests can be integrated with interviews and background information to yield indicators for parenting ability, indicators for potential change in psychotherapy, and indicators that change has occurred.

CHAPTER 9

PARENTS WITH DRUG AND ALCOHOL PROBLEMS: CHANGE TAKES TIME AND THE DILEMMA OF TIMESCALES

John Castleton

CONTEXT[1]

9.1   In 2011–2012, it was estimated that in the UK:[2]

- 8% of parents had taken illegal drugs.
- 7% of parents had taken legal highs.
- 82% of parents had drunk alcohol.

9.2   With regard to substance *use*, it should be recognised that: 'alcohol, and to a lesser extent drug use, is well integrated into the lives of many parents. For example, drinking alcohol is an intrinsic element of most religious ceremonies, festive celebrations, meals, and everyday entertainment ... The occasional use of alcohol or some ... drugs ... results in few, if any, lasting adverse effects'.[3]

9.3   The risks associated with parental substance *misuse* have been documented[4] and the emerging picture indicates that during 2011–2012:[5]

- 7% of parents drank every day.
- 700,000 children were living with a dependent drinker.
- 250,000–350,000 children were living with a problem drug user.
- 50% of adults in drug treatment were parents or lived with children.

---

[1]   In this chapter, I will use the terms drug or substance to refer to: 'a psychoactive ... chemical [including alcohol] ... whether of natural or synthetic origin, which can be used to alter perception, mood or other psychological states'. Gossop *Living with drugs* (Ashgate, 6th edn, 2007).

[2]   www.nta.nhs.uk; www.alcoholconcern.org.uk.

[3]   Cleaver et al *Children's Needs – Parenting Capacity* (TSO, 2nd edn, 2011).

[4]   Advisory Council on the Misuse of Drugs (ACMD) *Hidden Harm* (TSO, 2003); Brandon et al *Understanding Serious Case Reviews* (DCSF, 2009); Cleaver et al (2011).

[5]   www.nta.nhs.uk; www.alcoholconcern.org.uk; eg NTA, *Parents with drug problems* (NTA, 2012).

- 6% of women starting drug treatment were pregnant.

9.4   The focus of this chapter is parents who have substance use problems, including those whose substance use has become dependent.[6] As Galvani and Forrester note, 'terminology is important as this can be stigmatising with the potential to cause further disempowerment'. Using the terms 'substance use problems', 'problem drug and/or alcohol use' or 'substance misuse' will 'reflect the complex relationships with a range of substances and distinguish this type of use from the non-problematic use of alcohol and/or drugs'.[7]

9.5   Services and the courts deal with parents who are dependent on alcohol or drugs. They also intervene with parents who may not meet the criteria for dependence, but whose substance use is evidently problematic. In most cases, there will be a combination of adverse factors, eg substance misuse, domestic violence and mental health difficulties; 'the toxic trio'.[8]

PROBLEMATIC SUBSTANCE USE, ADDICTION, DEPENDENCE

9.6   The Advisory Council on the Misuse of Drugs (ACMD) defined *problem* substance use as that which has: 'serious negative consequences of a physical, psychological, social and interpersonal, financial or legal nature for users and those around them'.[9]

9.7   By definition, dependent use is also problematic, as the person will manifest dysfunction in many areas of their life (*domains*). In contrast, a problematic substance user may not be dependent, for example, someone whose behaviour is generally appropriate, but who occasionally binge drinks and gets into fights while drunk. (It must be recognised that the risk of acting inappropriately is increased by the disinhibiting effects of substances.)

9.8   There are many different models of dependence, which take contrasting perspectives on this issue (with a focus that ranges from biology, genetics, psychology, personality, culture and/or social factors) and, thereby, ways to resolve it. Crudely summarised below are two examples that appear to be at opposite ends of this spectrum.

9.9   Within the 12-step movement (based on Alcoholics Anonymous (AA), Narcotics Anonymous (NA))[10], addiction is seen as 'a progressive illness that

---

[6]   See Cleaver et al (2011) and ACMD (2003) for a detailed account of the implications of parental substance misuse, including the effects of different substances, at various stages of a child's life.

[7]   Galvani and Forrester *Social Work Services and Recovery* (Assoc Dir Soc Work, 2011, p 2).

[8]   Brandon et al *Building on the learning from serious case reviews 2007–2009 Research Report* (DFE-RR040 209).

[9]   Advisory Council on the Misuse of Drugs *Hidden Harm: Needs of children of problem drug users* (TSO/HMSO, 2003), p 7.

[10]   www.alcoholics-anonymous.org.uk; http://ukna.org/.

can never be "cured" but which, like some other illnesses, can be arrested ... "Once an alcoholic – always an alcoholic" is a simple fact we have to live with ... The only alternative is to stop drinking completely and to abstain from even the smallest quantity of alcohol in any form'.[11]

9.10 In contrast, social learning theory suggests that substance misuse is learned behaviour, which has a functional value to the individual, but can be modified and unlearned. It is possible, therefore, to overcome dependence and to develop skills and techniques for controlling behaviour.[12] This model is utilised by SMART (Self-Management And Recovery Training), 'a programme to help people manage their recovery from any type of addictive behavior ... SMART helps participants decide whether they have a problem, builds up their motivation to change and offers a set of proven tools and techniques to support recovery'.[13]

9.11 In practice, most services now utilise a combination of techniques derived from various models, including social learning and 12-step approaches, that is, adopting a *bio-psycho-social* model of substance misuse, which has been described as an excessive appetite.[14]

9.12 Dependence (or addiction)[15] is defined according to a cluster of biological, social and psychological factors. Dependence, describes a compulsion to take substances and:[16]

> 'is characterised by an individual pathologically pursuing reward and/or relief by substance use ... that leads to ... biological, psychological, social and spiritual manifestations ... [including] inability to consistently abstain, impairment in behavioral control, craving, diminished recognition of significant problems with one's behaviors and interpersonal relationships, and a dysfunctional emotional response.'

9.13 In the UK,[17] the *International Classification of Diseases*[18] defines substance dependence as the presence of three or more of the following criteria, occurring together repeatedly, within a 12-month period:

- A strong desire or sense of compulsion to consume substances.

---

[11] Quotation taken from www.alcoholics-anonymous.org.uk, 2014.
[12] Raistrick et al *Tackling alcohol together* (Free Association, 1999).
[13] Quotation taken from www.smartrecovery.org.uk, 2014.
[14] Orford *Excessive Appetites* (Wiley, 2nd edn, 2001).
[15] In general use, the terms 'dependence' and 'addiction' appear to be interchangeable.
[16] American Society of Addiction *Medicine Public Policy Statement*.
     http://www.asam.org/DefinitionofAddiction-LongVersion.html (2011).
[17] The US framework is the *Diagnostic & Statistical Manual of Mental Disorders [DSM-5]* (American Psychiatric Association, 5th edn, 2013).
[18] *International Classification of Diseases [ICD-10]* (World Health Organisation, 10th edn). Non-medical staff may be trained to use psychometric instruments that have been developed from ICD-10 and/or DSM-5 criteria to assess for dependent/problematic substance use, such as AUDIT (Babor et al Alcohol Use Disorders Identification Test; WHO, 2001) and SASSI (Miller et al Substance Abuse Subtle Screening Inventory, SASSI Institute, 2003).

- Impaired capacity to control substance use.

- A physiological withdrawal state when use is reduced or ceased.

- Evidence of tolerance to the effects of substances.

- Preoccupation with substance use.

- Persistent use despite clear evidence of harmful consequences.

9.14 As the diagnostic criteria indicate, dependence is perhaps best understood as the product of a variety of contributory factors: 'biology plays some part, in as much as certain drugs have physical withdrawal symptoms; but one also needs to acknowledge the role [of] other phenomena such as learned behaviour, cultural and social influences.'[19]

9.15 In other words, 'environmental factors interact with the person's biology and affect the extent to which genetic factors exert their influence. Resiliencies the individual acquires (through parenting or later life experiences) can affect the extent to which genetic predispositions lead to the behavioral and other manifestations of addiction. Culture also plays a role in how addiction becomes actualised in persons with biological vulnerabilities to the development of addiction.'[20]

9.16 Substances 'change the way we feel. If they make us feel better, relax us, give us a lift, make us feel powerful, energise us, excite us, let us escape, make the world go away, bring relief ... we tend to go back to them ... What can start out as casual experimentation, normal social behaviour or even doctor prescribed can lead to repeating the behaviour more frequently and with greater quantities involved ... The body's chemistry may start to adapt, demanding ever more ... and fiercely resisting the discomfort of withdrawal. The behaviour takes on a self-perpetuating life of its own.'[21]

9.17 To understand the development of problematic use, it is important to consider the interacting influences of *substance, set and setting*.[22] That is, the physical effects of the substance; the person's frame of mind, or psychological set; and the social setting in which they use substances.

9.18 For example, substance use may be pleasurable, or give relief from anxiety or depression (initially, at least). This can be attractive for someone who has had poor life experience (eg inconsistent parenting, neglect) and presents as vulnerable, with low resilience and relatively few protective factors (eg supportive family, success in education or employment). They may be living in a situation where substance use is normalised and there is relative social isolation.

---

[19] Reid *Theories of addiction and dependence* (MMU, unpublished paper, 1996).
[20] See footnote 16.
[21] Barton *Why do people become addicted?* (BBC, 2003).
[22] Zinberg *Drug, set and setting* (Yale University Press, 1984).

9.19 It should be acknowledged, also, that most people do not start to use drugs or alcohol for *obviously* negative reasons. In the Phoenix Futures survey of people in treatment for drug and alcohol dependence, most people were introduced to drugs by someone they knew (ie a friend or a relative) and the most common reason (58%) for first taking drugs heavily was for fun.[23] Then, after a period of dabbling, they may drift into dependence, 'taking weeks, months, or even years' and 'virtually every addict started out believing s/he could boss the drug'.[24]

9.20 Where substance misuse is found, it will often be *poly-substance* use, as we now live in a 'pick 'n' mix' culture,[25] where people use combinations of substances together, or over a relatively short period to achieve the desired effect (eg cocaine to 'get in the mood' for socialising, then alcohol or cannabis to 'mellow' when they get home).

9.21 Some of the identifiable risks factors associated with the development of problematic substance use include; a family history of substance misuse and modelling of this behaviour, dysfunction and/or conflict, childhood neglect or abuse, social deprivation and anti-social behaviour.[26] It should be noted, however: 'there is no typical ... adolescent and no specific personality type, family situation, socio-economic group or stressful experience that has been found to predict categorically the development of substance misuse.'[27]

9.22 There are also protective factors, for example, the impact of parental alcohol misuse will be reduced if there is a positive relationship with a parent or significant adult. Velleman and Orford[28] also found that the children of problem drinkers are more affected by inappropriate behaviour (arguments, aggression, etc) than parental drinking as such.[29]

9.23 A range of personality problems has been linked with substance misuse and dependence. Substance misusers may present with personality characteristics, such as poor impulse control, impatience, poor frustration tolerance, resentment and difficulty deferring gratification. For some people, these traits *precede* substance misuse and the associated lifestyle, for others they result *from* it.[30]

9.24 As NTA[31] have pointed out, problematic substance users present 'with a range of problems', for example, mood disorders (eg depression, anxiety) are

---

[23] Phoenix Futures *Dependent on a Future* (Phoenix Futures, 2006).

[24] Tyler *Street drugs* (Coronet, 2nd edn, 1986), p 288.

[25] Parker and Measham *Pick 'n' Mix* (Drugs: education prevention and policy 1994, 1, 5–1).

[26] Castleton and Shaw *Working with Young Substance Misusers* (Representing Children, 2001, 12 (2), pp 111–126); Castleton & Britton Taking care with drugs (DrugScope, 2002).

[27] Health Advisory Service (HAS) *Children and Young People: Substance Misuse* (HMSO, 1996).

[28] Velleman and Orford *Risk and resilience* (Harwood, 1999).

[29] See footnote 28.

[30] HAS, 1996; DSM-5, 2013.

[31] NTA *Enhancing outcomes* (NTA, 2004).

common among substance misusers. Weaver et al[32] reported that 67.6% of people in a drug treatment population and 85.5% of users of alcohol services experienced depression and/or anxiety disorder.

9.25 There is an association between substance use and self-medication to ease the distress from a range of problems. 'Drinking or drug use can … be used to alter undesirable states such as depression, anxiety … or the low self-esteem resulting from domestic violence.'[33] 'Self-medication is … a useful way to describe many of the reasons we [take] … a mood-altering substance that is used to mask other problems, or to deal with emotions … The first drink [or drug] … depresses the parts of the brain … associated with inhibition, increasing talking and self-confidence and reducing social anxiety. As more enters the bloodstream, the areas of the brain associated with emotions are affected.'[34]

9.26 Substance use results in emotional suppression and impaired information processing (ie not thinking clearly), so it provides 'relief from negative emotional states … which constitutes negative reinforcement',[35] even if this is short-lived. For example, using heroin and feeling wrapped in cotton wool, detached from physical or emotional discomfort or pain. Conversely, symptoms of anxiety or depression may be precipitated by cessation of heavy or long-term use of substances, setting up a vicious circle of abstinence, distress and further intoxication.

9.27 Unfortunately, while self medicating may initially assist the person to cope, it may become a contributing factor to their distress; that is, a maladaptive pattern. 'People try to self-medicate symptoms … and find that taking substances [initially] makes them feel better … But this ultimately just perpetuates the disorder, stops them from processing their problems, so they end up worse.'[36]

9.28 Continued substance use may be perceived as an appealing option, despite negative consequences. A significant amount of people in drug and alcohol treatment report they had previously relapsed because they could not face their emotions in a substance-free state.[37] Ambivalence, which is common, may be indicative of fear (implicit or explicit) that they will be overwhelmed if they open the Pandora's Box of their emotional world.

9.29 The risk factors raised by parental substance misuse have been covered in detail.[38] The 'SCODA Guidelines'[39] provide a framework for assessment of

---

[32] Weaver et al *Co-morbidity of substance misuse and mental illness* (NTA/DoH, 2004).
[33] Cleaver et al *Children's Needs – Parenting Capacity* (TSO, 1st edn, 1999, p 26).
[34] Mental Health Foundation *Cheers? Alcohol and mental health* (MHF, 2006).
[35] American Society of Addiction Medicine Public Policy Statement.
      http://www.asam.org/DefinitionofAddiction-LongVersion.html (2011).
[36] Mills et al 'Trauma, PTSD, and substance use disorders' [2006] Am J Psychiat, 163, 652–658.
[37] Phoenix Futures, 2006.
[38] Cleaver et al (1999/2011); Harbin & Murphy *Substance misuse and child care* (RHP, 2000).

substance using parents and risk to their children, in addition to broader assessments that will be undertaken by social care agencies.

9.30 It is possible for substance using parents to manage their home life effectively and this is more likely if they have a partner with whom they are able to make appropriate arrangements, for child care, etc. Unfortunately, parents may be physically or emotionally unavailable, or their behaviour may be inconsistent, for example, making a commitment to activities with, or for, their children, which they do not complete.

9.31 'The conventional prescription for good parenting ... is two parents in the home ... In the case of a drug-abusing mother, the situation calls for an heroic father who can fill the roles of both mother and father when needed ... Sad to say ... the heroic father is a rare breed. More often than not the fathers of these children are absent or drug-abusers themselves.'[40]

9.32 Kroll and Taylor[41] noted that substance misusing parents:

'have a range of problems to manage, in terms of accessing substances, and behaviour may be characterised by inconsistency, irritability, lack of energy and impaired judgement. This together with social context and the absence of family or friendship support systems ... can result in increased risks.'

9.33 In relationships where substance misuse is a common denominator, through which experiences have been filtered, the dynamics will be adversely affected. Partners can find it difficult to challenge each other and each partner knows how to manipulate the other. When facing the pressures of the world, the distorted sense of loyalty may result in a tendency to collude against the perceived threat, rather than look at how their behaviour may have brought about these challenges. When substance misuse becomes integral to a relationship, it will become both a trigger of difficulties and a perceived coping strategy.

9.34 These dynamics will also make it more difficult for the partners to achieve change. For example, someone who is trying to abstain will find it difficult if their partner continues to bring alcohol or drugs into the home. When change has been achieved, it is possible that one partner may relapse and this will present difficulty for the other, again including temptation to use substances, or how to deal with situations appropriately.

9.35 Parents who are involved in substance misuse may associate primarily with other people who would be supportive of this behaviour and lifestyle (eg 'drinking buddies'). In families affected by substance misuse, there may be attempts to conceal parental engagement in unacceptable activities (often

[39] Hogg et al *Drug Using Parents* [SCODA Guidelines] (LGDF & SCODA, 1989/1997).
[40] Klee et al *Drug misuse & motherhood* (Routledge, 2002, p 94).
[41] Kroll and Taylor *Parental substance misuse and child welfare* (JKP, 2003, p 38).

resulting in a pattern of deceit or denial). The consequent social isolation may adversely affect a child's development of pro-social views or behaviour.

9.36 Parents may have difficulty controlling the home environment, which may have frequent visits from acquaintances or strangers seeking drugs, or a place to use drugs. Substance misusers may put their children at risk by leaving them in the care of inappropriate adults, or taking children with them when they visit dealers or engage in acquisitive crimes, such as shop-lifting.

9.37 There may be many house moves for the family, as a result of which children may move schools, affecting opportunities to fully engage in education and establish friendships.

9.38 Substance misusing parents may have no discernible pattern to their day, when routines and boundaries are disrupted or absent, with adverse implications for children in developing settled meal-times, bed-times, school attendance, etc. A significant proportion of the parents' time will be spent on substance-related activities; income generation (including committing offences), buying and using drugs, etc. In addition, finances may be diverted from household requirements, or paying bills. Possessions may be sold, or family members may provide finances, supposedly for other purposes.

9.39 Even if they are too young to fully understand what is happening, children often have greater awareness of their parents' behaviour than the adults realise or openly acknowledge.[42] Children in such families may take on responsibilities that are not age appropriate; role reversal. Substance misusing parents may genuinely believe they have tried to prevent their children from being exposed to adult difficulties, but it is often not achieved.

9.40 There is sometimes condemnation of women who misuse substances during pregnancy. This can lead to reluctance to access services at a time when they are most needed and initial contacts and experiences may determine future uptake of services.[43] 'They often book late and their associated lifestyle may mean that there are more urgent demands on their time.'[44]

9.41 In terms of specific substances, one side effect of dependent heroin use is that periods may become irregular. Consequently, contraception may not be considered necessary, in the mistaken belief that the woman has become infertile. Similarly, the initial signs of pregnancy may not be apparent, as they are masked by the opiate effects, or they may be misattributed to other physical processes. Thirdly, the foetus may be small for dates, as a combination of substance effects and the woman's lifestyle (poor nutrition, etc).[45]

---

[42] Advisory Council on the Misuse of Drugs Hidden Harm *Needs of children of problem drug users* (TSO/HMSO, 2003), p 7.

[43] Pugh *Women, drugs & parenting* (Warwick University, 1996, unpublished MA Dissertation).

[44] Harrington and Stubbs *Women, pregnancy & substance misuse* (NHS Scotland, 2006), p 11.

[45] Hepburn *Drug use in pregnancy* (Druglink, 1996, 11/4).

9.42 As NICE have reported 'pregnant women who misuse substances may be anxious about the attitudes of healthcare staff and the potential role of social services. They may also be overwhelmed by the involvement of multiple agencies. These women need supportive and coordinated care during pregnancy.'[46]

TREATMENT/INTERVENTIONS AND RECOVERY[47]

9.43 In addition to the many ACMD reports,[48] there is evidence-based guidance around problem substance use from the NTA (National Treatment Agency for Substance Misuse, now incorporated into Public Health England)[49] and NICE (National Institute for Health and Clinical Excellence)[50] with which workers in generic social and health care organisations should be familiar.

9.44 The main outcomes according to which the effectiveness of treatment is usually measured are: substance use behaviour (substance type, frequency and quantity of use), psychological and physical health, and social functioning (employment, accommodation, offending).[51] From a *treatment* perspective, the demonstration of appropriate functioning in a broad sense is more important than a focus on total abstinence.

9.45 Abstinence may refer to a person being drug-free, that is, not using *any* substance, whether alcohol, licit or illicit drugs, or a prescribed substitute (for example, in the 12-step model, where abstinence is seen as a necessity for progress in recovery). But, in the context of some treatment programmes, the term may also be used to describe someone who has stopped using illicit drugs with the support of treatment that includes a prescribed substitute. For example, someone taking only prescribed methadone is not *drug*-free, but they are *illicit* drug-free, therefore, they may be referred to as abstinent.

9.46 It is important that professionals are clear about what they mean by abstinence, as this will have significant implications for the level of change expected of parents. It must also be recognised that *total* abstinence is unusual in the adult UK population.

9.47 For heroin addiction, for example, the daily dose of methadone should be enough to prevent withdrawal, but not enough to cause intoxication.[52] In

---

[46] NICE *Pregnancy and complex social factors* (NICE, 2010, p 13).
[47] For a detailed description of treatment see: Gossop *Treating drug misuse problems* (NTA, 2006).
[48] https://www.gov.uk/government/organisations/advisory-council-on-the-misuse-of-drugs.
[49] NTA *Models of care* (2002/2005/2007); Enhancing outcomes (2004); Gossop (2006); Development of joint local protocols (2011).
[50] NICE *Drug misuse: Psychosocial interventions & detoxification* (2007); *Methadone and buprenorphine for opioid dependence* (2007); *Pregnancy and complex social factors* (2010); *Alcohol-use disorders* (2011).
[51] Gossop *Treating drug misuse problems* (NTA, 2006).
[52] Preston *The Methadone Briefing* (ISDD, 1996).

comparison to street heroin, this provides a clean product, of known concentration (dosage), which produces a gradual, consistent release of the opiate into the person's bloodstream, rather than the relatively short peaks of heroin.

9.48 Prescribing can support the person to make changes in behaviour and drug-focussed lifestyle, unfortunately, this is only likely to be achieved if they abstain from heroin or achieve controlled use.

9.49 In the treatment of alcohol dependence, Antabuse (disulfiram) may be prescribed to assist the person to abstain. This is not an alcohol blocker, but:[53]

> 'causes an unpleasant reaction 15–20 minutes after alcohol enters the body ... [It] enables the individual to get used to life without alcohol ... [But] it only works if taken consistently ... [which] has been improved by ... having a partner or supervisor to aid compliance.'

9.50 It must be recognised, however, that a prescription is not a panacea and should be offered as part of a co-ordinated treatment programme, supporting the person to make changes in their behaviour and lifestyle.

9.51 A range of psychological interventions target a client's substance using behaviour, such as motivational interviewing, 'which directs people to explore and resolve their ambivalence about their substance use (the 'good things' versus the 'less good things') and move through the stages of change',[54] relapse prevention and contingency management, but it cannot be said that one form is better for all clients than any other.[55]

9.52 Although dependence is 'a chronic condition with a variable course and no known cure',[56] treatment works in terms of improved outcomes. There does not appear to be consensus, however, on which treatment works best, or matching clients to different treatments.

9.53 Large-scale studies in the UK and USA[57] covering various modalities (one-to-one, residential, etc), from a range of models (12-step, motivational interviewing, etc) have broadly found that all well-delivered interventions seem effective, but also found that matching effects were few and modest. Moreover, it has been suggested that the therapeutic relationship between worker and client was more important than which therapy was practised.[58]

---

[53] Chick 'Pharmacological treatments' in Heather and Stockwell (eds) *Treatment and prevention of alcohol problems* (Wiley, 2004), p 55.

[54] Humeniuk et al *Brief interventions manual; ASSIST* (WHO, 2010, p 13).

[55] Winigaratne et al *Effectiveness of psychological therapies on drug misusing clients* (NTA, 2005).

[56] McLellan et al *Is drug dependence a chronic medical illness* (TRI, undated, p 4).

[57] Drug Abuse Treatment Outcome Studies (DATOS); National Treatment Outcome Research Study (NTORS); Project MATCH; UK Alcohol Treatment Trial (UKAAT).

[58] Karno et al *Does matching matter?* (2007, 102), pp 587–596).

9.54   There does not appear to be consensus on the optimum treatment period and level of input (ie episode and dose), however, treated individuals achieve higher remission rates than do untreated individuals[59] and outcomes tend to improve as retention in treatment increases.

9.55   If treatment is to produce improved outcomes, clients should stay for long enough to be exposed to, and actively participate in, interventions of sufficient quality and intensity (in terms of dose, therapeutic relationship and engagement) to bring about change.[60]

9.56   Equally important is the after-care which someone receives. With regard to heroin addiction, for example, it has been recommended that: 'after successful ... detoxification ... offer ... continued treatment, support and monitoring ... for at least 6 months ... to help maintain abstinence.'[61] In addition, mutual aid (eg AA, NA, SMART Recovery) can play an important role in sustaining changes.

9.57   In addition to substance-focused interventions, psychological therapies (eg CBT) should be offered to clients who experience emotional difficulties (eg anxiety, depression, etc). A Cochrane Review also recommended that for people with *co-morbid conditions* (also referred to as *dual diagnosis*), co-ordination across substance misuse and mental health services is essential to maximise impact, efficiently utilise resources, and avoid the client having to negotiate multiple care systems (or risk 'falling between stools').[62]

THE PROCESS OF CHANGE

9.58   It is common to find that substance misusers are ambivalent about stopping using, as their motivation fluctuates. Objectively, there may be an accumulation of negative consequences from their actions. Despite this, however, the fear of having to cope with life without a psychoactive substance to cushion the interface with the world may be a much more powerful subjective force to maintain the status quo. They may react with hostility or obstruction in an attempt to resist what is perceived as unwelcome, or unwarranted, interference in their lives.

9.59   The process of addressing dependence is illustrated in the stages of change model,[63] which describes the cyclical nature of change in human behaviour, including substance misuse.

---

[59]   Moos and Moos 'Rates and predictors of relapse' [2006] *Addiction*, 101, 212–22.
[60]   Gossop *Treating drug misuse problems* (NTA, 2006).
[61]   NICE Drug misuse: Psychosocial interventions & detoxification (NICE, 2007).
[62]   Gossop *Treating drug misuse problems* (NTA, 2006); Cleary et al *Cochrane Review of psychosocial interventions for people with dual diagnosis* (2008).
[63]   Prochaska and Diclemente *Towards a Comprehensive Model of Change* (Plenum, 1986).

9.60　The stages of the model are:

- *Pre-contemplation*: Where substance users are not aware that they have a problem, and therefore do not seriously think about change. It is others who recognise that there are problems and change is required.

- *Contemplation*: A stage where the individual begins to weigh up the pros and cons of their substance use; they feel somewhat ambivalent about their behaviour. The person considers that there might be a problem and that change might be necessary.

- *Decision*: A stage where the balance of change is influenced and a point is reached where a decision is made by the person to do something, or possibly nothing, about their attendant behaviour.

- *Action*: The process or stage of doing something. The person chooses a strategy for change and pursues it, taking steps to put their decision into effect. This is traditionally where 'motivation' for treatment would begin.

- *Maintenance*: During this stage the task is to maintain the gains that have been made in order to avoid a return to undesired previous behaviours. Failure to consolidate progress may result in a relapse; consolidation will assist progress to a life without problem substance use.
  The model also indicates that problem substance users will usually pass through this cycle several times and that they are then more likely to implement self-directed modifications to their behaviour, or to engage and succeed in treatment that results in lasting change. 'Like other chronic diseases, addiction often involves cycles of relapse and remission.'[64]

- *Relapse* means that the person has returned to dependence-type behaviour. A *lapse* is an instance of substance use that does not result in a return to dependence. Relapse does not, in itself, indicate lack of motivation or ability to change, but it does show that the person needs to engage with services and/or mutual support to promote and sustain change.

9.61　It is recognised that 'substance dependence is hard to overcome [and] ... people often have numerous setbacks before gaining control over this problem', entering remission and, later, achieving recovery.[65] In other words, substance misuse is 'a chronic, relapsing condition ... and at each stage of treatment misusers may relapse and return to previous phases'.[66]

9.62　Permanent abstinence is unusual and 'one-year follow-up studies have typically shown that only about 40–60% of treated patients are continuously abstinent: although an additional 15–30% have not resumed dependent use during this period.'[67]

---

[64]　American Society of Addiction Medicine Public Policy Statement.
　　http://www.asam.org/DefinitionofAddiction-LongVersion.html (2011).
[65]　Frances et al *DSM-IV Guidebook* (APP, 1995, pp 134–135).
[66]　DoH *Task Force to Review Services for Drug Misusers* (DoH, 1996, p 13).
[67]　McLellan et al 'Drug dependence, a chronic medical illness' [2000] JAMA, 284, 1689–95.

9.63 When McLellan et al compared dependence with other common chronic health conditions, they noted:[68]

> 'outcome studies in adult-onset hypertension, diabetes and asthma ... [have] important parallels with the treatment of drug dependence. In all these disorders, lack of patient adherence to the treatment regimen is a major contributor to the reoccurrence of symptoms; and ... adherence is poorest among those with co-morbid medical, psychiatric, family and social problems.'

9.64 For many substance misusers, the hardest part of overcoming their problem is: 'not coming off but staying off.'[69] That is, not physical detoxification, but the psycho-social transformation of beliefs, thoughts and lifestyle that have become intricately linked to substance use.

9.65 Social learning theory suggests that substance misuse is learned behaviour and the person can develop skills to achieve controlled substance use. In practise, however, this may be difficult to achieve and, if so, a period of abstinence may help the person to address their difficulties.

9.66 As noted above, the 12-step model views abstinence as essential, but it is recognised that 'abstinence is not recovery ... Recovery is about building a satisfying and meaningful life, as defined by the person themselves, not simply about ceasing problem substance use ... A process, not a single event.'[70]

9.67 Those who are trying to extricate themselves from a substance-focussed lifestyle often find that there is a vacuum in their lives when their time is not taken up with these activities.

9.68 As Preble and Casey found, substance misusers may have skills that they have developed and deployed in 'wheeling and dealing', but that can be re-directed towards pro-social achievements.[71]

9.69 Family involvement has been found to be effective in motivating problem substance users to enter treatment and produces improved outcomes, when compared to individual treatment.[72]

9.70 It is fundamental to this process that the parent understands their position. I frequently hear from parents that they were not told by 'the authorities' what was expected of them at an early stage in proceedings. This may be indicative of the problem substance user's difficulty absorbing information, or acknowledging their responsibilities. It is important, however, that there are clear expectations and working agreements.

---

[68] See footnote 67.
[69] Orford *Excessive Appetites* (Wiley, 2001, p 237).
[70] Strang and Drummond *Addictions: an evidence-based orientation* (NAC, 2012).
[71] Preble and Casey *Taking care of business* [1996] Int J Addict, 4.
[72] Orford et al *Coping with alcohol and drug problems* (Routledge, 2005); Winigaratne et al *The effectiveness of psychological therapies on drug misusing clients* (NTA, 2005).

9.71   For example, drug or alcohol testing may be used by treatment providers and is important in a clinical context, however, intervention programmes will also take into consideration other aspects of the person's behaviour and lifestyle. When test results are used in care proceedings, there is a risk that this information dominates at the expense of a wider focus on behavioural and social change.

9.72   In addition, there are often conflicts for the professionals involved with parents who misuse substances: is it a therapeutic or supportive relationship, or is it mainly for monitoring? The reality is that it is probably both, therefore, role clarity is essential.

THE DILEMMA OF TIMESCALES

9.73   Change takes time,[73] but as noted by many in this volume, and stated by Pipe and Richardson (chapter 10), 'the introduction of the 26 week timescale for the completion of care proceedings generates new and complex dilemmas'. Flynn and Kelly (chapter 11) point out that 'one can no longer … expect a case to be adjourned in order to monitor a rehabilitation plan'.

9.74   In terms of the current diagnostic guidelines (eg ICD-10 and DSM-5), the prognosis improves – that is the risk of relapse reduces – when the person has achieved a consecutive period of 12 months without evidence of substance misuse (ie *sustained remission*) and during which they make progress in other domains towards the resolution of dependence.

9.75   To enable the person to achieve sustained recovery by making substantial life-style changes, time and support are required, as they progress through the phases described by Sellman (2009)[74] as:

- Treatment (picking up the pieces of a failed life-style).
- Rehabilitation (assembling a new life-style).
- Aftercare (practising the new life-style).
- Self-management (living the new life-style).

9.76   In other words: 'full recovery can only be achieved through working with education, training, employment, housing, family support services, wider health services.'[75]

9.77   Even after a long period in recovery, people may relapse. Consequently, in my opinion, it is not possible to give a definite prognosis or a precise timescale for recovery.

---

[73]   Sellman (2009).
[74]   Sellman *The 10 most important things known about addiction* (Addiction, 2009, 105).
[75]   Home Office *Putting Full Recovery First* (UK Home Office, 2012).

9.78 Sellman argues 'miraculous (long-term continuous abstinence) cures are still an expected standard for people entering addiction treatment ... Unrealistic expectations are likely to inhibit people initially presenting for help, but more importantly put them off re-presenting when a recurrence has occurred.'[76]

9.79 'Substance misuse is rarely the sole cause of family difficulties. It is usually part of a complex web of co-existing problems.'[77] Consistent with this, Cleaver, et al, point out, for 'multi-problem families ... short term interventions ... are rarely effective'.[78] It has also been reported that 'having children at home may be a factor in preventing parents from developing more serious drug-related problems'.[79]

9.80 Parents who have substance use problems, generally, do not present with many of the protective factors that appear to reduce the risk of relapse. These include: personal and social resources such as supportive relationships with family members and friends, education, employment, self-efficacy to resist substance use in high-risk situations, absence of depressive symptoms and less reliance on avoidance coping, or substance-use to reduce tension.[80]

9.81 The situation within the family can be much improved by collaboration across organisations, working in a person-centred, holistic way that takes into account all of the diverse issues that affect the family, rather focusing on reduction or cessation of substance misuse.[81]

9.82 Some of the most successful family interventions for parental substance misuse, as measured by the length of time children spend in care and the likelihood of family reunification, are based on appropriate goal-setting in the context of 'developing and sustaining a therapeutic relationship with service users' and case management approaches to providing and co-ordinating appropriate service provision to match the needs of the service users. But the more complex the needs, the more intensive and long-term case management will usually need to be,[82] indicating the need for early interventions (perhaps in pre-proceedings).

9.83 Family drug and alcohol courts (FDAC) offer intensive specialist support to parents of children at risk due to parental substance misuse by incorporating a multi-disciplinary service, working to a designated judge who actively manages the case. An evaluation of the first FDAC in Britain found better parental and child outcomes at lower cost than in comparison non-specialist

---

[76] Sellman (2009, p 8).
[77] NTA *Parents with drug problems: How treatment helps families* (NTA, 2012, p 3).
[78] Cleaver, et al, 1999, p 101.
[79] NTA, 2012, p 5.
[80] Moos & Moos.
[81] SCIE *Alcohol, Drug & Mental Health Problems in Families* (SCIE, 2003); Copello et al *Family interventions in the treatment of alcohol & drug problems* (Drug & Alc Rev, 2005, 24, p 369); Velleman & Templeton *Understanding & modifying the impact of parents' substance misuse on children* (Adv in Psych Treat, 2007, 13, p 79).
[82] Galvani & Forrester (2011, p 3).

courts. On average it took a few weeks longer for specialist court children to be reunited with their parents but less time for them to be placed in a permanent alternative home.[83]

9.84 Case management also involves negotiation with the client to agree a care plan that sets out which aspects of work can be undertaken in parallel and which should happen in sequence. This may go beyond the 26 week limit, with the implication that work and monitoring will continue after a final order has been made.

9.85 It has been reported also that: 'one of the key challenges ... in the context of parental substance misuse is the existence of many competing needs, including those of the parent, the child and the family as a whole ... Evidence points time and again to the tension between the timescales of the outcomes for the substance-misusing parent which may involve treatment and recovery over a long period of time, and those of the child who may be at more immediate risk ... Working in an appropriate way with the parent can lead to improvements in the outcomes for the child.'[84]

9.86 Unfortunately, it has been argued, current social policy initiatives have relied too much on neuroscientific knowledge that:[85]

> 'is not "policy ready" ... [but] has created a now-or-never imperative to intervene before irreparable damage is done to the developing infant brain ... [when] plasticity and resilience seem to be the general rule ... Too much has been taken on trust ... [and] the co-option of neuroscience has medicalised policy discourse, silencing vital moral debate and pushing practice in the direction of standardised, targeted interventions rather than simpler forms of family and community support, which can yield more sustainable results.'

9.87 An understanding of this position is fundamental to current policy of the UK Government, with a coalition commitment: 'to develop a new approach to supporting families ... where substance misuse is a factor ... [There is an] expectation that services work together to deliver effective services to families affected by substance misuse.'[86]

---

[83]   Harwin et al *The family drug and alcohol court evaluation project: final report* (Brunel, 2011).
[84]   Inst for Res & Innovation, *Leading for outcomes; parental substance misuse* (IRISS, 2011, p 7).
[85]   Wastell & White *Blinded by neuroscience* (Families, Relationships & Societies, 2012, 1, pp 397–414).
[86]   NTA *Supporting information for the development of joint local protocols between drug and alcohol partnerships, children and family services* (NTA, 2011, p 1 and p 10).

CHAPTER 10

THE CHALLENGE OF COLLABORATIVE PRACTICE IN PARENTING ASSESSMENTS

Caroline Pipe and Kathy Richardson

INTRODUCTION

10.1 Conducting parenting assessments is a key aspect of social work practice in statutory social care contexts. Increasingly, social workers are required to produce definitive accounts of parent's abilities to meet their children's needs for the duration of their minority. The introduction of the 26 week timescale for the completion of care proceedings generates new and complex dilemmas regarding the assessment process. With a lessening reliance on expert witnesses, social workers are required to produce fair and robust reports regarding parenting capacity whilst attending to multiple factors including high case loads, risk management and limited resources.

10.2 This chapter will provide an account how we are addressing these issues in our current employment in the children and families division of a local authority in inner London. A description will be provided of how we are utilising key principals of systemic theory to shape and inform the content and the process of our parenting assessments. It is our intention to demonstrate how our connection with systemic practice contributes to an approach to assessing parenting which is both rigorous and appreciative.

10.3 With regard to the use of language, in this chapter we have used the terms 'families' and 'parents' to refer to the service users we work with. We have given much thought to this and it is fair to conclude we have struggled to identify terminology that is both clear and respectful. In our context, the terms service user and client feel somewhat disingenuous, due to the implication of choice in these terms. We have used the terms families and parents to assist us in remaining oriented to who we work with and why.

MANAGING COMPLEXITY

10.4 The task of working within a 26 week timescale produces significant challenges for professionals involved in this process, particularly children and families social workers who are responsible for numerous aspects of case management, from completing assessments to co-ordinating contact arrangements. Unlike other professionals, social workers are likely to have high levels of contact with family members and need to be considerate in how they position themselves in relation to children, parents and the professional network.

10.5 The introduction of new timescales in care proceedings imposes strict limitations in terms of assessing and evidencing parental capacity to change when presenting difficulties are likely to be multi-faceted, entrenched and sustained by trans-generational patterns of behaviours. In addition, it is likely families will have experienced profoundly difficult relationships with professional agencies throughout their lives, contributing to difficulties in communication, trust and motivation.

10.6 Given these factors, the potential for errors within the assessment process appear very apparent. In explorations of failings in social work assessments[1] much emphasis has been placed on how unhelpful relationships between workers and families have led to skewed and deficient analysis.

10.7 In addition, in reviewing the work of Munro[2] and Sheppard, Newstead, DiCaccavo and Ryan,[3] Forrester comments that mistakes in assessments mostly occur 'when individuals form an opinion too swiftly … are no longer open to alternative hypotheses'.[4] It is our intention to document how we are attempting to address these matters by combining our knowledge and experience as social workers with our interest and belief in systemic practice.

KEY ISSUES

10.8 In accepting a fundamental flaw in traditional assessments is the way in which professionals and parents communicate and understand each other, we have been keen to consider how we may adapt our practice to address this issue. It is our position that in failing to attend to the relationship between professionals and parents, there is a danger of engaging in a superficial level of assessment which both fails to elicit potential strengths and bypasses potential risks.

10.9 In addition, we would highlight that increased pressures on social care staff, including the 26 week timescale may contribute to either punitive judgementalism or blinkered minimisation. Therefore the need appears

---

[1]   Laming *The Protection of children in England: A progress report* (The Stationary Office, 2009).

[2]   Munro *The Munro review of child protection: Final report. A child centred system* (2011).

[3]   Sheppard et al 'Comparative Hypothesis Assessment and Quasi Triangulation as Process Knowledge Assessment Strategies in Social Work Practice' [2001] Brit J Soc Work, 39(6), 863–885.

[4]   Forrester et al *Reclaiming Social Work? An Evaluation of Systemic Units as an approach to Delivering Children's Services. Final report of a comparative study of practice and the factors shaping it in three local authorities* (Tilda Goldberg Centre for Social Work and Social Care, 2013).

apparent to revise approaches to assessments which both adhere to newly established legislation and the human rights of children and parents.

10.10 The basic model for our assessments remains the *Framework for the Assessment of Need for Children and their Families*.[5] Our choice to retain this frame work is linked to the universal recognition of this template, its strong evidence base and its compatibility with systemic theory.

10.11 At the centre of our assessment model is a series of semi structured interviews that we conduct in pairs. The interviews relate to specific domains within the framework and are adapted to accommodate variables in family composition and identity. Prior to each interview we compile a list of questions, a practice that enables us to retain a focus and manage time effectively. The planned questions are not entirely prescriptive however, and it is our aim to be responsive to opportunities to explore specific matters that may arise unexpectedly.

10.12 In terms of how many interviews we conduct, this will depend largely on our prior knowledge of the case and current relationship with the family. Assessment involving large sibling groups and families with extensive social care histories are likely to entail a greater number of sessions, as are assessments requiring interpreters and those involving parents with specific needs such as learning difficulties. In general, we usually conduct between five and seven interviews, which are complimented by observations of parent/child interactions. In addition we rely on feedback from other members of the network, including contact supervisor and foster carers, which often alerts us to specific areas of interest or concern.

10.13 Whilst the structure and the evidence base for our assessments is probably familiar to the majority of children and families social workers, it is the stance or postures we adopt in our relationships with the families that we work with that has generated significant differences in our practice. This chapter will now detail how adopting a systemic lens to parenting assessments has radically altered our approach, and the experiences of families we work with.

SYSTEMIC APPROACHES

10.14 In considering effective theoretical approaches to operating in social care contexts, a growing emphasis has been placed on systemic thinking and practice.[6] The introduction of the framework for the assessment of children in need and their families[7] outlined the importance of adopting holistic, relational

---

[5]   Department of Health *Framework for the Assessment of Need for Children and their Families* (DoH, 2001).

[6]   Munro *The Munro review of child protection: Final report. A child centred system* (2011).

[7]   Department of Health *Framework for the Assessment of Children in Need and their Families* (DoH, 2000).

perspectives when assessing the needs of children and their families. An invitation was issued to focus on the connections between parent/child relationships, the family's cultural and social history and the contexts in which the family currently existed.

10.15 This mode of practice prompted a shift in focus from traditional linear and intrapsychic conceptualisations of family dysfunction to consideration of patterns of relational functioning along with contextual issues of power and difference. An understanding of systemic theory allows practitioners to adopt a broader, less assumptive approach to assessments and interventions, generating opportunities for new possibilities to emerge in terms of understanding and analysis.

10.16 Systemic practice in social care contexts links strongly to systemic psychotherapy and family therapy, the origins of which are situated in the theoretical domains of systems theory and cybernetics.[8] The notion of a cybernetic system, that is, a self regulating system in which an information feedback loop enable the maintenance of stability (or homeostasis) was adopted by Bateson,[9] an early pioneer of systemic conceptualisations of family functioning.

10.17 Bateson postulated that patterns of interaction within families serve to maintain a state of homeostasis, thus sustaining circular, recursive processes enabled through a process of mutual influence. This account of interactive functioning appears particularly salient when considering issues associated with multi stressed families[10] experiencing entrenched difficulties apparently unassisted by professional interventions.[11]

10.18 A central complexity of assessing parental capacity and capacity to change is the degree to which families present with problem saturated narratives in which constellations of significant difficulties are interlinked and mutually sustaining. Such cases may engender a sense of hopelessness and failure in both families and the professionals working with them and interventions based on addressing single causative factors are likely to be unproductive in terms of promoting sustained and meaningful change.[12]

10.19 It would therefore appear that adopting a systemic lens when working with families in need may orientate professionals to adopt a more curious

---

[8]   Wiener *Cybernetics* (MIT Press, 1961).

[9]   Bateson *Steps to an Ecology of Mind* (1972).

[10] Van Lawick and Bom 'Building bridges: Home visits to multi-stressed families where professional help reached a deadlock' [2008] J Fam Ther, 30, 504–516.

[11] Cabinet Office *Think Family: Improving the life chances of families at risk* (Cabinet Office, Social Exclusion Task Force, 2008).

[12] Pendry 'Systemic Practice in a Risk Management Context' in Goodman and Trowler (eds) *Social Work Reclaimed – Innovative Frameworks for child and Family Social Work Practice* (Jessica Kingsley Publishing, 2012).

stance[13] encouraging the deconstruction of problem maintaining behaviours and the relationships that sustain them. A central aspect of this process is the concept of second order practice.[14]

10.20   Second order practice is a constructivist concept postulating the notion that 'knowledge' is a construction formulated in a social domain. What is known in the external world is shaped and determined by language and context. In abandoning the premise of an objective reality.[15] Practitioners are positioned as co-creators of meanings and beliefs, situated within the family's broader contextual system.

10.21   Inhabiting such a position compels practitioners to adopt a stance of self reflexivity, in which personal biases and beliefs are made explicit and attended to. It is this process, necessitating rigorous self scrutiny that protects practitioners from assumptive thinking and unintentional seductions. Attention is given to the meaning and influence of the relationship between practitioners and families, specifically regarding power, difference and the process of social control.

10.22   A fundamental aspect of second order practice and of particular relevance to this chapter is the idea of first and second order change. Much emphasis has been placed on the need for practitioner to be vigilant to the process of 'disguised compliance'[16] and to evidence that changes observed are both genuine and sustainable. First order change refers to a process by which changes occur within a system. Such changes are usually behavioural and do not involve significant shifts in thinking, and the system itself is not altered. An example of first order change is a parent who ceases smacking their child as a social worker has told them to. The change is externally motivated and the belief system remains unaltered. Such changes are unlikely to be sustained and will often not be replicated in different contexts.

10.23   By contrast, second order change involves change at the level of belief. In an example of second order change a parent ceases smacking their child as they realise it scares and distresses them. The parent appreciates it is important their child can trust them and believes they have skills in their repertoire to deal manage their child's behaviour more constructively. In this instance 'the focus of change is in the meaning and the ideas which are held about the behaviour, rather than the behaviours themselves'.[17] In assessing parental capacity to change, evidence of second order thinking indicates changes are more likely to be embedded as shifts have occurred in terms of thinking, belief and action. The

---

[13]   Cecchin 'Hypothesising, circularity and Neutrality revisited: an invitation to curiosity' [1987] Fam Proc, 26,405–4110.

[14]   Hoffman 'Beyond Power and Control: Towards a 'Second Order' Family Systems Therapy' [1985] Fam Sys Med, 3, 381–396.

[15]   Ibid.

[16]   Howarth *The Child's World. Assessing Children in Need and their Families* (Jessica Kingsley Publishers, 2001).

[17]   Gross 'Systemic Thinking and the Practitioners Dilemma in Child Sex Abuse: Smooth Travelling Between Domains' [1991] Human Systems: J Sys Consult Man, 2, 263–277, p 265.

relational nature of the change is also apparent, in the understanding of how one's actions may be felt and experienced by others.

10.24 Whilst an appreciation of the effectiveness of systemic practice in social care contexts continues to grow,[18] it is crucial to consider the tensions that exist in using such approaches in a statutory setting and how this may be managed. This is particularly important in the sphere of parenting assessments given the gravity of their impact and the implications of their outcomes.

10.25 Operating in our organisational context involves significant complexity in terms of professional responsibilities, ethics and human rights. We are responsible for producing evidence-based assessments which provide recommendations for the long term care of children and young people. This is an onerous task undertaken in a context which involves the management of significant risk regarding emotive subjects. As practitioners, we are embedded in the lives of our families, and they in ours, in a manner many other professionals would not experience. We are often required to adopt numerous roles in relation to the families we work with, presenting dilemmas in terms of how we relate to the concepts of power, transparency and compassion.

10.26 In accepting our position as agents of social control, and our family's experiences of scrutiny and judgement[19] we have explored the concept of positioning theory[20] as a mechanism for managing this complexity. A central tenet of positioning theory is to offer a critique of the concept of role theory in social psychology. Harre and Davies postulate that the term 'role' denotes a sense of formality and stasis, inhibiting the consideration of dynamic, social constructionist perspectives regarding language and reality.

10.27 Positioning theory suggests that identities are constituted and re-constituted through conversation and the context in which they occur. Positioning theory is specifically attentive to the idea of power and dominance and how individuals may be positioned due to pervasive discourses and privileged narratives. This concept is of particular relevance when working in the field of children's social care. Given the majority of families connected with this service will experience marginalisation as a consequence of such factors as poverty, racism, abuse and low educational attainment[21] it appears apparent that the families we work with are likely to be positioned by discourses that are dominated by deficit and concern.

---

[18] Forrester et al *Reclaiming Social Work? An Evaluation of Systemic Units as an approach to Delivering Children's Services. Final report of a comparative study of practice and the factors shaping it in three local authorities* (Tilda Goldberg Centre for Social Work and Social Care, 2013).

[19] Foucault *Discipline and Punishment* (Vintage Books, 1979).

[20] Davies and Harre 'Positioning: The discursive Production of Selves' [1990] J Theo Soc Beh, 20(1), 43–610.

[21] Aggett et al '"Seeking Permission": an interviewing stance for finding connection with hard to reach families' [2011] J of Family Ther (published online).

10.28 Davies and Harre[22] use the terms 'intended meanings' and 'hearable meanings' to define processes in which the intentionality of a speech act may be perceived and understood very differently due to the complex social, political and personal contexts in which the act takes place. An example of this may be a parent vociferously advocating for their child's educational or health needs to be met. Such a parent may be perceived as protective and proactive, or as an aggressive trouble maker depending on how they may be positioned in terms of class, culture, ability and a myriad of other classification tools we utilise in social interactions.

10.29 In the process of assessing parenting capacity and capacity to change, our interest in positioning theory has promoted our understanding of both intentional and inadvertent discriminatory practice and provided us with scope to consider the part we may play in the creation of new and more useful positions, both for ourselves and the families we work with.

10.30 Connected with these themes is the matter of client's relationships with help[23] and how experiences of the misuse of authority may influence and encumber relationships with families in need of assistance. Literature regarding parental functioning and managing risk often focuses on difficulties families appear to have forming and sustaining relationships with professional agencies[24] and an implicit emphasis appears to be placed on the hope and expectation that families will develop the capacity to join with the culture and logic of formal helping agencies.

10.31 Given that many families linked to such services may be affected by trans-generational patterns of functioning which may have been experienced as traumatic, abusive or neglectful, it would appear fitting that the attachment narratives currently available to them focus on distrust, anxiety and powerlessness.[25] Opportunities for families to constructively assert themselves are therefore consistently limited, and many families report being unclear of what was expected of them, and how this may be measured and assessed.

10.32 In addition, experiences of social exclusion may persuade families to 'see the outside world as threatening, unreliable and antagonistic'.[26] In such instances 'strange loops'[27] are created in interactions between families and professional currently unable to trust each other and stuck in recursive patterns of criticism and hostility.

---

22 Davies and Harre 'Positioning: The discursive Production of Selves' [1990] J Theo Soc Beh, 20(1), 43–610.

23 Mason 'Six aspects of supervision and the training of supervisors' [2010] J Fam Ther, 32, 436–439.

24 Reder and Duncan *Lost Innocents: A follow-up study of fatal child abuse* (Routledge, 1999).

25 Dallos and Vetere *Systemic Therapy and Attachment Narratives: Applications in a range of Clinical Settings* (Routledge, 2009).

26 Van Lawick and Bom 'Building bridges: Home visits to multi-stressed families where professional help reached a deadlock' [2008] J Fam Ther, 30, 504–516, p 512.

27 Cronen et al 'Paradoxes, double binds and reflexive loops: an alternative theoretical perspective' [1982] Fam Proc, 21, 91–112.

10.33 In our practice, it is our intention to explicitly acknowledge these positions and create scope to generate more 'useful and fitting'[28] relationships in which possibilities may emerge regarding the creation of meaningful and sustained differences in family functioning. By deconstructing the notion of difficult to engage families and instead focussing on ways in which services being hard to engage with,[29] we are invited to think more creatively about our approaches to working with families. It is our experience that commencing our work with families by initiating conversations about prior experiences of 'helping' agencies generates a climate of transparency and allows us scope to consider how we may adapt our practice to facilitate more productive interactions.

10.34 The acronym Social GRRAACCES (gender, race, religion, age, ability, class, culture ethnicity and sexuality)[30] provides a key organising principle of second order practice and links strongly with positioning theory and the use of self in systemic practice. The Social GRRAACCES are of particular relevance to work in social care contexts where interventions are mandated in regard of families in positions of marginalisation and disenfranchisement. By holding in mind the concept of the Social GRRAACCES, our practice has moved beyond a position of cultural awareness to a position of cultural sensitivity.[31]

10.35 By adopting this frame, we hold a position of genuine curiosity regarding the families we work with, and have moved away from reductionist descriptions of identity shaping constructs. We are particularly keen to deconstruct diagnosis and descriptions given to individuals by professionals and establish how these have been formulated and maintained. This is particularly central to our work with families affected by mental health issues. The opportunity to explore their relationship to their diagnosis and the meaning it holds for them appears to be a particularly illuminating area for exploration.

10.36 Our connection with the Social GRRAACCES provides a natural pathway to considering our position in the family/professional system and our commitment to self-reflexivity in our practice. By adopting a second order stance in our practice, we remain mindful of how we are organised by both our own values and beliefs and those of the agency we represent. We appreciate our judgements and decisions are shaped largely by social discourse which are historically and culturally specific and openly share this belief with the families we work with. It appears acknowledgement of this matter decreases the adoption of binary positions and adversarial relationships. At all times

---

[28] Freedman and Combs *Narrative Therapy: The Social Construction of Preferred Realities* (Norton, 1996).

[29] Aggett et al '"Seeking Permission": an interviewing stance for finding connection with hard to reach families' [2011] J Fam Ther (published online).

[30] Burnham 'Systemic Supervision: The evolution of reflexivity in the context of the supervisory relationship' [1993] Hum Sys, 4, 349–381.

[31] Hardy and Laszloffy 'The Cultural Genogram; Key to training culturally competent family therapist' [1995] J Mar Fam, The 21, 227–237.

however, we remain explicit regarding our professional responsibilities and clearly reiterate the purpose of our work together.

10.37 A central element of conducting assessments in social care contexts is the issue of risk in an organisational culture strongly orientated to the 'domain of production'.[32] Drawing on Maturana's[33] idea that human interactions take place in three different domains, the domain of production, the domain of explanation and the domain of aesthetics we have looked to the work of Lang, Little and Crohen[34] to assist us in considering how we may operate ethically and consistently when assessing parenting capacity.

10.38 In simplified terms, the domain of production can be viewed as where objective truths are situated and prioritised. The domain of production involves activity and attending to tasks. In our experience as workers in a social care context, we often feel we are constantly required to inhabit this domain, which is characterised by procedures, timescales and the discovery of fact.

10.39 The domain of explanation is the domain of 'questions and questioning'[35] and presents opportunities to contemplate the generation of multiple versions of reality. In this domain, we may retain a sense of curiosity and openness towards alternative perspectives and meanings, providing opportunities to be reflexive regarding our beliefs and how they are being created. The domain of aesthetics involves such concepts as morality, consistency and ethics. This domain promotes attention to the coherence of our practice, and how we may remain grounded and accountable in our actions.

10.40 Connecting with Maturana's notion of existing in the domains of aesthetics, explanation and production simultaneously,[36] it is our intention to adopt a 'both/and' position in relation to risk,[37] with the aim of promoting the development of multiple narratives regarding the families we work with.[38] As we have developed our practice, we have examined the challenge to retain a posture of curiosity[39] whilst attending to safeguarding and statutory duties.

10.41 It is important to highlight that many of our practices have generated concerns regarding if our quest to adopt collaborative, transparent practice may contribute to collusion and false optimism. In order to address this, we focussed

---

[32] Lang et al ' The Systemic Professional: Domains of Action and the Question of Neutrality' [1990] Human Systems: J Sys Consult Man, 1, 39–55.

[33] Maturana 'Maturana's basic notions' [1991] Human Systems: J Sys Consult Man, 2, 71–78.

[34] See footnote 32.

[35] Lang et al 'The Systemic Professional: Domains of Action and the Question of Neutrality' [1990] Human Systems: J Sys Consult Man, 1, p 36.

[36] Maturana 'Maturana's basic notions' [1991] Human Systems: J Sys Consult Man, 2, 71–78.

[37] Andersen 'The Reflecting Team: Dialogue and Meta-Dialogue in Clinical Work' [1987] Fam Proc, 26, 415–428.

[38] Nielson 'Working in the grey zone: The challenge for supervision in the area between therapy and social control' in Campbell and Mason (eds) *Perspectives on Supervision* (Karnac, 2002).

[39] Cecchin 'Hypothesising, circularity and Neutrality revisited: an invitation to curiosity' [1987] Fam Proc 26, 405–413.

on our inner conversations[40] relating to risk and observed how they were often shaped by feelings of fear, inadequacy and negativity. By deconstructing these conversations, we cultivated an awareness of how our practice has been inhibited by well-established discourses regarding the failings of social care staff. This led us to understand that our audiences (managers, the court, colleagues) were also governed and organised by these beliefs, contributing to a culture of defensiveness and risk aversion. It is therefore our intention to make public our inner conversations *(monologues)* and invite comment and discussion. It is through this transformative process *dialogues* are generated, thus introducing difference and new possibilities in our thinking.

10.42 In order to consider such dilemmas further, we have looked to the work of Mason[41] and the concept of safe uncertainty. Mason challenges the usefulness of the notion of certainty and instead encourages an examination of how adopting a stance of certainty can be limiting and at times dangerous.

10.43 It is argued that whilst great emphasis may be placed on 'being certain' (particularly in social care settings) certainty is an illusionary state, which can never actually be achieved. Mason suggests that by 'understanding too quickly',[42] we adopt a restrictive and concrete viewpoints which fails to accommodate possibilities of change, evolution and surprise.

10.44 The importance of considering these ideas is of particular relevance to our work. Embedded in a context in which formula and checklists have been increasingly prioritised; little space exists for deconstruction, reflection and thoughtfulness. Practitioners are persuaded to adopt a ridged sense of 'knowing', a counterproductive stance that increases rather than diminishes risk.

10.45 In adopting a manner of practice which mindfully embraces professional knowledge, reflexivity, experience and intuitions, practitioners are enabled to demonstrate robust flexibility in their understanding of family functioning. By inhabiting a position of safe uncertainty, we can be receptive to notions of change and possibility whilst retaining a sense of expertise and authority in our judgements and decisions.

10.46 Throughout our careers in children's social care, we have wondered a great deal about the emotional content of the cases we are involved in and how we may continue to function safely and compassionately in climates of stress and distress. Often we are required to work with families where serious abuse has occurred and expressions of anger and contempt are live and present within the professional network. Much consideration has been given to how we

---

[40] Aggett 'Responsiveness, permission seeking and risk: three motifs in the development of outreach family therapy services and therapist reflexivity' [2012] Context, 120.

[41] Mason 'Towards Positions of Safe Uncertainty' [1993] Human Systems: J Sys Consult Man, 4, 189–200.

[42] Anderson and Goolishian 'Human Systems as Linguistic Systems: Preliminary and Evolving Ideas about Implications for Clinical Theory' [1988] Fam Proc, 27(4) 371–3910.

manage both our own feelings and those of others in a way which is both congruent and constructive: to this end we have looked to the work of Glenda Fredman[43] and the idea of emotional postures.

10.47   In a pressurised working environment where an emphasis is placed on completing assessments within brief timescales, our focus on collaborative, inquisitive practice can wane, and we find ourselves thinking about families in hostile and judgemental ways. If unattended to, these feelings govern our interactions with our families and we become ensnared in patterns of relating governed by disrespect and distrust. Fredman describes how practitioners may adopt a 'posture of mobilisation' characterised by an outward focus of attention, concerned with maintain protective defensiveness though distancing, controlling or shaming others. We are aware when we adopt a posture of mobilisation: our interviews become antagonistic, confrontational or sarcastic. We notice we sigh a great deal and interrupt. In these instances we have lost touch with our curiosity and frequently feel hopeless or overwhelmed.

10.48   In an effort to address this matter, we attempt to engage in the practice of emotional presupposing.[44] This involves preparing for assessment interviews with families by identifying our feelings regarding the session, the family and how we relate to them. We hypothesise how the family may be feeling about meeting us and attempt to orientate ourselves to their position. Through asking each other questions (or questioning ourselves when working alone) we have adopted this process as an integral aspect of our work with families. Often we will begin our sessions by speaking to the family about our thoughts and inviting them to respond. Our aim in this process is to develop a posture of tranquillity,[45] a stance characterised by openness and wondering.

10.49   The process of emotional presupposing is a fundamental aspect of our assessment model: when we inhabit a position of tranquillity we are receptive, engaged and attentive. This is not to say we readily accept our families' versions of events or accounts of their parenting. Whilst we aim to remain respectful, adopting a position of tranquillity enables us to constructively challenge, and attend to inconsistencies and contradictions in the moment. By attending to our emotional postures, we are well positioned to be responsive and connected to the conversations we take part in. We are less likely to become confused, dismissive or unquestioning. In summary, our critical rigour is protected and enhanced.

10.50   In order to demonstrate our approach, we will now focus on examples from our practice. A key aspect of systemic practice is the cultivation of a specific way of thinking and viewing the world. Therefore, much less focus is placed on formats and techniques. With this in mind, it is our intention to

---

[43]   Fredman *Transforming Emotion – Conversation in Counselling and Psychology* (Karnac, 2004).

[44]   Ibid.

[45]   Ibid.

describe how we aim to retain a stance of respectful curiosity, whilst promoting our families capacity to develop reflexive appreciation of their thinking and behaviours.

10.51   We begin our assessment process by discussing together our immediate thoughts and feelings regarding the proposed assessment. This includes sharing our initial 'gut' feelings about the case, our biases and prejudices and our predications for outcomes. By externalising these thoughts prior to meeting the family, we have commenced the process of thinking about ourselves in the family/professional system and what may influence and shape our work.

10.56   Such conversations demand a great deal of trust between colleagues: we need to be secure enough to make explicit our judgmental and fears. This practice of relational risk taking[46] has become a discipline which we are keen to incorporate in each stage of the assessment process. In understanding such transparency can be strange or intimating to both families and other professionals, we will often preface its usage by speaking about our own (developing) relationship with the concept and how we manage it. Feedback indicates our honesty is appreciated, and stories of our own struggles with this aspect of practice have been reassuring to others.

10.57   We are conscious of the fact that we usually conduct our assessments as a pair. Co-working is a concept privileged in our work context, partly as a response to the potential for collusive relationships and a myopic gaze and partly to privilege the systemic notion of the existence of multiple perspectives. It is clear not all social care staff will be in this position, and with growing pressures of timescale and workload, it is possible this practice will become less possible.

10.58   We would strongly argue that pair working is both cost effective and time saving. By co-working, practice becomes more dynamic and analytical. Momentum and interest is sustained by pre and post session discussions, and interviews become shared, co constructed processes in which multiple ideas and viewpoints are exposed. It is this process which ensures the richness and depth of our assessments: by exercising creativity in the positions adopted during interviews we are liberated from impasses and may attend to nuance. We retain a position of active participation which promotes critical thinking. In this process, information is generated which surprises both us, and the families we work with. It is this information which elevates the assessment from being a mundane re-telling of well-established stories to the creation of the new.

10.59   As discussed earlier, families involved in the assessment process are likely to have poor experiences of working with professionals. In our initial meetings with families we will make enquiries regarding this matter and think together about how we may do things differently. Our experience has led us to

---

[46]   Mason 'Relational risk-taking and the training of supervisors' [2005] J Fam Ther, 27, 298–301.

understand that in many instances, families have been unclear regarding the concerns of the local authority and what is expected of them.

10.60 With this in mind, we have adopted a process of formulating an assessment contract with families, including an explicit statement of concerns, what we will be assessing and how, the format and structure of interviews, how feedback will be given, and a code of conduct. The contract is a document signed by the family and ourselves: a sense of equity and agency is introduced into the process as the family sees us signing a contract regarding *our* timekeeping, cancellation procedures and commitment to anti discriminatory practice. van Lawick and Bom write 'In this process a culture of on-going feedback is crucial. This feedback helps clients keep a sense of agency over the process of change and can formulate the core values they want to be met in their lives'.[47] A short example of this process is documented below:

> Caroline 'What are your initial thoughts?'
>
> Matti 'Its okay, but you know sometimes I forget appointments because I've got so many'
>
> Caroline 'Okay, what ideas do you have about how we may get round that?'
>
> Matti 'I don't know'
>
> Kathy 'Well, some families we know like us to text them the day before, or some people stick the dates up on the fridge door ...'
>
> Matti 'Yeah a text would be good'
>
> Caroline 'Okay, we'll do that – and what about telling us how it's going for you – do you think you'd be able to do that?'
>
> Matti 'No way! I'd feel too embarrassed'
>
> Kathy 'So how are we going to know if it's really not feeling right for you, or you don't get what we're asking?'
>
> Matti 'I don't know'
>
> Caroline 'What might you do? What might we notice that makes us think "we need to do things a bit differently here?"'
>
> Matti 'Ummm, I'd probably go really quiet, then start fiddling' (laughs)
>
> Caroline 'Okay, that's helpful, so maybe if we see some of those things we need to stop and check things out a bit'

---

[47] Van Lawick and Bom 'Building bridges: Home visits to multi-stressed families where professional help reached a deadlock' [2008] J Fam Ther, 30, 504–516, p 516.

Kathy 'What else?'

Matti 'I don't agree with this bit that says about emotional abuse'

Caroline 'Say a bit more'

Matti 'Well, when it says abuse it sounds like I was doing it on purpose, and I wasn't but I do know what I did was harming her – so I'd call it more like emotional harm'

Kathy 'Okay – sometimes Caroline and me might still say emotional abuse, because it's a legal term, and it's what we call it, as professionals, but we'll do our best to remember it makes more sense to you if we talk about emotional harm'

Matti 'Alright'.

10.61 By engaging in these joining processes, it is our intention to generate opportunities to deconstruct pre formulated ideas regarding client's motivation and understanding of concerns. Had this conversation not taken place Matti may have been viewed as a parent in denial who will not engage. We adhere to the systemic notion that there is logic to all actions, and it is our responsibility as professionals to join with this logic in a manner which opens up new possibilities.

10.62 The basis of our assessment model is a series of semi structured interviews related to a specific aspect of parenting, such as emotional warmth, or guidance and boundaries. As our practice has developed we have become consistently more interested in the concept of interventive interviewing.[48] The purpose of questioning in this approach is to generate gateways to alternative experiences as opposed to focussing on linear information gathering processes. As a consequence of employing this approach, the assessment process itself often becomes a vehicle for change, in which motivation can be stimulated and newer ways of thinking emerge.

10.63 Of particular significance is the utilisation of reflexive questioning, an approach used with the intention of enabling interviewees to make sense of their situation through organising lived experiences into coherent narratives. By asking questions that 'require internal involvement and exploration to find their answers'[49] we attempt to elicit deeper and more illuminating accounts of current parenting and capacity to change.

10.64 In discussing our connection with reflexive questioning, it is important to highlight that whilst the intent of asking specific questions may be clear in the mind of the assessors, the actual meaning and effect of the questions will always be determined by the interviewee. In the initial stages of our work

---

[48] Tomm 'Interventive Interviewing: Part II. Reflexive Questioning as a Means to Enabling Self-Healing' [1987] Fam Proc, 26, 167–1810.
[49] Freedman and Combs *Narrative Therapy: The Social Construction of Preferred Realities* (Norton, 1996).

together, we were sometimes surprised and disappointed that questions used to great effect in some interviews appeared meaningless in others.

10.65 These experiences orientated us to the necessity of remaining attuned and responsive to feedback. This includes making distinctions between when a certain question may be difficult to our interviewees due to a lack of connection in language or social mores, and when interviews may experience disconnection due to emotional resonances such as guilt shame or denial. It is our role to attempt to deconstruct such episodes and establish some sense of shared meaning. This does not necessarily mean agreement, but a mutual acknowledgement of each other's experiences.

10.66 Due to fundamental reliance on the recursive process between interviewer and interviewee, it is unhelpful for us to provide numerous examples of the questions we use. It is however salient to consider the *type* of questions we use, our intention in doing so and their possible effect.

10.67 Freedman and Combes[50] defined three key categories of reflexive questioning which we employ routinely in our assessment interviews. We will discuss them below.

10.68 *Opening space questions* include questions that actively challenge dominant narratives and seek to uncover subjugated accounts or experiences. Such questions may involve exploring exceptions to problematic patterns and actions. For example: 'Can you remember in 2011 when you were clean for 10 months? What was enabling you to do this?'. Or 'Although you always maintain you don't trust professionals, you've got an excellent relationship with Grace, the health visitor. What is it about your relationship that allows you to trust her?'.

10.69 The effect of such questions is to orientate both the narrator and audience to a position of difference which can then be enriched and amplified. Future orientated questions such as: 'What stories would you like Benny to tell about you as his Mum when he's an adult?' can be very useful in terms of generating ideas about opportunity and change, as well as orientating parents to their child's position.

10.70 Indeed, evoking a sense of 'internalised others'[51] and generating scope for parents to see the world through their child's eyes is perhaps the most critical aspect of our assessments: it is through this process we assess a parent's capacity to emotionally connect with their child and demonstrate a sense of empathy. We have noticed that many parents currently exhibiting high criticism/low warmth styles of parenting have been strongly affected by this

---

[50] Freedman and Combs *Narrative Therapy: The Social Construction of Preferred Realities* (Norton, 1996).

[51] Tomm 'Interventive Interviewing: Part II. Reflexive Questioning as a Means to Enabling Self-Healing' [1987] Fam Proc, 26, 167–1810.

type of question, identifying for the first time the difficulties in their relationships with their children and the pain and grief this generates.

10.71 *Story development questions* create opportunities to cultivate the alternative possibilities generated by opening space questions. To many families, patterns of functioning are well established and reliable, even if that reliability is abusive or destructive. The prospect of change therefore is often experienced as frightening, generating defeatism and rejection. Story development questions allow us to unpick these ideas, often revealing patterns of that have held families in positions of vulnerability and failure for extended periods of time. Through this process we can begin to think collaboratively about how these patterns may be reconfigured to more constructive forms.

10.72 For some families, this may not be achievable in the timescale relevant to the children's needs. In this instance, our intent is to generate some level of understanding regarding the parent's difficulties in meeting their children's needs, which may create foundations for promoting ongoing contact and assisting children in coming to terms with permanent separation.

10.73 Finally, we utilise *meaning questions* with the intention of facilitating and identifying examples of second order change. By encouraging a reflexive stance regarding beliefs, we are seeking examples of how shifts in thinking are informing perceptions and relational interactions as well as actions and behaviour. Using meaning questions such as 'What does this new idea tell you about yourself?' creates opportunities for expressions of agency, responsibility and acknowledgement of difference. Evidence of these factors contributes to the likelihood of substantial developments in functioning, indicating sustainable changes with the possibility of replication in future contexts.

10.74 It is our experience that using reflexive questioning has assisted us in navigating the ethical complexities of making judgements regarding parent's abilities to permanently care for their children. The work of Karl Tomm[52] has encouraged us to consider how we may attempt to foster a sense of transparency in our interviews and remain mindful of the power imbalances in our endeavour. By using normative – comparison questions for example,[53] we are able to develop discussions regarding culturally and socially determined norms.

10.75 Through using this type of question, such as 'Do you think Tyler is particularly badly behaved or do you think most three year old boys do what he does?', we are able to gain a sense of the values and beliefs of the families we work with. Often we use this process to share our ideas and beliefs and how these have been established.

---

[52] Tomm 'Interventive Interviewing: Part II. Reflexive Questioning as a Means to Enabling Self-Healing' [1987] Fam Proc, 26, 167–1810.

[53] Ibid.

10.76 It is our experience that normative comparison questions are of particular use when working cross culturally and in instances where families have felt misunderstood or disconnected from the concerns of the professional network. Using these questions appears to develop a climate of respectful appreciation, whilst generating opportunities to challenge and debate.

10.77 As discussed previously, our assessment sessions are not always constructive and thoughtful despite our best efforts, and at times we find ourselves locked into unproductive battles or forced politeness. It is in these instances we would seek to use 'process interruption questions'[54] in an attempt to name our experience and think of possible resolutions. Sometimes we are sufficiently attuned to attend to this in the moment, pausing the interview in an attempt to unravel what has been created.

10.78 At other times we may lack awareness or be too enmeshed in the process to adopt a meta position. This is less common when we co-work, as we negotiate permission with each other and the families we work with to engage in 'in the room' reflections,[55] a process valued by families as an active demonstration of our use of self and capacity to hold multiple perspectives.

10.79 In other instances we may enlist the assistance of a colleague to consult with retrospectively. This can be particularly helpful when we hold significantly different views regarding prognosis. We often find such impasses can be overcome by revisiting our own core beliefs and family of origin narratives. We are also often struck by how our past experiences of working with families with specific issues, such as drug abuse, honour based violence or sexual exploitation affects and organises us at a very personal level. Such instances dramatically re-affirm our commitment to self-reflexivity and to conduct our work in a context that actively supports this process.

ACCEPTING REALITY

10.80 Whilst we remain clear in the belief that the process of our assessments provides parents to think differently about helping agencies, and allows them to develop more constructive beliefs regarding themselves and their children, we acknowledge that many parents will be unable to demonstrate sufficient capacity to change within timescales relevant to their children's needs.

10.81 Whilst we do not intend to minimise the shock and grief parents and children experience when decisions regarding permanent separation are made, we do notice that since adopting systemic approaches, our relationships with parent's post care proceedings tend to be less hostile. This is a recent observation and we are reluctant to draw significant conclusions. Currently, we

---

[54]   Ibid.
[55]   Malley and Hurst '"Alice and Alice not through the looking glass": therapeutic transparency and the therapeutic and supervisory relationship' in Flaskas et al (eds) *The Space Between: Experience, context and process in the therapeutic relationship* (Karnac, 2005).

hypothesise this may be connected to the respectful stance of appreciation we adopt, specifically regarding our responses to different belief systems.

10.82 This is an area of our work we wish to investigate further as it has significant implications for family's futures. We are hopeful that by initiating opportunities for parents to cultivate alternative perspectives, choices are increased, along with potential to develop a sense of agency and self-determination. It is our hope this may provide scope to perturb repetitive cycles of abuse and disconnection and allow families and professionals to contemplate pathways to preferred futures.

CONCLUSION

10.83 In this chapter, we have attempted to highlight the complexities of creating fair and robust parenting assessments in social care context. Our model of working is newly established and yet to be thoroughly researched. However, anecdotal evidence and our experience as practitioners leads us to believe a systemic approach to parenting assessments promotes both rigour and appreciation, allowing both ourselves and the families we work with opportunities to consider alternative perspectives and think differently.

10.84 In a climate of increasing demand and diminishing resources, it is imperative to contemplate how we may retain high standards of professional practice whilst responding to vulnerable families in ethical and compassionate ways. Systemic theory provides a road map to these aims, orientating professionals to the importance of self-reflexivity in practice and highlighting themes of power and positioning.

10.85 Completing this chapter has provided us with the opportunity to reflect upon evolutions in our practice to date and to contemplate how we may respond to future challenges and developments. We are hopeful our work may encourage other practitioners to evaluate their practice and the role they play in life changing episodes for the children and families we work with.

CHAPTER 11

UNDERSTANDING THE LEGAL PROCESS IN THE ASSESSMENT OF CAPACITY TO CHANGE IN THE CHILD'S TIMESCALES

Michelle Flynn and Siobhan F Kelly

11.1 This chapter intends to alert experts to the current circumstances and considerations operating in the family jurisdiction. It looks at those matters that are relevant for practitioners and judges alike and which an instructed expert must also be aware of in order to assist the court process and understand what is needed and expected of them. The particular focus is on public law cases where historically the greatest reliance has been placed on instructed experts.

11.2 This has been and continues to be a time of dramatic change within the family justice system. Sir James Munby, the President of the Family Division, has described it as a 'cultural revolution'.[1] The central tenet of the reform is that, save for 'exceptional' matters, all public law proceedings under Part 4 of the Children Act 1989[2] will conclude within 26 weeks of issue. Those elements of reform that have not had to wait for primary legislation have been introduced by amendments to the Family Procedure Rules 2010,[3] the imposition of changes to working practice and new practice guidance that has been in place since July 2013, initially under the form of a 'pilot scheme' PLO.[4] This was introduced to all courts in England and Wales between July and October 2013. Whilst what follows relates specifically to the jurisdiction of England and Wales there are important messages and guidance that may be equally applicable in other jurisdictions.

11.3 Since April 2014[5] and the commencement of the Children and Families Act 2014 the necessary legislation has been in place to underpin those reforms that have been born out of the Norgrove Review.[6] That review was published in

---

1   Remarks by Sir James Munby, President of the Family Division and Head of Family Justice in *The President's Court* (29 April 2014) http://www.judiciary.gov.uk/wp-content/uploads/2014/05/family-justice-reforms-29042014.pdf.

2   http://www.legislation.gov.uk/ukpga/1989/41/contents.

3   https://www.justice.gov.uk/courts/procedure-rules/family/rules_pd_menu.

4   *View from the President's Chambers (2)* http://www.judiciary.gov.uk/wpcontent/uploads/JCO/Documents/FJC/Publications/VIEW+FROM+THE+PRESIDENT.pdf.

5   http://www.legislation.gov.uk/ukpga/2014/6/contents/enacted.

6   https://www.gov.uk/government/uploads/system/uploads/attachment_data/file/217343/family-justice-review-final-report.pdf.

2011. As of April 2014, the 26 week limit has been made statutory by s 32 of the Children Act 1989; there is a revised Public Law Outline 2014 (PLO)[7] and there is a unified, single Family Court.

11.4 The 26 week time limit is a mandatory limit which must be complied with, subject to the statutory exception set out in s 32(5). Whilst the overarching aim of the revision of the family justice system is the completion of cases within 26 weeks, one of the main planks of that intention is greater regulation on the use of, and reliance upon, expert witnesses.

11.5 The statutory provision in this respect is found at s 13 of the Children and Families Act 2014:

> **13 Control of expert evidence, and of assessments, in children proceedings**
>
> (1) A person may not without the permission of the court instruct a person to provide expert evidence for use in children proceedings.
>
> (2) Where in contravention of subsection (1) a person is instructed to provide expert evidence, evidence resulting from the instructions is inadmissible in children proceedings unless the court rules that it is admissible.
>
> (3) A person may not without the permission of the court cause a child to be medically or psychiatrically examined or otherwise assessed for the purposes of the provision of expert evidence in children proceedings.
>
> (4) Where in contravention of subsection (3) a child is medically or psychiatrically examined or otherwise assessed, evidence resulting from the examination or other assessment is inadmissible in children proceedings unless the court rules that it is admissible.
>
> (5) In children proceedings, a person may not without the permission of the court put expert evidence (in any form) before the court.
>
> (6) The court may give permission as mentioned in subsection (1), (3) or (5) only if the court is of the opinion that the expert evidence is necessary to assist the court to resolve the proceedings justly.
>
> (7) When deciding whether to give permission as mentioned in subsection (1), (3) or (5) the court is to have regard in particular to –
>
> > (a) any impact which giving permission would be likely to have on the welfare of the children concerned, including in the case of permission as mentioned in subsection (3) any impact which any examination or other assessment would be likely to have on the welfare of the child who would be examined or otherwise assessed,
> >
> > (b) the issues to which the expert evidence would relate,
> >
> > (c) the questions which the court would require the expert to answer,
> >
> > (d) what other expert evidence is available (whether obtained before or after the start of proceedings),
> >
> > (e) whether evidence could be given by another person on the matters on which the expert would give evidence,

---

[7]   https://www.justice.gov.uk/protecting-the-vulnerable/care-proceedings-reform.

(f)   the impact which giving permission would be likely to have on the timetable for, and duration and conduct of, the proceedings,

(g)   the cost of the expert evidence, and

(h)   any matters prescribed by Family Procedure Rules.

(8) References in this section to providing expert evidence, or to putting expert evidence before a court, do not include references to –

(a)   the provision or giving of evidence –

     (i)   by a person who is a member of the staff of a local authority or of an authorised applicant,

     (ii)   in proceedings to which the authority or authorised applicant is a party, and

     (iii)   n the course of the person's work for the authority or authorised applicant,

(b)   the provision or giving of evidence –

     (i)   by a person within a description prescribed for the purposes of subsection (1) of section 94 of the Adoption and Children Act 2002 (suitability for adoption etc.), and

     (ii)   about the matters mentioned in that subsection,

(c)   the provision or giving of evidence by an officer of the Children and Family Court Advisory and Support Service when acting in that capacity, or

(d)   the provision or giving of evidence by a Welsh family proceedings officer (as defined by section 35(4) of the Children Act 2004) when acting in that capacity.

(9) In this section –

"authorised applicant" means –

     (a)   the National Society for the Prevention of Cruelty to Children, or

     (b)   a person authorised by an order under section 31 of the Children Act 1989 to bring proceedings under that section;

"child" means a person under the age of 18;

"children proceedings" has such meaning as may be prescribed by Family Procedure Rules;

"the court", in relation to any children proceedings, means the court in which the proceedings are taking place;

"local authority" –

     (a)   in relation to England means –

         (i)   a county council,

         (ii)   a district council for an area for which there is no county council,

         (iii)   a London borough council,

         (iv)   the Common Council of the City of London, or

         (v)   the Council of the Isles of Scilly, and

     (b)   in relation to Wales means a county council or a county borough council.

(10) The preceding provisions of this section are without prejudice to sections 75 and 76 of the Courts Act 2003 (power to make Family Procedure Rules).

(11) In section 38 of the Children Act 1989 (court's power to make interim care and supervision orders, and to give directions as to medical examination etc. of children) after subsection (7) insert –

"(7A) A direction under subsection (6) to the effect that there is to be a medical or psychiatric examination or other assessment of the child may be given only if the court is of the opinion that the examination or other assessment is necessary to assist the court to resolve the proceedings justly.

(7B)   When deciding whether to give a direction under subsection (6) to that effect the court is to have regard in particular to –

    (a)   any impact which any examination or other assessment would be likely to have on the welfare of the child, and any other impact which giving the direction would be likely to have on the welfare of the child,

    (b)   the issues with which the examination or other assessment would assist the court,

    (c)   the questions which the examination or other assessment would enable the court to answer,

    (d)   the evidence otherwise available,

    (e)   the impact which the direction would be likely to have on the timetable, duration and conduct of the proceedings,

    (f)   the cost of the examination or other assessment, and

    (g)   any matters prescribed by Family Procedure Rules."

11.6   The timeframe that we must work within is now 26 weeks but it is still important to remember that s 1 of the Children Act 1989 (the welfare principle and checklist) remains firmly in place:

1 Welfare of the child

(1) When a court determines any question with respect to –

    (a)   the upbringing of a child; or

    (b)   the administration of a child's property or the application of any income arising from it,

the child's welfare shall be the court's paramount consideration.

(2) In any proceedings in which any question with respect to the upbringing of a child arises, the court shall have regard to the general principle that any delay in determining the question is likely to prejudice the welfare of the child.

(3) In the circumstances mentioned in subsection (4), a court shall have regard in particular to –

    (a)   the ascertainable wishes and feelings of the child concerned (considered in the light of his age and understanding); his physical, emotional and educational needs;

    (b)   the likely effect on him of any change in his circumstances;

    (c)   his age, sex, background and any characteristics of his, which the court considers relevant;

    (d)   any harm, which he has suffered or is at risk of suffering;

    (e)   how capable each of his parents, and any other person in relation to whom the court considers the question to be relevant, is of meeting his needs;

    (f)   the range of powers available to the court under this Act in the proceedings in question.

(4) The circumstances are that –

    (a)   the court is considering whether to make, vary or discharge a section 8 order, and the making, variation or discharge of the order is opposed by any party to the proceedings; or

    (b)   the court is considering whether to make, vary or discharge a special guardianship order or an order under Part IV.

(5) Where a court is considering whether or not to make one or more orders under this Act with respect to a child, it shall not make the order or any of the orders unless it considers that doing so would be better for the child than making no order at all.

11.7   The welfare principle remains the umbrella under which we continue to operate and be guided. It is not varied nor its intention diluted in any way by the reforms. It remains the primary ambition of the court to seek to maintain or reunify a family if it is at all safe and possible and if a good enough standard of parenting can be achieved for the subject child within their birth family.

11.8   The introduction of the set timeframe requires us all to be evermore alert to the need to balance a swifter decision-making process against the continuing essential components of fairness and diligence. One must hope that fairness to parents, who face the most serious of prospects, that being the permanent removal or adoption of their children, will not be trampled over in these progressive times.

11.9   It was never anticipated or intended that litigation under the Children Act 1989 would evolve in a way that has led to such heavy reliance upon expert witnesses. The courts decisions about a case are made within a framework of legal principles, statute and case law. These decisions are not based solely on expert evidence. Historically the court has required assistance from experts when there has been a gap in the courts knowledge base that required that input. However the court arena and those within it have changed and evolved over the years. We now have a judiciary that has better, more focused and more specialised training than ever before. The same is true of the practitioners. As such automatic recourse to expert instruction in many (not all) circumstances should be revisited. Indeed in more recent times there has been a lessening of the use of experts.

11.10   A review of approximately 400 sample public law case files where an order was made in 2009 found that expert reports were commissioned in 87% of cases and in 74% of cases more than one expert was commissioned.[8] In these cases, the most common type of instructions were adult psychiatric (35% of cases), independent social workers (33%) and parents psychological (33%). The same study indicates that expert reports were ordered less frequently in private law proceedings concerning children (37% of cases, with an average of two reports in those cases). The most commonly requested reports were drug

---

[8]   Family Justice Review: Government Response
https://www.gov.uk/government/uploads/system/uploads/attachment_data/file/217337/fjr-eia.pdf.

tests (10% of all private law cases), independent social worker (8% of all private cases) and adult psychiatric reports (6% of all private cases).[9]

11.11 Extensive research published by Cafcass (Children and Family Court Advisory and Support Service) *The Instruction of Expert Witnesses in Care Applications* published in June 2013 indicates that the instruction of expert witnesses in care applications is decreasing. Experts were instructed in 70% of the Cafcass study sample cases. This is a significant downward shift from their previous study of care applications in 2009, which found that experts were instructed in 92% of cases.[10]

11.12 Cafcass points out that this finding is in line with government-approved recommendations from the 2011 Norgrove Review, which acknowledged the positive contribution of expert evidence, but highlighted a 'trend towards an increasing and, we believe, unjustified use of expert witness reports, with consequent delay for children'. The Cafcass survey found that adult psychologists were the most commonly instructed type of expert, accounting for 30% of all the experts instructed in the sample cases. Adult psychiatrists were next, comprising 20% of all the experts instructed. These two types of experts account for half of all experts instructed in the care cases that made up the sample. Child psychologists and psychiatrists made up 10% of all the experts instructed, and paediatricians 6%.

11.13 The Cafcass study also found an association between the duration of the sample cases and the instruction of experts: those with experts instructed lasted an average of 12 weeks longer than those without. The most common causes of delay seemed to be the late instruction and completion of reports and time taken waiting for results of assessments. This is a particularly important statistic when reducing delay in care cases and the introduction of the 26 week timeframe being a key aim of the reforms. It has previously been common practice for most experts to require 12–16 weeks to complete an assessment.

11.14 In *Re Avon, North Somerset and Gloucestershire Public Law Case (2013) No 1* [2013] EWCC 4 (Fam) much of the blame for the case lasting an unacceptable 58 weeks falls at the door of excessive use of expert witnesses. 'There was far too much expert evidence. How could it be said to be a reasonable requirement (to use old money language) or, in modern and current parlance, necessary for there to be so many experts (psychologist, independent social worker, special guardianship social worker, local authority social worker and guardian)? An understanding of the mother's dyspraxia was necessary but why were so many professionals instructed on basic welfare issues?'

11.15 Cafcass research in November 2013 showed a drop in care applications year on year. Cafcass received a total of 816 applications to November 2013.[11]

---

[9]   Ministry of Justice Impact Assessment, January 2013 http://www.legislation.gov.uk/ukia/2013/28.

[10] http://www.cafcass.gov.uk/media/149859/cafcass_expert_witness_research_6.2013.pdf.

[11] http://www.cafcass.gov.uk/news/2013/december/november-2013-care-demand-statistics.aspx.

This figure represents a 15% decrease compared to the 947 received in November 2012.[12] This reduction in cases may have had the benefit of freeing up court space to ease the path to meeting the 26 week limit for other cases. It may also have balanced the feared reduction in availability of expert witnesses caused by the changes (reductions) to Legal Aid Agency (LAA) funding rates.

11.16 However, the comparable Cafcass research from October 2014[13] shows there has been 999 applications which shows a significant increase on the year and is in excess of the 2012 level of issuing. So any prospect of spare capacity in the system to ease the path to 26 weeks has vanished again.

11.17 So, when and why will an expert witness be needed and used in the future?

11.18 The Ministry of Justice and the Family Justice Council jointly published the May 2013 government consultation document *Standards for Expert Witnesses in the Family Courts in England and Wales*.[14] It set out the intention for experts under the new regime.

- Experts are required to provide high quality robust reports that help judges move forward quickly and ensure children spend as little time as necessary waiting for their futures to become clear.

- Properly formulated reports can contribute to reducing delays in the system where others lack the skills or time to undertake the work immediately.

- Experts have specialist knowledge and skills needed by the courts in the more complex cases.

- Experts also provide courts with a genuinely independent expert view in cases that have become intractable and need a robust, analytical assessment in order to be moved on.

- Most expert reports commissioned were highly experienced practitioners with specialist skills, highly articulate, and with effective and with detailed knowledge of public law, child development and the needs of the court.

- Children and proceedings cannot wait. When the necessity is identified immediate availability of high quality and timely expert assessment is imperative if timescales are to take precedence. Avenues must remain open to courts, guardians and local authorities to obtain the best evidence; no option should be immune from question or bypassed in that exercise.

11.19 These intentions and aims are now encapsulated in PD25B *The Duties of an Expert, the Expert's Report and Arrangements for an Expert to Come to*

---

12 http://www.cafcass.gov.uk/news/archive/2012/november-care-application-statistics-released. aspx.

13 http://www.cafcass.gov.uk/news/2014/november/october-2014-care-demand-statistics.aspx.

14 https://consult.justice.gov.uk/digital-communications/expert-witnesses.

Court.[15] It is essential that any instructed expert within the family law arena is familiar with this practice direction and all of FPR Part 25. These national standards for family court experts were developed in partnership with the Family Justice Council.

11.20 The practical effect of the tighter controls on the use of expert witnesses reminds us that their use is not automatic. We should not revert to the instruction of an expert as a matter of course or some default setting. We must remember that cases should not and will not be expert driven.

11.21 In his *View From the President's Chambers (3)* released in June 2013[16] Sir James Munby P says:

> 'My focus here is on the use of experts in care cases. My starting point is the proposed statutory requirement that care cases are to be concluded within 26 weeks and that expert evidence is to be restricted to what is 'necessary'. My call to everyone in the family justice system is simple and clear. We can and must reduce the excessive length of far too many care cases. In order to achieve this we must get a grip on our excessive and in many instances unnecessary use of experts. I emphasise a point I have previously made: The problem does not lie with the experts themselves. It lies in the use we make of them.'

11.22 An expert will be required, and their instruction approved by the court, when the expertise and knowledge base they can bring to a case would not be readily available without their input. Judges are encouraged to greater scrutiny of any application to instruct experts and to assess in far greater detail whether or not the proposed instruction will bring additional, purposeful knowledge. The Children and Families Act 2014 statutory framework includes provisions relating to tighter control by the courts on expert evidence in family proceedings relating to children (both private and public law).

11.23 In considering whether any expert evidence falls within the definition of 'necessary', it will be an essential exercise of the court to evaluate the other evidence that is or will be available to it. This is in order to assess if it will be fair and proper to make such findings of fact or conclusions as are necessary without the use of an expert. The court will evaluate and consider the sufficiency and quality of evidence including that of social workers and guardians.

11.24 In public law court proceedings relating to children, when seeking the court's permission to instruct an expert one must provide full details as to the discipline, qualifications and expertise of the proposed expert. This is to assist the court in determining whether the proposed expert is appropriate. It is anticipated that the court will only give permission if it is satisfied that the

---

[15] https://www.justice.gov.uk/courts/procedure-rules/family/practice_directions/practice-direction-25b-the-duties-of-an-expert,-the-experts-report-and-arrangements-for-an-expert-to-attend-court.

[16] http://www.judiciary.gov.uk/wp-content/uploads/JCO/Documents/FJC/Publications/VIEW+President+Expert%283%29.pdf.

expert meets the requirements of the case, on the basis of information supplied. In publicly funded cases where one or more of the instructing parties is in receipt of legal aid, solicitors will only be permitted to instruct experts who meet the relevant standards as set out in the Annex to PD25B. Instructing solicitors will need to confirm to the Legal Aid Agency (LAA) when making an application for payment and/or prior authority that the expert meets the standards or why (exceptionally) they do not. Before agreeing payment, the LAA will expect to see evidence that the instructing solicitor has made reasonable efforts to assure themselves that the expert meets the standards and that they will accept the LAA codified rates for their discipline. When all the information has been gathered to meet the requirements of the LAA for funding and it is before the court, permission will only be given to instruct an expert if it is 'necessary'.

11.25 The President held in *Re TG (A Child)* [2013] EWCA Civ 5:

> 'It is a matter for another day to determine what exactly is meant in this context by the word "necessary", but clearly the new test is intended to be significantly more stringent than the old. The text of what is "necessary" sets a hurdle, which is on any view significantly higher than the old test of what is reasonably required.'

11.26 Pauffley J in *MR (A Child)* [2013] EWHC 1156 (Fam) reminded herself:

> 'that with effect from 31 January 2013, the Family Procedure Rules as amended by the Family Procedure (Amendment) (No 5) Rules 2012 provide that active case management includes "controlling the use of expert evidence." By r 25.1, as amended, "Expert evidence will be restricted to that which in the opinion of the court is necessary to assist the court to resolve the proceedings".'

11.27 In *Re H-L (A Child)* [2013] EWCA Civ 655 guidance was given by the President as to the test for permitting expert evidence pursuant to r 25.1 FPR 2010. The President recognised that the point left open in *Re TG (A Child)* [2013] EWCA Civ 5, now had to be determined. In *Re TG* what was meant by 'necessary' was not determined.

11.28 So in *Re H-L* the issue for the court to determine was the change in test for the instruction of expert evidence from 'reasonably required to resolve the proceedings' to whether it is 'necessary to assist the court to resolve the proceedings'. The President held:

> 'We now have to decide what is meant by "necessary". The short answer is that "necessary" means necessary. It is, after all, an ordinary English word. It is a familiar expression nowadays in family law, not least because of the central role it plays, for example, in Art 8 of the European Convention and the wider Strasbourg jurisprudence. If elaboration is required, what precisely does it mean? That was a question considered, albeit in a rather different context, in *Re P (Placement Orders. Parental Consent)* [2008] EWCA Civ 535, [2008] 2 FLR 625, paras [120], [125]. This court said it:

"has a meaning lying somewhere between 'indispensable' on the one hand and 'useful', 'reasonable' or 'desirable' on the other hand", having "the connotation of the imperative, what is demanded rather than what is merely optional or reasonable or desirable."

In my judgment, that is the meaning, the connotation, the word "necessary" has in rule 25.1.'

11.29 Experts will continue to be instructed in suitable cases, but the likelihood is that choices will have to be made. It has recently been common practice to instruct both a psychiatrist and a psychologist to assess a parent. This will no longer be so readily done. The precise nature of the most valuable assessment will need determining at the earliest possible stage. The requirements under the rules for 'necessity' (Family Procedure (Amendment) (No 3) Rules 2014, r 25.1) are for representatives and courts to think very carefully about the type of expert required and the specific expertise needed in reference to the issues to be addressed.

11.30 The timing of an application for an expert to be instructed will now be critical. A Part 25 application must be set out in writing with detailed reasoning. It must be issued, requiring a fee to be paid. It is expected in the 26 week timeframe that any application will be made at the first case management hearing, on day 12 of proceedings. Two days in advance of that there will have been an advocates meeting and it is at that meeting that identity, costings, timescales and draft questions in respect of the proposed expert will need to be made available. For this to work, experts will be expected to respond swiftly to requests for such information and to have up to date CVs and availability to hand. When the request comes in from a solicitor be assured it will be time sensitive.

11.31 There is provision for a repeat case management hearing by no later than week 4 of proceedings. However the further into proceedings and the more of the timetable used up, the harder it will be to assert 'necessary'. The time allowed for an assessment is also reduced. LA final evidence is due at week 16; this will require all assessments to be in at week 14. Therefore the longest an assessment can ever take is 12 weeks and that will be the exception and not the norm.

11.32 These time constraints also mean the days of split hearings and of fact-finding hearings prior to assessment are on the way out. We will all have to re-accustom ourselves to working on a contingency basis when there are factual disputes. Ryder LJ in *Re S (A Child)* [2014] EWCA Civ 25:

'It ought to be recollected that split hearings became fashionable as a means of expediting the most simple cases where there was only one factual issue to be decided and where the threshold for jurisdiction in section 31 CA 1989 would not be satisfied if a finding could not be made thereby concluding the proceedings (see *Re S (A Child)* [1996] 2 FLR 773 at 775B per Bracewell J). Over time, they also came to be used for the most complex medical causation cases where death or very serious medical issues had arisen and where an accurate medical diagnosis was integral to the future care of the child concerned. For almost all other cases, the procedure is inappropriate. The oft repeated but erroneous justification for them that a split hearing enables a social care assessment to be undertaken is simply poor social work and forensic practice. The justification comes from an era before the present Rules and Practice Directions came into force and can safely be discounted in public law children proceedings save in the most exceptional case.'

11.33   Each case needs to be considered on its own merits and decisions about the use of expert evidence in individual cases are ones for the court. Judicial scrutiny of the nature of expertise sought and the contents of the letter of instruction has increased dramatically. The draft letter of instruction must accompany a Part 25 application and will be considered and approved by the court in the event the application is granted. The increased commitment to judicial continuity means that the allocated judge will be able to determine the evidence and the assistance they will need to carry out their judicial function in the particular case. It will be they who determine the evidence that will assist them in reaching the decisions necessary in that case. In considering the letter of instruction the legal process asking for the information will have to be astute to ask the right questions and to ensure that correct language and terminology in respect of the relevant area of expertise is used. (In Annex A to PD25C[17] some helpful suggested questions for a letter of instruction can be found.) In some cases, such as those involving allegations of non-accidental injury, expert evidence will remain essential in order to reach a proper resolution.

11.34   None of what is said here of the tighter regulations is intended to underestimate or undermine the importance of the role of experts within proceedings.

11.35   Although the reforms seek to limit the use of experts, this is not an indication that expert evidence has become any less relevant or critical to ensuring fair conclusions for families. The ambition remains to make the right decision, for the relevant child, at the right time. However, poor quality evidence may mean that the court does not have the best information on which to make a decision; it could have the exact opposite affect to that which the instruction sought.

11.36   In the case of *Re CtL and CmL (Children) (Welfare Hearing: Expert Report)* [2013] EWHC 2134 (Fam) the court was critical of a 75-page report prepared by the child and adolescent psychiatrist in the case, when he had been directed to limit his report to 10 pages. The judge referred to an 'abundance of tedious, even mind-numbing detail' in the report (para 32). This should serve as a salient reminder for an expert of what they need to give the court. A regurgitation of the information already contained within the court papers is unnecessary. A re-potting of the history of the family or the path into

---

[17]   https://www.justice.gov.uk/courts/procedure-rules/family/practice_directions/practice-direction-25c-children-proceedings-the-use-of-single-joint-experts-and-the-process-leading-to-an-expert-being-instructed-or-expert-evidence-being-put-before-the-court.

proceedings serves little if any purpose in an expert assessment. Where there are matters that are relevant they can be flagged up quite succinctly. The same applies to including a verbatim account of interviews and discussions with the subject of the assessment.

11.37 A meandering narrative of the time spent with the subject means there is a possibility that salient points and key issues become lost. The courts want and need an overview of the assessment process. The courts want and need a concise critical analysis of the case in hand. The courts want and need the questions asked of an expert to be the questions answered by that expert. The courts want and need conclusions and recommendations as specific as can be achieved.

11.38 Under the new regime local authority evidence is to be filed at week 16 of proceedings so not only will assessment timescales need to recalibrate to allow for that but also report authors. The document received from an expert at week 14 (for example) will need to be in a format that is readily digestible for those whose care planning and case progress it must inform (ideally with pagination and paragraph numbers). Few if any social work professionals have the luxury of time to allow a leisurely read of a 75-page report before they are able to mull over the conclusions and recommendation and formulate their response. Length does not necessarily equate to quality.

11.39 Furthermore, there is new guidance from the President as to bundle size for any hearing. The draft format was issued on 14 January 2014 and says, 'Unless the court has specifically directed otherwise the bundle shall be contained in one A4 size ring binder or lever arch file limited to no more than 350 pages'. This has now been incorporated into Practice Direction 27A[18] which supplements Family Proceeding Rules Part 27.

11.40 This clearly underpins the expectation that expert reports will henceforth be pithy and succinct.

11.41 If one is to consider that the most recent LAA guidance suggests, for example, that a parenting assessment by an independent social worker can be done within 30 hours where one parent to be considered and 40 hours for two or more including assessment, analysis, consideration and report writing the days of voluminous reports may well be behind us for a plethora of reasons. Of course in particular circumstances one can seek to justify greater time allowances for a given case. Seeking prior authority is time consuming and can easily cut into the time frame of proceedings and the length allowed for an assessment. It is important to bear this in mind. If more hours are necessary the instructing parties will need to be told why and given very clear detail as to the reason as soon as possible in order to seek prior authority.

---

[18] https://www.justice.gov.uk/courts/procedure-rules/family/practice_directions/pd_part_27a.

11.42 It will be at the IRH at week 20[19] that the decision is made whether or not there will be a contested final hearing and whether an expert will be called to give evidence. It is the expectation that in future more use will be made of written questions to an expert and there will be increasingly less reliance on court attendance. This will require experts to strictly adhere to deadlines for filing responses. There will only be a narrow window of opportunity for the court to determine whether or not the written responses are sufficient or there remains a need for attendance.

11.43 A feared consequence of the new LAA funding is a reduction in the availability and/or quality of available experts or the willingness of experts to continue with LAA funded work. A survey of members of the Consortium of Expert Witnesses to the Family Courts suggests that reductions in the legal aided fees payable to expert witnesses from 2 December 2013 is causing experts to decline to undertake such work in the future.[20]

11.44 These are the most recent figures of this type available and relate to a survey that was conducted in November 2013 in anticipation of the introduction of new rates of remuneration for experts.[21] Those rates and the maximum numbers of hours per case (above which prior authority is required) are set out in the Legal Aid Agency's *Guidance on the Remuneration of Expert Witnesses*.

11.45 Two hundred and forty members (or 42%) of the membership responded to the survey. Ninety per cent of the respondents were experts who have worked in the courts for 10 years or more. The majority of the respondents were psychologists or psychiatrists although the Consortium includes a wide range of health and other professions.

11.46 A quarter of the respondents stated they no longer undertake family court work. The concern is that this figure will continue to grow and there will be a consequential qualitative effect on the experts available to the family justice system.

11.47 The case of *Re B (A Child)* [2013] UKSC 33 signalled a reconsideration of the way evidence before the court is analysed in cases that may lead to the permanent removal of a child from their birth family. The care plan in that case was adoption but the same principles apply in respect of long term foster care (see McFarlane J below in *Re G*).

11.48 In *Re B* Lord Neuberger says:

'Whether or not article 8 has any part to play in the threshold decision, it certainly comes into full flower at the disposal stage. Lady Hale and Lord Wilson have both

---

[19] http://www.justice.gov.uk/downloads/protecting-the-vulnerable/care-proceeding-reform/public-law-outline-flowchart.pdf.
[20] http://www.familylawweek.co.uk/site.aspx?i=ed122540.
[21] https://www.gov.uk/expert-witnesses-in-legal-aid-cases.

referred to emphatic statements by ECtHR in such cases as *Johansen v Norway* (1996) 23 EHRR 33, *K and T v Finland* (2001) 36 EHRR 255, *R and H v United Kingdom* (2011) 54 EHRR 28, [2011] 2 FLR 1236 and *YC v United Kingdom* (2012) 55 EHRR 967 concerning the stringent requirements of the proportionality doctrine where family ties must be broken in order to allow adoption to take place. I agree with Lady Hale's statement (in para 198 of her judgment) that the test for severing the relationship between parent and child is very strict and that the test will be found to be satisfied only in exceptional circumstances and "where nothing else will do". I also agree with what Lord Wilson has said in para 34 of his judgment, that "a high degree of justification" is required before an order can properly be made.'

11.49   It is worth reminding ourselves at this point of our European identity and what Article 8 is:

> **'Right to respect for private and family life**
>
> Everyone has the right to respect for his private and family life, his home and his correspondence.
>
> There shall be no interference by a public authority with the exercise of this right except such as is in accordance with the law and is necessary in a democratic society in the interests of national security, public safety or the economic well-being of the country, for the prevention of disorder or crime, for the protection of health or morals, or for the protection of the rights and freedoms of others.'

11.50   This is an overarching consideration that must be borne in mind and must be the thread running through any decisions made or affecting the retention, reunification or destruction of a family unit.

11.51   The relevance of the United Kingdom's place in Europe and the context within which our family justice system is viewed was highlighted in In *Re E (A Child)* [2014] EWHC 6 (Fam). Sir James Munby P said:

> 'It would be idle to ignore the fact that these concerns [relating to children from other jurisdictions being the subject of care proceedings within the UK] are only exacerbated by the fact that the United Kingdom is unusual in Europe in permitting the total severance of family ties without parental consent. We need to recognise that the judicial and other State authorities in some countries that are members of the European Union and parties to the BIIR regime may take a very different view and may indeed look askance at our whole approach to such cases ...
>
> The English family justice system is now part of a much wider system of international family justice exemplified by such instruments as the various Hague Conventions and, in the purely European context, by BIIR. Looking no further afield, we are part of the European family of nations. We share common values. In particular in this context we share the values enshrined in BIIR.'

11.52   *Re G (A Child)* [2013] EWCA Civ 965 McFarlane LJ considered what the judicial approach should now be to the welfare balancing exercise when deciding whether to make a care order on a care plan of adoption or permanent removal from the family (including long term foster care). This case identifies that a care plan for removal requires the court to approach the question not in a linear way but as a single holistic question. 'The judicial task is to undertake a global, holistic evaluation of each of the options available for the child's future upbringing before deciding which of those options best meets the duty to afford paramount consideration of the child's welfare.'

11.53 *Re G* impressed upon us that each of the competing options presented to the court must have 'an evaluation of its internal merits and de-merits'. This defines the court's task as being to address all the options and analyse the internal positives and negatives for each one. Thereafter the court must balance each option against the other in order that it reach a proper determination.

11.54 Pauffley J cautions us, in *Re LRP (A Child) (Care Proceedings: Placement Order)* [2013] EWHC 3974 (Fam) the focus of the competing options should be '… upon the sensible and practical possibilities rather than every potential outcome, however far-fetched'. It will of course be vital for any instructed expert in making a recommendation to bear this in mind. The court should not be distracted by the wholly 'fanciful'. The court will need to know the range of options that are within a wide definition of realistic or achievable.

11.55 *Re B-S (Children)* [2013] EWCA Civ 1146 is essential reading for anyone involved in care proceedings as it provides an exhaustive analysis of the law post-*Re B* to that point. It determined that the court's assessment of a parents' capacity to care for the child should include consideration of the support that the authorities could offer them in doing so and that information should be available to the court whether or not it is the path commended to the court by the local authority. The court had:

> 'real concerns, shared by other judges, about the recurrent inadequacy of the analysis and reasoning put forward in support of the case for adoption, both in the materials put before the court by local authorities and guardians and also in too many judgments. This is nothing new. But it is time to call a halt.'

11.56 In *W (a Child) v Neath Port Talbot County Borough Council* [2013] EWCA Civ 1225 Ryder LJ commended adopting a balance sheet approach in which the positives and negatives of the competing placement prospects before the court were set out by reference to the welfare checklist factors. He described this as:

> 'an illuminating and essential intellectual and forensic exercise that will highlight the evidential conclusions and their implications and how they are to weighed in the evaluative balance that is the value judgment of the Court. It is to be noted that this exercise is different in substance and form from a mechanical recitation of the welfare checklist with stereotypical commentary that is neither case specific nor helpful.'

11.57 *Re S, K v The London Borough of Brent* [2013] EWCA Civ 926, para 21, states that what is needed is: 'An assessment of the benefits and detriments of each option for placement and in particular the nature and extent of the risk of harm involved in each of the options.'

11.58 Turning again to *Re B-S* we find a commitment to the imposition of the 26 week time frame but with an acknowledgement of circumstances in which we may need to depart from the rigid structure:

> 'We do not envisage that proper compliance with what we are demanding, which may well impose a more onerous burden on practitioners and judges, will conflict with the requirement, soon to be imposed by statute, that care cases are to be concluded within a maximum of 26 weeks. Critical to the success of the reforms is robust judicial case management from the outset of every care case. Case management judges must be astute to ensure that the directions they give are apt to the task and also to ensure that their directions are complied with. Never is this more important than in cases where the local authority's plan envisages adoption. *If, despite all, the court does not have the kind of evidence we have identified, and is therefore not properly equipped to decide these issues, then an adjournment must be directed, even if this takes the case over 26 weeks.* Where the proposal before the court is for non-consensual adoption, the issues are too grave, the stakes for all are too high, for the outcome to be determined by rigorous adherence to an inflexible timetable and justice thereby potentially denied.'

11.59 In the case of *Re R (A Child)* [2014] EWCA Civ 1625, the President sought to set right some 'myths and misconceptions' that may have arisen as a consequence of *Re B-S*. This case provides a useful analysis of key decisions following on from *Re B-S*. Importantly, the President says:

> 'I wish to emphasise, with as much force as possible, that *Re B-S* was not intended to change and has not changed the law. Where adoption is in the child's best interests, local authorities must not shy away from seeking, nor courts from making, care orders with a plan for adoption, placement orders and adoption orders. The fact is that there are occasions when nothing but adoption will do, and it is essential in such cases that a child's welfare should not be compromised by keeping them within their family at all costs.'

11.60 The President, in *M-F (Children)* [2104] EWCA Civ 991 when considering an appeal 67 weeks after care proceedings began stated that 'the 26 weeks rule "is not, and must never be allowed to become, a straightjacket"'. In *Re S (A Child)* [2014] EWCC B44 the President, gave further guidance as to the factors that the court may consider when determining whether to extend care proceedings beyond 26 weeks.

11.61 The President in *Re S* reasserts his view that this timeframe can and will be met whilst also approving Pauffley J's view in *Re NL (A child) (Appeal: Interim Care Order: Facts and Reasons)* [2014] EWHC 270 (Fam) that 'justice must never be sacrificed upon the altar of speed'.

11.62 The President makes clear that the need or otherwise to extend the 26 week limit will need to be considered on a case by case basis and that as far as relevant considerations go 'Only the imperative demands of justice – fair process – or of the child's welfare will suffice'.

11.63 He envisages three types of scenario in which extension may be justified:

'This is not the occasion for any elaborate discussion of a question which, in the final analysis, can be determined only on a case by case basis. But some preliminary and necessarily tentative observations are appropriate.

There will, as it seems to me, be three different forensic contexts in which an extension of the 26 week time limit in accordance with section 32(5) may be "necessary":

(i)   The first is where the case can be identified from the outset, or at least very early on, as one which it may not be possible to resolve justly within 26 weeks. Experience will no doubt identify the kind of cases that may fall within this category. Four examples which readily spring to mind (no doubt others will emerge) are (a) very heavy cases involving the most complex medical evidence where a separate fact finding hearing is directed in accordance with *Re S (Split Hearing)* [2014] EWCA Civ 25, [2014] 2 FLR (forthcoming), para 29, (b) FDAC type cases (see further below), (c) cases with an international element where investigations or assessments have to be carried out abroad and (d) cases where the parent's disabilities require recourse to special assessments or measures (as to which see *Re C (A Child)* [2014] EWCA Civ 128, para 34).

(ii)   The second is where, despite appropriately robust and vigorous judicial case management, something unexpectedly emerges to change the nature of the proceedings too late in the day to enable the case to be concluded justly within 26 weeks. Examples which come to mind are (a) cases proceeding on allegations of neglect or emotional harm where allegations of sexual abuse subsequently surface, (b) cases which are unexpectedly "derailed" because of the death, serious illness or imprisonment of the proposed carer, and (c) cases where a realistic alternative family carer emerges late in the day.

(iii)   The third is where litigation failure on the part of one or more of the parties makes it impossible to complete the case justly within 26 weeks (the type of situation addressed in *In re B-S*, para 49).'

11.64 When the court is making an appraisal of a case and the need to go beyond 26 weeks:

'Typically three questions will have to be addressed. First, is there some solid, evidence based, reason to believe that the parent is committed to making the necessary changes? If so, secondly, is there some solid, evidence based, reason to believe that the parent will be able to maintain that commitment? If so, thirdly, is there some solid, evidence based, reason to believe that the parent will be able to make the necessary changes within the child's timescale?'

11.65 *Re S (A Child)* [2014] EWCC B44 also usefully highlights the changes to s 38 of the Children Act and the meaning of necessary in that section:

'Later this month, the amendments to section 38 of the 1989 Act affected by the Children and Families Act 2014 will be brought into force. Sections 38(7A) and (7B), inserted by section 13(11) of the 2014 Act, provide as follows: (7A) A direction under subsection (6) to the effect that there is to be a medical or psychiatric examination or other assessment of the child may be given only if the court is of the opinion that the examination or other assessment is necessary to assist the court to resolve the proceedings justly. The factors that the court should have regards to are set out in the new s 38(7B).'

11.66   And:

'For present purposes the key point is the use in common in section 38(7A) of the 1989 Act, section 13(6) of the 2014 Act and FPR 25.1 of the qualifying requirement that the court may direct the assessment or expert evidence only if it is "necessary" to assist the court to resolve the proceedings. This phrase must have the same meaning in both contexts. The addition of the word "justly" only makes explicit what was necessarily implicit, for it goes without saying that any court must always act justly rather than unjustly. So "necessary" in section 38(7A) has the same meaning as the same word in section 13(6), as to which see *Re TG (Care Proceedings: Case Management: Expert Evidence)* [2013] EWCA Civ 5, [2013] 1 FLR 1250, para 30, and *In re H-L (A Child) (Care Proceedings: Expert Evidence)* [2013] EWCA Civ 655, [2014] 1 WLR 1160, [2013] 2 FLR 1434, para 3.'

REQUIREMENTS OF EXPERTS

11.67   So we turn now to consider what the court and practitioners require of an expert. First and perhaps most obvious is the standard and quality that is expected.

11.68   Experts need to be aware of the task and thought process required of professionals in a case – including the social worker and guardian – when they are making their recommendations to the court and formulating a care plan. The judge will have to carry out their own balancing exercise in making a final determination. They have to balance the indicators of success and failure of each competing option. However before that the social workers and guardians in drafting or commenting upon a care plan will have carried out a similar task in their own right.

11.69   For the court and professionals consideration must be given to all competing options. That does not in any way displace the welfare principle: that remains the paramount consideration. In all these matters the welfare checklist remains the same.

11.70   The court must be satisfied that the care plan is proportionate and nothing else will do in all the circumstances of the subject child's life experiences and needs. We will reasonably expect an expert to know more than the court and practitioners about their relevant subject area – that, of course, is the reason they are instructed.

11.71 An expert will be expected to give insight into a relevant issue above and beyond the common knowledge and experience of others in the court arena. The instructed expert will need to show themselves to be someone with special knowledge, skill or training. It is those qualities and proficiencies which must be conveyed to the court as a tool for it to then use in its decision making exercise.

11.72 The instructed expert will be expected to give a well formed and rational conclusion and one which can be explained to and inform the court. It is the expectation that the recommendation and conclusion of any report is the definitive answer from that expert. If the expert feels there is insufficient data or detail to give that definitive answer they must, as soon as the issue arises, request what they feel is needed and, failing receipt of such for whatever reason, indicate if the then expressed opinion and conclusion is therefore provisional.

11.73 As is already the standard practice the instructed expert must cite any study or literature relied upon. It is vital that the expert identifies the factual nexus upon which their opinion is based. This will form part of the basis upon which the court will evaluate their evidence and assess the weight to give it. This does not alter the fact that it is the sole domain of the court to determine any factual disputes that occur in the evidence. If there is any factual dispute or discrepancy that has a direct impact on an experts work they should notify the instructing parties as soon as possible so that the appropriate course of action can be taken and if necessary the allocated judge be notified (although bear in mind what is set out by Ryder LJ in *Re S* above). The expert must consider all relevant facts contained within the court papers including those that could detract from their recommendation.

11.74 The expert report and recommendation is expected to be uninfluenced by the demands of the proceedings and court process. It is vital the expert is clear when questions or issues addressed in their letter of instruction fall outside their area of expertise or in the event that there is a need for input from another area of expertise.

11.75 What the court and professionals need an expert to say is what the prospective carer can actually do, what they need in order to do this, how long this will take and with what support. Within that an expert report will need to identify the measures that will need to be taken in order to achieve or maintain a family placement. The markers and predictors of sustained change need to be identified, as do the markers and predictors of failure. The time frame each prospective carer will need to be given in order to address the difficulties under which they labour is fundamental information for the court.

11.76 This is where the 26 week parameter becomes relevant. In many circumstances one can anticipate that a recommendation of work and support will go far beyond the 26 weeks allowed for in the court process. There is no longer the luxury of time available to the court process. One can no longer hope for or expect a case to be adjourned in order to monitor a rehabilitation plan. Instead, if a process of support or rehabilitation has a decent prospect of success that goes past the 26 week limit, the work and monitoring necessary will form part of the care plan and to be implemented under a final order. The consequence of this is that the markers and predictors of success or failure become vital pieces of information for the court to base a decision upon.

11.77   There will be an increasing demand on experts to quantify their level of optimism or pessimism about a particular course of action. They will be increasingly expected to give percentages and to define the prospects numerically. Whilst a reluctance to do this is understandable given the differing ways in which each discipline assesses the needs of a child, at the very least they will be expected to be very clear about their view of the outcome on a balance of probabilities.

11.78   The court will need to be told what the key stages will be along the path to any given placement succeeding or failing. For example, no longer will the court be satisfied if told by an addiction expert that a parent needs to be 'clean for a year' to give an indication of long term success. Now the court will want to know what the positive and negative markers are after, perhaps, 3 months and 6 months. The relevance of each of those markers will need to be identified, as will how they influence the overall prospects of a successful outcome. At what point can one assume things will turn out well? At what point can one assume the placement or work towards the placement should be terminated despite all intervention?

11.79   Another key piece of guidance sought from an expert is whether or not any work, therapy or treatment that is required can be done with the subject child being in placement with the potential carer? If not, at what stage can the child be placed with them and what are the targets that need to be met in order to sanction such a move? There will also need to be consideration of how any plan for reunification would take place. Does there need to be a gradual increase in contact or can it take place more swiftly?

11.80   The court will expect a clear recommendation as to the nature, duration and availability of any necessary or identified treatment. If at all possible the identity of a suitable resource provider would be of great assistance, as will any information as to how the nature of such intervention will evolve over the course of treatment or during any predicted period of assessment or rehabilitation.

11.81   Consideration will also need to be given to how different, if at all, the recommendations are if there are expected to be two carers in the prospective placement. A clear recommendation will be needed as to whether or not the second carer (if not labouring under any relevant difficulties) can be a protective factor during any process of assessment of rehabilitation. An opinion may well be required as to what if any stressors will impact on the second adult, how they will manage and function in those circumstances? To what extent will that be a determining factor? The support, treatment or guidance that the second adult will need should be identified.

11.82 If a shared care arrangement is a realistic prospect, or if it is not, the competing benefits and negatives must be identified.

11.83 The court will always want to be astute to explore all avenues before resorting to any separation of a child from their birth parent(s). With that in mind realistic alternatives will need to be identified to the court and the positives and negatives about those prospects identified. Each possibility will need to be considered and as appropriate discounted or supported with clear reasoning given.

11.84 If a recommendation amounts to needing a 'team around the child' the various essential components of that team will need to be identified.

11.85 The court will need clear recommendations as to what the relevant time frame is for each subject child. (An issue that is further explored in other chapters in this book.) How long can or should this particular child wait for a decision or final determination in respect of placement to be achieved? In the event that their prospective carer is not yet ready (and potentially won't be ready within the 26 weeks' timeframe) how long could or should a decision be delayed or adjourned pending resolution? If the recommendation is to wait but that proceedings would be deemed necessary to continue, very clear opinion will be needed as to why that delay should be entertained. It will need to be made very clear what makes the case 'exceptional' to justify an extension of the 26 week limit. These extensions will not be given freely.

11.86 It will be necessary for each instructed expert, within the ambit of their area of expertise, to identify the pros and cons of the subject child returning or remaining within the care of their parent. In the alternative it will be necessary to identify the consequences of their removal from and remaining away from their parents and/or their family of origin. In the event that a child will not be returned to their parents then specific recommendations of a similar nature will need to be given for contact in the short, medium or long term.

11.87 Indications as to the qualities of a carer required for each subject child also need to be identified to the court. The parenting that the court will seek to achieve for a child is 'good enough'. In the event that any form of reparative parenting is needed or any reason that something above 'good enough' would be needed for a child must be clearly and specifically identified and explained.

11.88 As referred to earlier, experts are under a duty to comply with Part 25 (Experts and Assessors) of the Family Procedure Rules and all the associated Practice Directions relating to expert evidence. These make clear that the expert's overriding duty is to the court and that they are independent regardless of the party who instructs them.

11.89 Experts should be receiving feedback from the court arena in respect of any case they are involved in to enable them to improve their own practice, however experts more commonly report that this does not happen or happens rarely. It is assumed that many experts would welcome feedback in order to learn and continuously improve their practice and as such both expert witnesses and legal professionals should be astute to ensure this channel of communication is open. If you as an expert do not get feedback as a matter of course, ask.

11.90 In January 2014 Sir James Munby P issued a Practice Direction entitled *Transparency in the Family Courts*. The guidance within that practice direction took effect as of 3 February 2014.[22] The intention of the guidance is:

> 'There is a need for greater transparency in order to improve public understanding of the court process and confidence in the court system. At present too few judgments are made available to the public, which has a legitimate interest in being able to read what is being done by the judges in its name. The Guidance will have the effect of increasing the number of judgments available for publication (even if they will often need to be published in appropriately annonymised form).'

11.91 This guidance is clearly a shift in emphasis and a stark intention to achieve greater openness and transparency. The guidance is to be the first of several incremental steps towards greater transparency. This is aimed at reassuring the public as to what goes on in both Family Division and Court of Protection hearings. This also has a direct impact on instructed experts:

> 'In all cases where a judge gives permission for a judgment to be published:
>
> Public authorities and expert witnesses should be named in the judgment approved for publication, unless there are compelling reasons why they should not be so named.'

11.101 Expert reports need to fulfill the intended purpose. That is to help a judge move the case forward swiftly to ensure children spend as little time as possible waiting for their as yet undetermined future. The expert henceforth will be expected to give the court a route map out of and beyond proceedings to enable the court to reach its determination within 26 weeks. The report will also be expected to set out in the clearest possible terms when and if the expert opinion means that 26 weeks is not appropriate in a particular case and that such case should instead be considered 'exceptional' and freed of the 26 week limits.

11.102 The Ministry of Justice statistics published for April to June 2014[23] showed that the average time for the disposal of a care or supervision

---

[22] http://www.familylaw.co.uk/system/redactor_assets/documents/1171/transparency-in-the-family-courts.pdf.

[23] https://www.gov.uk/government/uploads/system/uploads/attachment_data/file/358230/court-statistics-quarterly-april-to-june-2014.pdf.

application had dropped to just under 30 weeks (down 28% from April to June 2013[24] and down 43% from April to June 2012[25]).

11.103   The introduction of the statutory 26 week limit is innovative and everyone in the family justice system is still trying to weave a path through the new requirements. How this will ultimately sit with instructed experts is yet to be seen. However, come what may, 26 weeks is here to stay. Though it may at times seem difficult and counter intuitive, these are the parameters in which we now function. The challenge is to make it work, not to try and change it.

Some useful resources

Family Justice Council	http://www.judiciary.gov.uk/related-offices-and-bodies/advisory-bodies/fjc/
Ministry of Justice	http://www.justice.gov.uk/
Court and Tribunals Judiciary	http://www.judiciary.gov.uk/
United Kingdom Legislation	http://www.legislation.gov.uk/
Legal Aid Agency	https://www.gov.uk/government/organisations/legal-aid-agency
CAFCASS	http://www.cafcass.gov.uk/
Family Court Guide	http://www.judiciary.gov.uk/related-offices-and-bodies/advisory-bodies/fjc/guidance/familycourtguide/

---

[24]   https://www.gov.uk/government/uploads/system/uploads/attachment_data/file/245095/court-stats-april-june-2013.pdf.

[25]   https://www.courtsni.gov.uk/en-GB/Publications/Targets_and_Performance/Documents/ChildOrderAprJun2012/p_tp_ChildrenOrderBulletin_AprJun12.html.

CHAPTER 12

CAPACITY TO CHANGE: PRIVATE LAW COALFACE

Ursula Rice

12.1 If legal proceedings are buildings, then public law is an edifice. A soaring fortress built of state funded functionaries. Professionals educated in psychology, education, medical specialties, legal specialties, social work, rehabilitation and so on. People who know what they are doing and how other experts can be channeled. Compared to that, the private law proceedings 'building' is a shed. On an allotment. Maintained by a man holding his trousers up with string (that is not a cheeky allusion to the President of the Family Division!).

12.2 Abandoning metaphor, there is a great contrast between the sense of system in public law and private law. There are buildings, people, IT, courts, money committed to the system, innovative projects being invested in like FDAC.[1] Public law cases take precedence in court listings and in almost all cases[2] each parent and the children is guaranteed legal representation at the expense of the public purse. Resources seem comparatively available and properly funded, no matter how the constraints of austerity have impacted upon them.

12.3 Families in public law proceedings are asked to perform supreme feats of mental strength by making changes to fit in the child's timetable. They have to change their core thinking and behaviour if they are to avoid the ultimate disaster, boiled down as the state removing their children forever. They rightly have help to do that if they can and such decisions are taken with the right to a family life at its centre.

12.4 Parents are told they must change by the courts daily. The majority of those parents are not in a public law setting, but there by their own motion, having launched legal action using s 8 of the Children Act 1989. Emotional

---

[1]   Family Drug and Alcohol Court. A multi-disciplinary service set up to deal with care proceedings when drugs or alcohol misuse are an identified cause of harm.

[2]   See in the matter of *Re D (A Child)* [2014] EWFC 39. A standalone placement order application currently does not attract legal aid, in spite of the fact that the outcome may be permanent removal of a child from a birth family. In this case, the parents have now been granted 'exceptional funding' from the legal aid agency but a cynic may say it took being embarrassed by the President of the Family Division to obtain it.

abuse is a certainty for a child if they experience sustained parental conflict over how much they see each parent or where they should live. This abuse is created by the negative angry thinking and amplified by negative angry reactions.

12.5 In this chapter, the capacity to change in the timetable of the child is explored in the private law context. When a child, as a subject of private law, needs his parents to change what factors come into play? What cards must be played? What gets in the way for him? Are there approaches or tactics a concerned practitioner – be it lawyer, Cafcass officer, social worker or judge, could use that would produce a better outcome?

12.6 All but the most optimistically proto-revolutionary lawyers will not be expecting increases in funding in this area of law anytime soon. This is no plea for an army of experts to be summoned up by the government. This chapter strives to be an assessment of how those professionals, particularly advisors, child social care practitioners and judges, with power in the arena of section 8 law could use it more wisely and to better effect. How can these parents be persuaded or coerced into a change of ways, what will push them into mending or reprogramming their parenting so that their children, in their turn, learn to deal with conflict in relationships without passing on the poisoned chalice.

LEGAL ARENA

12.7 Many readers will have an idea of the law but it seems polite to refresh the basis of the legal context.

12.8 If a person is a party in Children Act 1989, s 8 proceedings then they, not the state, have asked to be there. A request of the court is made by a person with parental responsibility (usually a natural birth parent) for an order against the other parent that must be obeyed. Punitive measures are there if acceptable obedience to the order is not forthcoming.

12.8 Currently almost all such applications have to be preceded by a meeting to find out about mediation (the state accepted alternative way of resolving family disputes). There are some limited exceptions to this mandate but they need not be set out for the purposes of this chapter.

12.9 Generally, whilst the applying parent may be asking for an order to be imposed on the other parent the other parent uses the application to either oppose the current status quo or refine it in some way.

12.10 The order will be about a child. With whom should a child live? How often should they see each parent? Can they go to this school or that school? Should they move to another area? Can they change names?

12.11 Big ticket questions that attract media attention are also dealt with in this legislation but s 8 of the Children Act 1989 for 99% of the time is prayed in aid of the basics and indeed on the minutiae of daily parenting.

12.12 The standard orders produced by the court are a 'child arrangements order' (the child will live with his Mum/or live with his Dad/) or a 'prohibited steps order' (The Dad cannot remove the child from the school) or a 'specific issue order' (the child has to go to this school). It is useful to know that up until April 2014 child arrangement orders were expressed as contact and residence orders and that in many documents, these expressions continue to crop up.

12.13 As in public law, ss 1–3 of the Children Act 1989 apply namely that the welfare of the child is paramount, delay is bad for children and the welfare checklist applies to the decision making process.

CAN THE THRESHOLD BE CROSSED?

12.14 Is there a concept of significant harm applicable to these cases?

12.15 Yes, as in all the Children Act proceedings. Where a child is experiencing or at risk of significant harm then protective measures are triggered.[3] It also brings in the involvement of the local authority who must investigate and take appropriate action. Starting out in private law proceedings but ending up in care proceedings is an unusual route but not unknown and generally stems from the emotional harm done by the high levels of parental conflict.[4] Children in s 8 proceedings become at risk of emotional harm as the dispute goes on. Professionals advising such parents become increasingly aware of this, as their client complains of the terrible symptoms their children exhibit after contact occurs. The irony is the complaining client considers it to be a result of dislike of the other parent, whereas frequently it is a result of the tension generates by the resident parent's dislike of the non-resident parent.

12.16 It follows that by definition, most children who are the subject of s 8 proceedings may sustain some emotional harm or be, at the least, potentially *at risk* of emotional harm. Most s 8 cases resolve themselves and parent find an equilibrium or a space in which to allow the child to cross from one parent to another without parental disharmony undermining the contact.

12.17 There are however cases that defy the efforts of the courts to resolve them and continue for years – and the children who are in the grip of their

---

[3] Section 31(2) provides as follows: 'A court may only make a care order or supervision order if it is satisfied (a) that the child concerned is suffering or is likely to suffer significant harm and (b) that the harm or likelihood of harm is attributable to the care being given to the child, or likely to be given to him if the order were not made, not being what it would be reasonable to expect a parent to give to him.'

[4] See the sorry tale of parental failure set out in *X County Council V M1 & M2 v F1 & F2 v A v B (by her children's Guardian)* [2014] EWHC 818 (Fam). It is worth tracking back through the three judgments connected to this case.

parents dispute present as sad and anxious, sometimes self-harming, eating disordered and depressed – and yet the family veers away from the legal threshold of significant harm, keeping the family away from the scrutiny and assistance of publically funded expert bounty.

12.18 This practitioner has heard many times from despairing district judges that if the parents don't shape up, care proceedings may be issued. However, the threshold to cross before the children will be subject to a care order is high. I am reminded by Hedley J in *Re L:*[5]

> 'Society must be willing to tolerate very diverse standards of parenting, including the eccentric, the barely adequate and the inconsistent. It follows too that children will inevitably have both very different experiences of parenting and very unequal consequences flowing from it. It means that some children will experience disadvantage and harm, whilst others flourish in atmospheres of loving security and emotional stability. These are the consequences of our fallible humanity and it is not the provenance of the State to spare children all the consequences of defective parenting. In any event, it simply could not be done ... It would be unwise to a degree to attempt an all embracing definition of significant harm. One never ceases to be surprised at the extent of complication and difficulty that human beings manage to introduce into family life.'

12.19 In public law, the 'delay is bad factor' is systemically tackled by using the 26 week timetable as the starting point for capacity to change. The lacuna in private law is that there is no corresponding time driven framework. Recently timetables were tightened a little, by imposing targets on the court service to list matters inside a certain timetable as well as discouraging review hearings. There is no specific outside timetable pushing the case along. A child in a sticky s 8 case is met with the problem that his parents will not be chivvied by a system that shows them a countdown to the abyss of removal from the family home by way of a care order. A child in s 8 proceedings is reliant upon the judge to bear in mind the delay problem. It is the role of the impartial tribunal to be robust about delay but that function can be frequently put under pressure through litigants' tactics which are self-serving.

THE INTRACTABLE DISPUTE

12.20 Practitioners have a term for these cases. They are often labelled as 'intractable disputes'[6] and the resident parent is badged up as 'implacably hostile'. They have a flavour all of their own with lengthy proceedings, breaches and allegations flying between the parties. Typical intractable cases progresses like this:

- A terrible relationship between the parents is exacerbated by detail orientated correspondence. Every failing by each person assumes a

---

[5]   *Re L (Care: Threshold Criteria)* [2007] 1 FLR 2050.
[6]   These are specifically NOT disputes where due to a factual circumstance, there is every good reason for contact to be limited or difficult.

disproportionate significance and is presented as proof of an underlying parental vice. Nothing is forgotten, everything is relevant.

- Mediation is entered into; it fails early due to already complete lack of trust between the parents.

- Proceedings are embarked upon and contact is started up or moved on by the court.

- It breaks down due to an expressed wish by the child to stop the contact.

- Enforcements or fresh proceedings are issued by the non-resident parent.

- Cafcass become involved and say in their report to the court that the parent's conflict is causing emotional damage.

- No parent changes their behaviour, instead blaming it on the other party.

- Desperate measures are employed by the parties – classics include referral to children's services about the sexual abuse of the child from an 'anonymous source', questioning parentage, recording handovers or conversations by telephone.

- Breaches of the order continue and it is brought back to court.

- Further hearings decide that the child itself should have a guardian and a lawyer.

- The guardian expresses the view that psychological assessment is necessary of the parents.

- The litigation extends for years.

12.21 More hearings, more professionals and more money is spent trying to get the parents to change even though the years of process they have endured makes them almost rock like in their resistance and denial that there is a problem.

SCREEN, RECOGNISES, REACT

12.22 'The fact that too often in such cases we only wake up to the fact that the case is intractable when it is too late for any effective intervention' – Munby J.[7]

12.23 Every experienced Cafcass officer and social worker in the field, as well as judges and legal practitioners can sniff the wind and realise when a case is likely to be intractable. As well as the litigation characteristics set out above there seem to be other regular common denominators that should sound the alarm.

- Single child to these birth parents.
- Older parents.

---

[7] Mr Justice Munby (as he then was) in *Re D (Intractable contact dispute: Publicity)* [2004] EWHC 727 (Fam).

- Parents come from a professional/ higher social division.
- Parent's liaison of short duration (less than 2 years from first meeting to separation of a parent from child and in reality often a separation of the parents before birth).
- Significant differential in living standards (usually poorer mother than father).
- Acrimonious relationship from or before birth of the child.
- Allegations of manipulation of the child's feelings by either or both parties.
- Multiple proceedings between the parties, often about money as well as child arrangements.

12.24 These parents are so often articulate, educated and have not had any kind of recognisably abusive personal history, or at least not often one that includes discrete serious trauma such as chronic neglect, or sexual abuse. They are very different to the parents of children who are the subject of public law proceedings. They often express extreme, uninsightful and illogical views in a persuasive and professional manner. The new practitioner should be on guard for these cases.

12.25 It is argued here that recognition of such a case at an early stage is crucial. If it is not identified or confronted in the lawyer's consultation then the subject child of the proceedings needs somebody to grasp the nettle as quickly as possible. It is advantageous to the child if that someone is the tribunal.

12.26 In order for the court to make an early finding of intractability or potential intractability there has to be an evidential basis. At the initial stages in the proceedings it may well be a term bandied about by one party but the court must take a balanced view.

12.27 The power to obtain that evidence is in the hands of the court. An option at the preliminary stage may be to direct a report from Cafcass with an emphasis on the possibility of emotional harm, rather than physical harm. The experienced legal practitioner will realise that the report will be scathing about the behaviour of both parents.

12.28 One of the difficulties with the expert led approach is that although there is no overt cost to the parties to asking a Cafcass officer to report, (that is nobody in the room has to write a cheque for that privilege) there is definite resource cost. It is obvious that the system is financed by a creaking treasury and using up Cafcass more frequently puts pressure on that resource. The court will be mindful of the use of the court's resources, in line with the overriding objective.[8]

12.29 Prior to the first hearing an initial safeguarding assessment is done as a matter of course before every first hearing in a s 8 case. This is carried out by

---

[8]   Family Procedure Rules 2010, r 1.1(2)(e).

the duty Caffcass officer. The officer will be sent a copy of the application as it is seen by the judge, as well as a copy of the response to the application, if available. Brief telephone interviews are had with the parents individually and a letter setting out any safeguarding concerns is produced for the hearing. Many such letters touch on potential for emotional harm but criminal records, domestic abuse and drug use tend to form the core of any safeguarding letter that causes interest to the court in the initial stages.

12.30 Sometimes it feels that the safeguarding letter process is simply a box tick in emotional harm cases. This is a bad use of a resource that is ready and waiting to be used to better effect. It is requires no extra resource deployment, being part of every case already. The safeguarding letter is the place to call out behaviour that looks, on the outside at least, to have an emotionally harmful impact.

12.31 Of course, a representative for a non-resident parent may well have instructions that flag up the intractable nature of the case. The early alarm can be sounded by being transparent about the problem on the application form. That said, it is inevitable that the client will have the spotlight turned upon their own behaviour, ie what are they doing to fuel the intractability? It is never a one way street but an application that is not afraid to raise the prospect of emotional harm, can hasten the need for change in behaviour on both sides.

THE TENSION AND LIMITATION IN THE LAWYER'S ROLE

12.32 There is a natural tension in the position of any advisor to the legal process, due to the adversarial nature of proceedings and the historical context that Children Act proceedings sit in.

12.33 Psychology as an inherent issue in s 8 cases is not where the conversation with a legal practitioner starts. No clients come in and say, 'My anxiety, caused in part by my own childhood experience, is stopping me from seeing the good in a relationship between my ex and my child. My ex by the way uses destructive negative behaviour that causes my anxiety to heighten, fuelling parental conflict which is aligning my child to me, further damaging her attachments'.

12.34 Inevitably the conversation in a nutshell is, 'My ex is a weirdo, my child hates him and he has only himself to blame. Can you stop contact as it's damaging my child?'

12.35 Occasionally the desire for change to the dynamic of the family is spontaneously expressed 'I just want us to get on'or 'it should not be like this' but it is a rare client indeed to express the insight that they may need to readjust their own behaviours or reactions. It is even rarer for a parent to then go on to see that the court may well be unable to do that and it is therapeutic work that can help.

12.36   The advisor is being asked to help the client win. They are going to be paid money to do that. The Solicitors Code of Conduct is specific about acting in the best interests of the client. Part of our training involves putting the client's case forward (so long as it is not known to be untrue) vigorously. We have no duty of care to the child who is the subject of the proceedings all though where a serious child protection issue arises and we are in possession of information that could prevent it, we may breach the duty of confidentiality to the client (only to be used in the rarest of occasions). The tragedy is that for the resident parent to obtain a 'win', they often to feel contact must stop. However, contact will only stop once the child has become damaged enough to be in an alienated state. To 'win', your client must participate in the emotional abuse and you must put forward their case. Being a 'good' solicitor does entail representing people whose cases are less than meritorious. However, the question can arise, what is the long term benefit that I am seeking for my client; should I not encourage them to explore the dynamics of the family as well as the underlying causes of disharmony? As a professional we have seen these cases before and know the toll it will take on the client and the children. It is exhausting for them both emotionally and financially. We have foresight and it should be used to be direct with the client about the road that is being embarked upon.

12.37   In spite of the changes to legal aid, many parents in a legal family dilemma will consult a solicitor before anyone else.[9] It is likely to be a solicitor who meets one of the parents long before a social worker, judge or psychotherapist. A solicitor is in a privileged position, having the authority to convince a client of the steps to be taken or to be resisted as well as the know how to navigate the punitive legal system.

12.38   Solicitors tend to be the most trusted of the professionals that form part of the family justice system. It is part of our duty that our clients can rely on their discussions being confidential and that we are on their side. Other professionals that are likely to be seen are rarely in that position. For example to discuss your mental health with a social work practitioner is often believed by a lay person to concede that your mental health is unhealthy, and to risk an inference that you cannot parent. Time-wise, mental health and wellbeing has only just stepped out of the cupboard of shame and it feels risky to be honest about anxiety or other disorders.

---

[9]   It is worth noting that solicitors as the legal advisor of choice are on the wane. There is a lack of legal aid for the majority of private law disputes and many litigants are self-representing or using cheaper options for assistance such as paid *McKenzie* friends. The genuinely neutral *McKenzie* friend service can be immensely supportive and helpful to the litigant and the court alike.

12.39 Solicitors will guide clients towards non legal dispute resolution, to a degree because they have to under new legislation but also because many practitioners sense that the law is unlikely to help in the long term without accompanying change of behaviour. An early recognition and deconstruction of problem causing behaviours is appropriate in our first meetings with clients and a more holistic and more curious approach serves the client and the practitioner better. Solicitors have great influence on a key protagonist and we should use it with more purpose and more powerfully if we want to influence change in them.

THE COMMON DAMAGE

12.40 The families involved in intractable hostile contact disputes becoming immensely damaged. The damage operates on a number of levels.

12.41 All infant humans seek attachment to a caregiver. Attachment is the psychological phenomenon that binds humans together in strong family ties. The mother child bond is usually the first and strongest attachment.

12.42 In conflict between two people the child has attachment to, a child will seek to be aligned with the caregiver who seems to be the most necessary and secure adult. This is a preservation and defence mechanism at an inbuilt level. It will be the person with whom the child spends the most time. It is often the mother who, after a separation, has taken on the traditional gendered role.

12.43 Eventually the conflict between the two parents or attachment figures will force the child into choosing a parent to stay aligned with. There is no choice for the child as the psychological discomfort caused by the emotional pressure of the conflict will always be too great.

12.44 Generally the disputes draws in the wider family, it becomes the overwhelming context in which the whole family operates. The next occasion of contact, the potential to breach contact, the child's expressions of distress start to mount up. They become the pervasive background colour to everything the family does. The disputes taints every bit of time that the family members have together.

12.45 A level of psychological disquiet is constantly present. It often leads to long term mental health conditions such as depression and anxiety in both the children and parents. Time leading up to court hearings is marked by behavioural disturbance and awareness on the part of the child.

12.46 The brass tacks cannot be ignored. The representation and expertise that is used costs a great deal, generally being almost unsustainable to the family financially.

12.47   The children end up suffering loss. If the change in the dynamic between the parents is not forthcoming, they are in an impossible position, the child must choose a parent and therefore loses the other parent. Usually the loss is completely unperceived by the parent in the 'winning' position and the bereavement goes uncomforted. The children will feel guilt and betrayal – both poisonous and damaging to self-esteem. The child under psychological pressure is unlikely to be permanently resilient. Eventually they develop their own anxiety problems and may self-medicate through troublesome behaviour, self-harm, substance abuse or eating disorders. Sometimes the damage done cannot be undone.

12.48   School becomes a haven of calm and respite from the psychological tension. Neither parent can offer respite from the focus on conflict. Body language will say things more loudly to a child than words ever can. It becomes obvious to the child that they are the object to be fought over, even from the best of motives. The parents cannot protect them from the damage and are in denial. Neither parent can just let it go.

12.49   Children become professional children inside the proceedings. Many meetings, new 'special people' to talk to, worried parents. Children become vigilant and stop sharing their feelings on the basis that to say nothing cannot do harm. It is no exaggeration to say that these disputes ruin childhoods. Change in the adults becomes urgent and necessary.

WHAT HELPS? WHAT HINDERS?

12.50   Numerous fragile conciliated agreements, crafted possibly more in hope than expectation, and endorsed by judges encouraging a collaborative outcome, have achieved at best no more than temporary solutions to a profound problem. For all the while that efforts have been made to promote contact without success, the children have become more enmeshed with the distorted thinking of their carers.[10]

12.51   There is rarely a single attractive party in private law disputes. Constantly courts find that balanced against the over anxious, unreasonable, brainwashing mother who is sabotaging court orders at every opportunity is the controlling, bullying attack dog father, baying for mother to be sent to prison and for residence to be transferred to him.

12.52   Intractable contact dispute always have lengthy statements from the parent parties. There is frequently a concentration on the minutiae and a constant totting up of sins of the other parent. If a lawyer or a judge or a social work professional want to set the stage for change then zooming out is what is required. How can this be achieved when wider concepts of fair play such as being able to put a case forward have to be considered?

---

[10]   *Re A & B (Children)* [2013] EWHC 2305 (Fam).

12.53 Fact finding the significant issues can prepare the ground for the psychological work to come. It can be fateful to a case to have factual hangovers that are unresolved. The court process is geared to an extent to encourage avoidance of evidence hearings but the court should not overlook the value of digging in the dirt with the facts where appropriate.[11] An early direction to have oral evidence about the facts can start firming up the boundaries so that the real underlying issues are addressed. The fact finding exercise will always need a direction for statements from the parties. In themselves they are likely to be long and verbose, but can give a fantastic pen portrait of character of the parties.

12.54 From the court's point of view, and certainly anyone instructed for a child, judicial continuity is required from the earliest stage possible. It ensures that the shifts in position by the parents are remembered. In one hearing a party may be putting forward a position based on cooperating with an expert and by the next hearing they may be found wanting. In the general fact flinging and complexities of the case it is easy for a new judge not to grasp nuances.

12.55 The widely perceived panacea of mediation does not move parties forward in these cases, at least not until some insight or change has been attempted in the dynamic between the parents. This may be counter to the current thinking, but those with experience of the intractable case know they are not suitable to mediate. The protagonist have an emotional difficulty in focussing on the needs of the child in a meaningful way. Usually mediation simply bolsters the internal ideas of each parent that the other is unreasonable and a person that cannot be worked with.

12.56 It is in the power of the court to impose early punishment. To advocate this as a positive is probably is even more controversial than suggesting mediation is ineffective in these cases. Frequently enforcement proceedings or costs orders are applied for by a party who has the benefit of an order that is being breached. There are therefore two aspects, costs orders and enforcement orders. On costs, the court applies a starting point of no order for costs. There is no 'winner's costs are paid by the loser' principal. However one of the effective uses of costs orders is to level the playing field between an unrepresented but difficult party and a represented party. It can remind parties that not having representation in Children Act proceedings does not necessarily come without the risk of costs. This is a useful tool to tackle the litigant in person who is either not sorry that the represented party is having to pay for help, or to discourage constant applications.

12.57 The second leg of punitive options comes through the court enforcing its orders through unpaid work orders, financial penalties or even committal to prison. It is the court's prerogative to insist on compliance with its orders but so often by the time this approach is considered the case is well and truly stuck. The child who is alienated will feel as if the court is punishing them and it is

---

[11] See *WX v YZ* [2013] EWHC 2877 (Fam) for a masterly fact finding example from Bodey J.

unlikely to be conducive to contact restarting, when the child knows the other parent put their carer in prison. If committal is to be used then it can and should be considered at an early stage, before the parties become complacent about enforcement and before the alienation is thoroughly set in. A very short period of committal, 2 or 3 days, can send the right signal.

12.58 The court on occasions considers the reversal of residence as an option. This is a draconian order. It can only be considered with an assessment of the emotional loss the child will suffer if they are put into the household of the non-resident parent, who of course will be a hate figure due to the alienation that has occurred. It cannot be considered without a full understanding of the psychological impact that it will have on the child and all the risks such an order will contain such as a child running away.

12.59 Insistence on contact: this is strongly advocated by Dr Kirk Wier. His seminal paper[12] was clear in his view that childrens' wishes and feelings are unreliable and therapy itself is unlikely to help. It causes delay while people wait to see if parents can change. In his startling research he was clear that if the court is firm on keeping contact going, an alienated child will turn around and start to engage with a non-resident parent quickly, within hours not days. Key factors in this being successful include not doing handovers from a resident parent's house or car. A quiet room from school was much less stressful for the child as it diminished the sense of visible disloyalty for the child.

12.60 This seems very counter intuitive but the research is sound. The writer has seen this method employed by the court and observed that it was the only thing that preserved the contact between the child and her father, notwithstanding that it was difficult for all the parties.

12.61 A case management technique that can be fruitful is an order for contact to be made, with a follow up direction for the parties to attend 48 hours after the cessation of contact; ie the Tuesday morning after the Saturday contact should have happened, in order to investigate the success of the order and the potential sanctions if the matter is otherwise than happy.

12.62 An early appointment of a guardian under s 16(4) of the Children Act 1989 is essential in such cases. The court is greatly assisted by having a neutral protagonist, gathering the children's thought and desires, considering the perspectives and reporting an independent view of the parties.

12.63 Care proceedings are sometimes floated early on in s 8 disputes. The practicalities are never easy. Resource is an issue, as well as a reluctance to initiate the conversation as to whether the tipping point of significant harm has been reached. Once that threshold is crossed then the court still needs to

---

12   *Intractable contact disputes – the extreme unreliability of children's ascertainable wishes and feelings* (Family Court Journal, Volume 2 No 1, 2011). A paper so short and so full of utility that it is worth an immediate diversion by the reader to the internet http://www.xm-ecosse.co.uk/Articles/Intractable_Contact_Disputes2011%20Published%20version.pdf.

consider care plans as well as whether the order it is proposing to make needs to pass the legal test that 'nothing else will do'.[13]

12.64 Finally the court can impose and order that no application can be made without the permission of the court.[14] These are not lightly made by courts as it necessarily impacts on a litigant's access to justice, but they are often a feature in final orders.

12.65 These techniques are in the hands of the tribunal, not the advocates or the parties. They are the most potent weapons and frequently not deployed at an early stage as there is a constant hope that change will happen and the personalities of the parents will magically transform when they see the misery they are causing to their child. We forget that that intractable contact disputes are characterised by parents in denial who cannot gain insight without realisations leading to a desire to change.

12.66 Therapeutic work is only going to be helpful after the situation has been stabilised. One parent may well need to have an appropriate therapy to say control their anxiety. Another may need to consider coaching to become better at communication. However, this is a remedy outside the power of the court to compel. It is more likely to be the advising practitioner who can drop the hint for change in this case.

12.67 Thus the court and the parties have a number of catalysts to produce change, some stick, some carrot. The trick for a child who needs his parents to change is likely to be how well the participants, including those with influence or power over the parents wield the various options.

HELPING THE HELPER

12.68 The professionals involved at the coalface of the decision making are rarely trained in psychology. We certainly become experienced in human dynamics through our fieldwork as well as having the benefit of reading numerous reports from qualified experts. Judges and lawyers have a legal expertise that can be manifestly dry. However, I argue that embracing a more holistic legal model would produce better outcomes for the children who are subject to these proceedings and by extension, our clients.

12.69 The lawyer who is recommended to deal with a contact dispute is often recommended because they emit empathy, as well as strength. However, people with a good bedside manner tend to be instructed in cases with psychological issues to resolve, underneath the legal ones. We are not well equipped by training to evaluate some of the more subtle issues, particularly in the early years of practice.[15]

---

[13] *Re B (Care Proceedings: Appeal)* [2013] UKSC 33.
[14] Children Act 1989, s 91(14).
[15] It may come as a surprise to some readers that no solicitor has any training in psychology,

12.70 Becoming more holistic in the private law practice can be achieved in a number of ways.

12.71 Unless psychology was part of a previous academic life, it is perfectly possible for a lawyer specialising in family work to have no formal knowledge of any of the basics of how humans interact with each other in their families. We should learn as a matter of formal CPD, about the psychology of children and their reaction to parental separation, including the basics of attachment theory, alignment and the interplay between those feelings in disputes between attachment figures.

12.72 We should remember that professional psychologists have, as a matter of professional propriety, 'supervision'. In legal speak, supervision means an overseer, someone to make sure you are 'doing it right'. For a therapist it does mean someone to discuss cases with and to check success/failure and direction of travel. However there is also another aspect, namely to reflect on the effect the emotional download from the client has on the therapist. Has the emotion of the client transferred itself onto the therapist? Has it affected objectivity or the ability to empathise rather than sympathise? Is the therapist still effective in resolving the psychological issue or are the waters becoming muddied? Replace the word 'therapist' with 'legal advisor' and you reflect the reality of practice for most family lawyers.

12.73 The theory of transference and counter transference suggests that feelings can be transferred in an intense social communication, such a therapy session or advice consultation. Transference is viewed as where the feelings that a client may feel about another person are transferred on to the therapist; counter transference is where the therapist has emotional feelings that are directed towards the client.

12.74 It is not difficult to see that an intense social communication takes place in a heartfelt discussion about a case involving a child. Consider the intense communication that takes place in trying to explain to a client why their assumptions about the other parent are either likely to be wrong, or unlikely to find favour with a court. If the client's belief system is outmoded, or just wrong, and it will damage their case the lawyer must advise them.

12.75 If (when) the advice is rejected, either overtly or through the sabotage mechanisms that clients often employ (saying yes, but then meaning no) it is not unusual to feel frustration or guilt or anger whilst trying to ignore those emotions or bat them away as they take up too much brain space and thinking time. That is client to lawyer counter-transference.

12.76 Clarity and acknowledgment over transference and counter-transference can help the professional stay useful to the client. It stops us becoming

---

attachment or family dynamics, outside that which is undertaken voluntarily (usually after interest is piqued through a difficult contact case).

complicit in their unsuccessful emotions and their desire to normalise damaging parenting patterns. It is so easy for a lawyer to go with the disguised compliance/imperfect contrition route. Agree that mum is right, but for the sake of looking good with the judge, the advice is to just keep quiet about it and try and keep the contact going. We have thereby appeased the client, given them the useful advice but missed an immense opportunity to support capacity to change.

12.77 The more honest route and one that allows the client to have a true reality check is the direct conversation that challenges her assumptions. Asking why she thinks the child hates contact if she hasn't asked him? How she reacts to the child's non-verbal communications? Challenging her about some of the more non-verbal cues that may causing alignment between the child and herself (for example faster breathing, unrelaxed facial expression and angry voice tone). Identifying feelings of anger that may be exposed when dad is mentioned by the child.

12.78 Lawyers operate in a high octane environment with the pressure of offering help for money. We are bound by serious deadlines. We have to remember the law and advise on it. We have to time record, bill and collect money. The clients that need the most help are the most difficult to deal with. They take up the time available and cause stress and anxiety. This can result in misplaced anger or fear towards the client, lessening our ability to be objective. Without some kind of reflective supervision inside the practice it is suggested that legal professionals cannot manage the necessary kinds of conversations that give productive rather than distorted advice, to a client. The capacity for a client to change their way of thinking is much more likely if the legal advice comes from a lawyer who is direct and as well as reflective about the emotional drivers in the case.

SUMMARY

12.79 'Making contact happen and, even more importantly, making contact work is one of the most difficult and contentious challenges in the whole of family law' – Lady Hale.[16]

12.80 It is hard to step outside of my own understanding of what it must feel like to be in need of such profound change. I can understand at an intellectual level the immense amount of cognitive dissonance that the pressures on parent in intractable contact disputes go though. I have done my best to explore the issues reflectively.

12.81 However, I have to question the importance that this problem is given by the family justice system. It feels as if the children in intractable cases are not as important as children who are in the public law system. Surely the capacity

---

[16] *Re A and B* [2013] EWHC 2305 (Fam).

to change of parents of intractable contact case children are equally important as parents whose needs take them to the public law system.

12.82 Tragically, however, it is my view that many lawyers collude with their clients, through ignorance, not malice, in the emotional harm of children by allowing the legal forum to be used as an extension of the argument, without challenge to the client of some of the underpinning premises of the client's instructions. The children in these proceedings deserve a system and an approach that is more robust.

CHAPTER 13

THE ASSESSMENT PROCESS

Emma Peart, Bryn Williams and Roger Young

13.1 Child protection 'scandals' arising from all parts of world, and the modest outcomes for 'looked after' children[1] are a good reminder of the importance of making the best decisions for children and families that find themselves within the family courts. Whilst the facts and the decision rest with the decision maker, typically a court or tribunal, psychological and other expert assessments can heavily influence the course of proceedings, and ultimately the future lives of those involved. Therefore, the evidence on which those decisions are made needs to be robust, balanced, and thorough.

13.2 When we consider that 20% of children in society are described as having mental health difficulties,[2] that there are 50,732 children on the Child Protection Registers or subject to child protection plans in England and Wales alone[3], and the 68,110 looked after children,[4] we must acknowledge the exponential problem that such families face.

13.3 Recognising that 'every child matters', we would argue the need to approach every case regarding 'each child' as unique with their own set of circumstances, as well as each parent and family as unique in their own way. We are reminded of the story of a man walking down a long beach, littered with starfish. He comes across another man who is throwing the starfish one at a time back into the sea. Aware of the gravity of the situation, he calls out to the man 'why bother, there are so many, what's the point?'. The man picks up another starfish, throws it into the sea and replies 'try telling that to this one'.

---

[1] Department of Education *Statistical First Release: Outcomes for Children Looked After by Local Authorities in England as at 31st March 2013* (2013).

[2] Mental Health Foundation *Lifetime Impacts: Childhood and Adolescents Mental Health, Understanding the Lifetime Impacts* (2005). Retrieved from www.mentalhealth.org.uk/help-information/mental-health-statistics/children-young-people/.

[3] NSPCC *Child Protection Statistics UK: 2009–2013*. Retrieved from www.nspcc.org.uk/globalassets/documents/statistics-and-information/child-protection-register-statistics-united-kingdom.pdf (2013).

[4] *BAAF Adoption and Fostering Statistics: England* Retrieved from www.baaf.org.uk/res/statengland, March 2014).

THE RELEVANT LITERATURE BASE

13.4 Each assessment must be completed with care and should reflect the complexity of people's lives, the traumas, the inter-generational issues, the risks that the family may be exposed to and the protective factors that mitigate those risks. It must provide the decision maker with an evidence-based 'algorithm' of the likelihood of change, not just risk and protective factors at a purely cross-sectional juncture. Therefore, any opinion about capacity to change in the timescales of the child should be generated from an integrated theoretical position, guided by psychological and social care models, and informed by best practice. This means that the assessor not only requires an in depth knowledge of the factors that influence parenting capacity, but they must also have an in depth knowledge of child development, resilience and have the capacity to identify risk in observations of parent-child interaction. Given the enormous weight placed on psychological models and evidence in separating children from their parents, it is only right that this evidence is subject to the most serious scrutiny. Whether this needs to remain within an extremely expensive litigious system in some jurisdictions, or a more collegiate multi-disciplinary, family and community based approach remains a subject for another day.

13.5 Research evidence is used routinely by the health and social care professionals in the formulation of cases involved in public and private law cases, and it is by using this material as part of the 'process' of completing our formulation that we begin to develop an opinion about timescales. Remembering that each 'child' and their family is individual and unique and requires their own psychological formulation.

13.6 Unfortunately, in the literature there is a remarkable paucity about the specifc 'capacity-timescales' issue, with a few important exceptions[5] such as Jones[6] and Howe.[7] There has been however, an entire generation of research that has emphasised the relationship between an adverse parenting experience and poor psychological outcomes (eg Rutter,[8] Woodcock and Shepherd,[9] Dixon et al,[10] Hindley et al,[11] Brandon et al[12]). Some important summaries detailing the evidence base that inform a psychological and social work assessment of the risk and protective factors for a vulnerable child, include those of Aldgate et al[13] and Horwath.[14] Through a series of edited chapters, these important books explore child development using research evidence to explain the influences of abuse and neglect on a child throughout their development.

13.7 Cleaver et al[15] produced an equally important summary of the current evidence regarding the vulnerabilities and needs of children at different developmental stages, measuring these against key risk factors affecting their parents, namely, mental illness, learning disability, substance misuse and the toxic issue of domestic violence. Stanley et al[16] provide a useful review of the impact of these risk factors on parenting capacity. Their message, supported by others, is clear that comorbidity between these issues is associated with greater risk and vulnerability, and the relationship between risk factors being causal. For example, a parent exposed to domestic violence may be at an increased risk of mental health difficulties, and possible substance misuse by way of self-medicating.

---

5   Ward et al *Safeguarding Babies and Very Young Children from Abuse and Neglect* (Jessica Kingsley Publishers, 2012).

6   Jones 'Assessment of Parenting' in Horwath (ed) *The Child's World. A comprehensive guide to assessing children in need* (Jessica Kingsley Publishers, 2nd edn, 2010).

7   Howe 'Attachment: Implications for Assessing Children's Needs and Parenting Capacity' in Horwath (ed) *The Child's World. A comprehensive guide to assessing children in need* (Jessica Kingsley Publishers, 2nd edn, 2010).

8   Rutter et al 'Attainment and adjustment in two geographical areas. 1. The prevalence of psychiatric disorders' [1975] *British Journal of Psychiatry*, 126, 493–509.

9   Woodcock and Sheppard 'Double trouble: Maternal depression and alcohol dependence as combined factors in child and family social work' [2002] Child Soc, 6, 232–45.

10 Dixon et al 'Risk factors of parents abused as children: national analysis of the interagency continuity of child maltreatment (Part 1)' [2005] J Psychol Psychiat, 46, 47–57.

11 Hindley et al 'Risk factors for recurrence of maltreatment: A systematic review' [2006] Arch Dis Child, 91(9), 744–7513.

12 Brandon et al *Building on the Learning from Serious Case Reviews: A Two-Year Analysis of Child Protection Database Notifications 2007–2009: Research Brief* (Department for Education, 2010).

13 Aldgate et al *The Developing World of the Child* (Jessica Kingsley Publishers, 2006).

14 Horwath (ed) *The Child's World. A comprehensive guide to assessing children in need* (Jessica Kingsley Publishers, 2nd edn, 2010).

15 Cleaver et al *Children's Needs – Parenting Capacity – Child Abuse: Parental Mental Illness, Learning Disability, Substance Misuse and Domestic Violence* (DoE, 2nd edn, 2011).

16 Stanley *Domestic Violence and Child Abuse: developing social work practice.* Child and Family Social Work, 2, 3, 135–146, 1997.

Capacity to Change

13.8 Many professionals will also be familiar with the Child Assessment Framework.[17] This framework provides a 'triangulation' model that conceptualises the child's needs from a developmental perspective alongside parenting capacity and the family and environmental factors. Similarly, Bentovim et al[18] provide, for example, a model for developing a systemic assessment of children living with trauma and violence within their family. These frameworks are useful for all professionals working within the family law system but have a slight bias towards longer term, or longitudinal assessments of the type that are usually completed by social workers within the child protection process. Further reference texts that are useful for both longitudinal and cross-sectional assessments include: Ostler[19], Reder et al,[20] Reder et al[21] and with an emphasis on Private Law assessments, Stahl[22] and Gilmour.[23]

13.9 Whilst these frameworks all have a focus on the assessment of risk, they all share an emphasis on the importance of assessing family strengths and the role of resilience. This may include a child with a temperament[24] that makes them innately more robust, **coupled with them having a stronger sense of self. Their ability to experience themselves as** a good and strong person at a young age may allow them to withstand exposure to harm, particularly if by the time they reach early adolescence they have begun to develop the beginnings of reflective thought and the capacity to mentalise.[25]

13.10 In addition to the literature reviews covering risk and protective factors, there are also some very useful and robust psychological models that directly address the issue of parenting capacity, the underpinning psychological difficulties and the effects on children.[26] These models are guided by neuro-scientific research that has outlined the impact of abuse and neglect on the development of the child, placing attachment theory at their core. Such

---

[17] DoH *Assessing children in need and their families: practice guidance* (HMSO, 2000).

[18] Bentovim et al *Safeguarding Children Living with Trauma and Family Violence: Evidence-Based Assessment, Analysis and Planning Interventions (Best Practice in Working with Children)* (Jessica Kingsley Publishers, 2009).

[19] Ostler *The assessment of parenting competence in mothers with mental illness* (Paul H Brooks Publishing Co, 2008).

[20] Reder and Lucey *Assessment of Parenting: Psychiatric and Psychological Contributions* (Routledge, 2008).

[21] Reder et al *Studies In The Assessment Of Parenting* (Routledge, 2003).

[22] Stahl *Conducting Child Custody Evaluations From Basic Complex Issues* (Sage Publications, 2011).

[23] Gilmour 'Shared parenting: the law and the evidence. Part 13' [2010] *Seen and Heard*, 20(1), 21–35.

[24] Chronis-Tuscano et al 'Very Early Predictors of Adolescent Depression and Suicide Attempts in Children With Attention-Deficit/Hyperactivity Disorder' [2010] Arch Gen Psychiat, 67(10), 1044–1051.

[25] Fonagy et al *Affect Regulation, Mentalisation and the Development of Self* (Karnac Books, 2004).

[26] Crittenden *Raising Parents* (Willan Publishing, 2008); Howe et al *Attachment Theory, Child Maltreatment and Family Support: a practice and assessment model* (Macmillan, 1999); Howe *Child Abuse and Neglect: Attachment, Development and Intervention* (Palgrave Macmillan, 2005).

models not only provide practitioners with a theoretical underpinning to guide a more detailed assessment, but the authors have also developed associated assessment frameworks with corresponding assessment tools or outlines to assist with family oriented, child centered and holistic assessments.

13.11 In the past social and psychological theories relating to child abuse and parenting capacity have seemed quite disparate to psychiatric systems for categorising mental illness. Many clinicians have found themselves reliant on the inadequate diagnosis of post-traumatic stress disorder for conceptualising observed trauma symptoms in abused and neglected individuals. However, the diagnostic category was not initially intended for conceptualising complex trauma and many professionals working within social care settings have found themselves at loggerheads with mental health services when attempting to obtain therapeutic intervention for the families with which they have been working. Fortunately, over the last decade Van Der Kolk and colleagues have been working on the development of a new system for assessing and categorising relational and developmental trauma.[27] This framework is useful for understanding the multi-dimensional difficulties experienced by abused and neglected children, and later the adults and parents they become, although as yet it has not been formally accepted as a diagnostic classification.

ASSESSMENT TOOLS

13.12 With respect to the tools that are needed to undertake such cross-sectional assessments, there are a number of extremely useful and effective standardised assessments that can assist with the timely gathering of data and provide an additional mechanism for ensuring some degree of emotional independence from the information being gathered. There are also multiple assessment tools and measures that can assist with various aspects of the assessment. These vary greatly and the choice of assessment tool will depend mostly on the development of an initial hypothesis about what might be occurring for the individual or family. For example the clinician may suspect that a mother is experiencing post-natal depression and therefore decide to use an assessment tool such as the Edinburgh Post-Natal Depression Scale to assess her symptoms. In addition, the clinician may be interested in the impact of the mother's post-natal depression on her interaction with her child and may therefore choose to use an assessment tool that assists with the assessment of the interaction such as the infant CARE-index.[28] Selection of the assessment measure is very important and assessment tools should not be used outside of

---

[27] Van der Kolk 'Developmental trauma disorder. Toward a rational diagnosis of children with complex trauma histories' [2005] Psychiat Ann, 35(5), 401–408; D'Andrea et al 'Understanding Interpersonal Trauma in Children: Why we need a developmentally appropriate trauma diagnosis' [2012] Am J Orthopsychiat, 82(2), 187–200; Ford et al 'Clinical Significance of a Proposed Developmental Trauma Disorder Diagnosis: Results of an International Survey of Clinicians' [2013] J Clin Psychiat, 74, 8; Kiesiel et al 'Constellations of Interpersonal Trauma and Symptoms in Child Welfare: Implications for Developmental Trauma Framework' [2014] J Fam Viol, 29, 1–14.

[28] Crittenden *CARE-Index: Infant Coding Manual* (unpublished manuscript, 1979–2005).

the population for which they have been intended. If there are no appropriate assessment tools or the tools have not been researched for the population they are being used, this needs to be cited within the final report and appropriate consideration given to how this may have impacted upon the validity of the results.

13.13 No assessment tool alone has sufficient predictive ability to indicate outcomes in child protection evaluations and they need to be interpreted within the context of a thorough assessment, based on multiple sources of information, gathered using multiple methods. This is particularly important, as many assessment tools that are used for assessing psychiatric symptoms have been developed with a different purpose in mind, often with the assumption that an individual will be truthful about their difficulties, due to their desire to alleviate their own distress. Sadly this is often not the case for the families being assessed within the family courts that may be held culpable for their actions.

13.14 It is important to sound a note of caution about the perception that the 'tools' are infallible. They are ultimately only someone's attempts to construct and measure someone else's reality. This point was made so beautifully by a young person involved in an assessment of their psychological well-being, who responded to a question about whether she had completed the 'forms' left for her during the previous appointment by saying 'I think you psychologists just hide behind all these numbers and questions, why don't you just ask me what is going on?' With such instruments it would be easy to suggest that a tick box exercise is all that is required. We hope we speak for our colleagues across professions when we say that the 'paperwork' only provides the structure and a means for checking out inconsistencies across the information gathered. What is perhaps far more important for the welfare of the child is looking beyond the obvious, and time, experience and familiarity with both normal and abnormal development is essential. Many of the parents we work with 'know' how to stack a pile of bricks, or pretend to engage the child in eating lunch for a short period of time.

13.15 The best assessments are those that also have 'colour'. In other words looking for the 'how' parents care for their children. Tuning into the high negative expressed emotion, for example whilst mixing a Cinderella ready-mix cake at the contact centre, there is a big difference between a depressed mother who is fighting to remain attuned to her daughter who is spilling the mixture on the floor, and does so with compassion and fun. Contrast that with the mother who is sharp, rejecting, pushes the child away so that she can clean the mess and get the cakes just right, so they look as they do on the box. We walk away feeling the exercise was more about the mother's needs, not the child. Of course this evidence is also critical as we question the mother's capacity to place her child's emotional needs above her own. In the latter scenario, were we witnessing a traumatised woman who we know was, as good as, tortured as a child, and wondering whether her own unresolved trauma renders her parenting as cold, critical and rejecting.

13.16 Given our interest in the 'change process', we would of course be curious about whether the mother had been able to reflect on her trauma, perhaps access therapeutic work, or take on board the contribution from the social work team who had been trying to facilitate change for the previous 18 months. The assessment tools therefore have a very important role, but like baking a cake, they are only part of the success in producing a cake that looks and tastes good, and priority should be given to getting to know the family within their own context.

TRIANGULATION AND A TEAM APPROACH

13.17 In order to test out inconsistencies further we also advocate the use of multi-disciplinary teams, a robust and important methodology, such as Bentovim et al.[29] It is common practice for the instruction of separate expert witnesses to assess the children and the adults. However, we have developed concerns about this practice due to the artificial nature of dichotomising families and we have found within our practice that we are missing important, if not vital information when the assessments are completed separately.

13.18 In our assessments we remain curious about the relationships children have with other people in the family and the extent to which they are able to rely on these people to help them feel safe, secure, stimulated and contained. We need to know how these relationships decrease or increase the risk to the child. Through observation of the child, reference to medical and other health and education records, reports from parents and professionals, we advocate gaining a thorough understanding of the child's developmental progress and needs. This typically covers:

- Pregnancy and birth history.
- Family history of physical, development or psychological difficulties.
- Development and progress of self-regulation (feeding, eating, sleeping, toileting).
- Development and progress of independence skills and adaptive functioning.
- Physical health and development (giving consideration to hearing and vision, use of medication, trauma).
- Development of fine and gross motor skills, and coordination.
- Development of sensory integration.
- Speech and language development and communication.
- Play and cognitive development, including learning and educational achievement and mastery over attention and concentration, executive function, memory and visuo-spatial skills.

---

[29] Bentovim et al *Safeguarding Children Living with Trauma and Family Violence: Evidence-Based Assessment, Analysis and Planning Interventions (Best Practice in Working with Children)* (Jessica Kingsley Publishers, 2009).

- Bonding and attachment history and family relationships.
- Social relationships with friends, peers, adults.
- Temperament, emerging identity and personality issues.
- Psychological health and behaviour.

13.19   We caution against the team 'staying put' in the clinic and highlight the enormous value in meeting the child and the parents in their own environment. Sitting on a little girl's urine-stained mattress, stepping over the sanitary towels in the bathroom, and experiencing the step-father's impulsive temper as the child spills their yoghurt down their school uniform, or witnessing the child kick another hole in the hall wall and rip out the banister, are just a few of the 'ecological' experiences that enable a real insight into the stressors within the family. It is also important that the time spent with the family, enables them sufficient time to relax. Spending a day with the family, observing and joining them as they complete the normal everyday tasks that cause stress such as meal times and shopping trips, both reduces the risk of false positives (where parents appear adequate because they can maintain good enough parenting for short periods) and false negative assessment outcomes that result from anxious family members performing poorly due to the pressure of the assessment process.

13.20   It takes time, and sometimes guts! One of the team called his partner after a visit to family's home; the opening remarks were 'I've been shot at'. The startled partner later recounted that he did not hear the words 'with a water pistol' and said that it reaffirmed all the fears he had about his partner going into someone's home with an agenda of 'taking the kids'. In reality, compared to our colleagues in the police and social work, the risks to the expert witness whilst real, are usually entirely peaceful and respectful experiences. It almost goes without saying that if we are not willing to take the risk, why on earth would we allow any child to stay in such an environment. Typically families have regarded us as impartial and often have a vested interest in remaining positive and involved with us. Nevertheless having a protocol for ensuring personal safety should be at the heart of what we all do, including the solicitor meeting their clients at home or in their offices.

13.21   A further issue relates to the timing of the assessment. We would also advocate getting involved in the process early, particularly in cases where the risks about capacity change are important. In the UK the Public Law Outline sets out a clear timetable for public law cases. The issues raised about the 26 week timetable for public law family cases in the England and Wales family court system, illustrates the value of entering the assessment process in the pre-proceedings phase. For us, as clinicians, this is an increasingly common and sometimes welcome development, given that on occasions it has felt our recommendations have come far too late in the process to have any chance at success. Ideally, we would welcome even further change that enables psychological assessment to be utilised even earlier in cases that are high risk or difficult to engage. We remain acutely aware, that no assessment can predict risk of an individual's capacity to change with absolute accuracy, as there are so many factors which influence peoples' lives, and families have the greatest chance of change and remaining together when appropriate intervention is offered as early as possible. Intervention can also act as the most reliable assessment of whether an individual or family has the capacity to change.

13.22 An important and useful clinical process to avoid creating 'castles in the sky' is to use the 'triangulation of evidence', achieved in such a way that we *do not try to prove a theory that is already developed*, but that we seek to explain risk by contemplating the influence of a set of variables on a particular problem. Triangulation is a method that supports cross validation of data through the gathering and verification of information from multiple sources. A critical part of the process is a loop back to test out the veracity of the formulation. Through a dialectical process, taking one idea (a thesis) and postulating an alternative position (an antithesis) from which a new position, or even new question, can be formulated (synthesis).

13.23 For example, we might begin to be curious when for the third time a family are not at home at the agreed time for a family observation as part of an assessment ordered by the court during care proceedings. The letter of instruction for the assessment summarised how the mother was hostile to professionals. Referring to the six-year social work chronology detailing child protection concerns, we also make a note of the 26 sessions that were cancelled, forgotten, not attended and aborted by the family with the social work team, health visitor, school and mental health service in the previous 18 months. We are also aware of the eight changes in social worker and the template letters from the mental health service 'closing the case' because the family 'did not attend', alongside the letters from the headteacher of the children's primary school and the health visitor repeatedly raising concerns about neglect. From our own experience of returning to the tube station on a wet winter morning with the visit abandoned, we could feel self-pity about how late we are now going to be in completing our assessment, how depressing our job is and how irritated we are with this 'neglectful' mother.

13.24 Undeterred we need to use the evidence to the advantage of the family and raise the issue of the families avoidance and their inability to access support, and incorporate what we experienced into the formulation. After a diligent reminder from the mother's solicitor to attend an interview with the psychologist, we finally get to meet the mother and over several appointments begin to learn more and understand her avoidance. With her own history of being in care, abused in care, separated from her siblings, returned to her violent father at 14 years of age, and raped by her step-brother at 15, she could not contemplate 'social workers or psychologists' and 'courts' having anything to do with her or her children. Yet she knew she could not cope, felt overwhelmed by her role as the mother, whilst continuing to experience domestic violence from the father of her youngest child.

13.25 This information was critical in reframing her sometimes hostile and avoidant behaviour, as one of seeking to deal with her own history of abuse and hurt and her determination to protect her children from a similar fate, albeit that she knew she was not coping. This marked a shift from the initial formulation that the mother was hostile and unwilling to work effectively with professionals to one of her trying what she could to protect her family.

13.26 A further case illustration regarding the process of formulation involved a teacher presenting material from a little girl who lived alone with her mother and who was thought to be at risk of significant harm as a result of neglect and the mother's inability to protect the child from abusive partners. The Year Two class had been exploring relationships and difference. On the work sheet there were 'stick' pictures of groups of children, boys and girls, with some suggestion that they were friends. The children had been invited to draw a picture of themselves and their friends in a box in the second half of the page to explore how they were the same and different from their friends. In the knowledge that the child had been heard talking about adult sexual behaviour, had presented with some unexplained physical injuries and had been found taking pictures of another child's bottom in the playground on her iphone, the teacher was alarmed by this little girl's depiction of her 'friends' and their potential differences.

13.27 Alongside a small picture of herself was a larger character with messy black hair, a long body and careful drawing of a penis and testicles. There appeared to be 'something' coming out the penis. The teacher acted in a safeguarding role and discussed the matter with other professionals, taking the opportunity to express her concern that she feared the child had been sexually abused. Without a narrative from the child about the drawing of genitals and any disclosure, the picture had the potential to mean multiple things.

13.28 A number of possible explanations could be offered, ranging from the child communicating to her teacher that her mother's friend was sexually abusing her to the other extreme where the little girl was simply observing that the boy she had drawn was a friend from her class with whom she had been friends since a very young age and she had learned one of the differences between them as friends is that they urinated differently. It was important in this case to test out the range of possibilities explaining the drawing. It was also essential to do so with reference to a broader formulation including other risk and protective factors. From a psychological perspective it required consideration of what we know about normal developmental behaviours of a 7 year old girl, growing up in a deprived community on the edge of a large city in England, giving thought to psychological evidence about the way in which children of this age think and talk about gender, sexuality, relationships, and at the other extreme using the evidence base to explore children's behaviour and actions when sexual abuse is suspected. This process of formulation, looking at what we see and what we know, and questioning causation is not only in our view essential in the cross sectional assessment of the child's and family's needs, but needs to be at the heart of our concern, capacity to change and timescales.

PAYING ATTENTION TO THE CONSTRUCTION OF MEANING

13.29 It is self-evident that 'diagnosis' can bring clarity to understanding of someone's difficulties: it provides a shared language and probably most importantly plays a gate-keeping role in accessing services and resources. From a psychological perspective it is also possible to observe how we risk constructing our narratives about families through a diagnostic lens and ignore the relational influences or vice versa. This manifests itself in our assessment work in one of two extremes. First it is not uncommon to be confronted by a scenario in which the parents, armed with a psychiatric diagnosis of attention deficit hyperactivity disorder (ADHD), seek to explain the child's behaviour difficulties as being entirely 'within' the child, whilst the school and social worker complain that the label has absolved the family of taking any responsibility for the lack of boundaries, stability and self-regulation within the family. Conversely, it is not unknown for us to be involved in family assessments where there have been long standing concerns about a child and the prevailing narrative is that the 'mother has failed'.

13.30 On closer examination of the child's needs, we have observed neuropsychological difficulties that have placed enormous stress on the parent, the school and particularly the child that have impacted in a dynamic and circular nature. It is also necessary to consider whether heritability also plays its role in this inter-generational matrix.

13.31 Similarly there is also evidence to suggest that raising a child with neurodevelopmental difficulties, such as autism or ADHD can have a profound impact on the psychological well-being of parents and families.[30] Where there is a combination of these risk factors, we have certainly observed in our clinical work that parents with their own vulnerabilities, perhaps related to their own abuse, learning difficulties or socio-economic vulnerability, do not have the personal resources to 'parent' a 'neuro-atypical' child. One useful contribution in the field of autism and attachment disorders is the Coventry Model.[31] The Child and Adolescent Mental Health Services in Coventry and the West Midlands have developed a tool for distinguishing between children with autistic spectrum conditions and attachment disorders. However, it is important to bear in mind that many neuro-atypical children may also have insecure attachments given that the added pressures of raising a child with such difficulties may reduce the parents' availability and responsiveness.

13.32 This remains particularly important when parents have received a diagnosis that is stigmatising, such as personality disorder. Diagnosis can be particularly helpful for clinicians when considering the evidence base for treatment and for researching new and effective treatment models. However, as

---

[30] Hatton and Simpson *Next Steps in Supporting People with Autistic Spectrum Conditions* (Sage, 2012).

[31] Moran 'Clinical Observations of the Differences between Children on the Autism Spectrum and those with Attachment Problems. The Coventry Grid' [2010] Good Aut Prac 11(2), 46–59.

with assessment tools, they should not be used as a single mechanism to predict parenting capacity without considering seriously the relational and interaction qualities between the parents and the child. One of our team members recollects working with a mother with a diagnosis of borderline personality disorder, whilst in a child protection context. Multiple professionals reported concerns based on her diagnosis and her fraught interactions since her child had been placed away from her (with the father who had decided to apply for custody) due to her recent hospital admission. However, closer inspection of the quality of her interaction with her daughter demonstrated her ability to read and respond to her daughter's cues and a level of comfort and joy from both mother and child that are not evident in abusive relationships. The woman had a good relationship with her adult-mental health services who were able to work in close liaison with child protective services. The woman was able to take on feedback about the high level of expressed emotion in front of her child, and access services to support her to reduce this resulting in a successful rehabilitation process.

13.33 In contrast however, adults without such diagnoses may present very well in some contexts, misleadingly so to professionals, but are unable to provide their child with the necessary environment they need to develop, sometimes being incredibly harmful to them. Given the greater cognitive maturity of the adult they are much more able than a child to behave deceptively and often the more dangerous an adult's past experiences, the more adept at deception they become,[32] highlighting again the dangers of assessing the adult alone without knowledge of the child's psychological functioning. Johnson and Elbogen[33] provide a very useful summary when considering some of the difficulties with the classification of personality disorder in legal contexts.

13.34 Emerging from this issue is also the fundamental matter of conducting the assessment within what we call 'an assessment therapeutic relationship'. A few years ago in the High Court in London one of us had been giving oral evidence to the court, describing a psychological formulation regarding the needs of six very vulnerable children. In short the mother's ability to parent her children had been reduced to 'impossible'. Having spent the best part of 3 hours giving evidence, making eye contact only with the judge, on leaving the court the mother calls out, 'bye, thanks very much, see you again', all delivered with a grateful smile.

13.35 Absolutely perplexed by her response, given what most observers would have thought was a 3 hour 'mother assassination', it was also possible that she had been able to hear something else. From the very first days of working with her the first task had been to develop an unconditional and respectful therapeutic relationship with her as a woman. Whilst always remaining aware

---

32 Crittenden and Landini *Assessing Adult Attachment: A Dynamic-Maturational Approach to Discourse Analysis* (Norton, 2011).

33 Johnson and Elbogen 'Personality Disorders at the interface of psychiatry and the law: legal use and clinical classification' [2013] Dialogues Clin Neurosci, 15(2), 203–2011.

of why the assessment was happening, being able to make sense of her own difficulties, to listen to her and learn how these problems impacted on her ability to parent, perhaps allowed her to see that it was not a character assassination of her as a person, but a respectful deconstruction of her difficulties in being a 'good enough' parent, as a result of her own difficult childhood experiences. We would suggest that to contribute to an assessment, developing a knowledge and respect for each child, adult and family is paramount, bearing in mind that the final report and evidence can either re-frame an individual's difficulties empathically or add to a re-traumatising narrative, that lives within a permanent document. Even if children are removed, the family's chances for change do not end with this generation and paying attention to how one constructs meaning with the family can create opportunities for change now and in the future.

CHAPTER 14

FORMULATION OF THE PARENT'S CAPACITY TO CHANGE IN THE TIMESCALES OF THEIR CHILD: 'CAPACITY – TIMESCALES ALGORITHM'

Bryn Williams, Emma Peart, Roger Young and David Briggs

14.1 Our aim for this chapter is to present a 'formulation algorithm' which provides a structure to refer to when deciding whether a parent who has placed their child at risk of harm has the capacity to meet the child's needs and can do so within the timescales of the child. We will have failed in our task to advocate for integrated formulations if this exercise is reduced to a 'tick-box exercise', and even more so if we are encouraged to attach a percentage to the bottom of the page. Our clinical experience suggests that our contribution to the discussion about the best interests of the child is served well when we undertake a balanced analysis of the factors that either support or undermine the child's place within their birth family. Whilst it may be of assistance to the decision maker to provide an opinion about what the outcome might be, our primary role is to put the algorithm of risk and protector factors before the person responsible for making the decision. We need to make the formulation accessible and manageable, but sufficiently inclusive so that we are guided towards a thorough psychological understanding of the child's situation.

14.2 We have to do our best for the child to ensure that we understand whether the 'vulnerable' parent has the capacity to change, and to do so in such a way that we are confident they are able to meet the needs and welfare of the child, appropriate to their developmental needs. In our assessments is important for us to be clear about what we mean by 'capacity to change to meet the needs of the child' and 'timescales for the child', and it becomes necessary for us to use psychological theory, models, practice experience, and evidence unique to the case in order to provide a balanced view of the risks to the child in the future. David Jones' table of factors associated with risk of future harm continues to provide a useful reference to the balance of evidence-based concerns that we need to build into our formulation.

Figure 1: Factors associated with future harm (Jones et al, 2006)

Factors	Future significant harm more likely	Future significant ham less likely
Abuse	Severe physical abuse including burns/scalds *Neglect* Mixed abuse *Previous maltreatment* Sexual abuse with penetration or over a long duration *Fabricated/ induced illness* Sadistic abuse	Less severe forms of abuse If severe, yet compliance and lack of denial, success still possible
Child	Developmental delay with special needs Mental health problems Very young – requiring rapid parental change	Healthy child Attributions (in sexual abuse) Later age of onset One good corrective relationship
Parent	*Personality disorder* • Anti-social • Sadistic • Aggressive Lack of compliance Denial of problems Learning disabilities plus *mental illness* Substance misuse *Paranoid psychosis* Abuse in childhood – not recognised as a problem	Non-abusive Willingness to engage with services Recognition of problem Responsibility taken Mental disorder, responsive to treatment Adaption to childhood abuse
Parenting and parent/ child interaction	Disordered attachment Lack of empathy for child Poor parenting competency Own needs before child	Normal attachment Empathy for child Competence in some areas

Factors	Future significant harm more likely	Future significant ham less likely
Family	*Inter-parental conflict and violence* Family stress Power problems: poor negotiation, autonomy and affect expression	Absence of intimate partner violence Non-abusive partner Capacity for change Supportive extended family
Professional	Lack of resources Ineptitude	Therapeutic relationship with child Outreach to family Partnership with parents
Social Setting	Social isolation Lack of social support Violent, unsupportive neighbourhood	Social support More local child care facilities Volunteer networks

THE CHILD AND THEIR TIMESCALES – DEVELOPMENT OF THE CHILD

14.3 Aldgate et al[1] rightly suggest that 'no one could question how that understanding of a child's development is absolutely crucial in shaping assessments and professional judgements about appropriate services to meet children's developmental needs'. In order for us to have an understanding of the child's needs at all stages of maturity, we need to have a culturally sensitive understanding of what is 'normal' in terms of development, and what risks undermine the child's success in maturing to adulthood with good psychological well-being. The iconic developmental theorists such as Erikson, Piaget and Freud sought to explain the process of maturity through the child's developmental accomplishments, measured in stages. Although it became somewhat unfashionable to be too stepwise in conceptualising development, the models of child development have provided an enduring template by which boys and girls, of different faiths and different cultures, with different parenting experiences, share some basic common similarities in achieving maturity. Alastair Barnett's exploration of the development of attachment behaviour and its significance in achieving adequate psychological adjustment offers a solid foundation on which to build a psychological formulation specific to case work.

14.4 Essentially, children learn (or not) to trust themselves as a good person, capable of individual thought and action. They explore the world, learn to

---

[1] Aldgate et al *The Developing World of the Child* (Jessica Kingsley Publishers, 2006).

walk, to hold, to run, to kick, to touch, to lick, to play, to talk, to listen, to make and keep friends, to experience joy and feel pain, fear and loss. Hopefully they learn through a selective relationship with a few key people in their lives that they will be cared for, nurtured, shown how to do things, told when they have gone to far, and critically, have someone to help them when they are lost, hurt or anxious. Observing mothers in their burkhah, sari, or denim jeans on a number 15 bus in South London or a father on the beach in Jersey, we witness the unique intimacy between a parent and their baby of shared attention, attunement, love and care that seems oblivious to the skin colour or faith that informs their parent's moral and spiritual compass.

14.5 Talay-Ongan[2] provides a very useful and accessible reference exploring normal development in early childhood. Others involved in understanding the impact of developmental psychopathology are equally helpful, for example Cicchetti[3] offers a description of the child's key developmental stages, which include:

- Birth to 12 months: Bonding and achieving a selective attachment.
- 12 to 36 months: Achieving a sense of autonomy and ability to explore the world.
- 3 to 7 years: Becoming involved in a social world.
- 7 to 12 years: Achieving an integrated sense of self, purpose and a place with others.

14.6 Central to our thesis is whether a parent has the capacity to enable, promote and sustain their child's well-being so that they reach maturity psychologically well. Madge Booth from the Windows Therapeutic Community for young children in Kent, England, provides an extremely useful illustration of the possible trajectories available to children and young people, using Erikson's model of identity of self-concept.[4]

---

[2] Talay-Ongan *Typical and Atypical Development in Early Childhood: The Fundamentals* (BPS Books, 1998).

[3] Cicchetti *Child Maltreatment: Theory and research on the causes and consequences of child abuse and neglect* (Cambridge University Press, 1989).

[4] Erikson *Identity and Society* (The Hogarth Press, 1965).

Figure 2 Madge Booth's illustration of Erikson's developmental model of identity and what may happen when the process if fractured from the beginning
(© Madge Booth, Windows, Kent, UK)

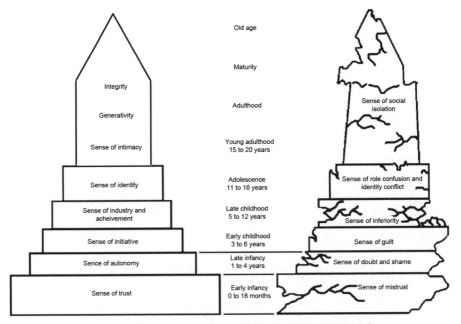

Without completing each stage, a child's emotional development is greatly impaired

14.7 Madge Booth (personal communication, 2014) suggested that nobody should underestimate the child's physical and in particular their sensory needs, particularly when they have been exposed to neglect and harm.

14.8 Essentially this model suggests that children who develop within a safe and secure parenting experience, when they have a good start, a sound foundation, especially during the time in their lives when they are learning to trust and learn that they are an effective 'self', know the world is exciting to explore, but sometimes scary. When frightened, anxious or stressed they have the opportunity to retreat to a safe base. The role of the parent being to send the child out to explore the world, but to be available to guide, support and protect when it becomes too much.[5]

14.9 As Gerhardt[6] suggests we are all born 'a blue print' and our environment, our experience and they way we are supported to manage 'trauma' will determine what the blue print becomes. A reconciled nature – nurture process. It is important for us in understanding how the child perceives and experiences their relationships with significant attachment figures.

---

5   Golding and Hughes *Creating Loving Attachments* (Jessica Kingsley Publications, 2012).
6   Gerhardt *Why Love Matters* (Routledge, 2004).

14.10 We use the evidence base to test out whether developmental delay is more likely to be associated with exposure to harm, always mindful of not determining the facts, but using our psychological skills to describe possible relationships between the child's presentation and their parenting experience. In this book the authors have sought to explore issues relevant to the formulation from a range of perspectives. We must not forget that children and young people, continue to live mostly in families throughout our assessment of capacity to change, be that birth family, kinship family or in foster care.

14.11 Caroline Pipe and Kathy Richardson explored what we can learn from intervention and from the experience of the 'process' of being involved with vulnerable families can have on the assessment of capacity to change. We are also mindful that children and young people are members of communities and understanding their experience of being cared for by teachers and managing and developing peer relationships and friendships is at the heart of the process of formulation has been explored by Louise Bombér. Judy Eaton's discussion about neurodevelopmental disorders has allowed us to consider the risks associated for the child and the parent, where developmental and learning difficulties are present.

THE CHILD'S EXPERIENCE OF ABUSE AND NEGLECT

14.12 Our curiosity about the child's development extends to our analysis of likelihood 'consequences' of having been exposed to neglect or harm. The most obvious signs of physical trauma, exemplified in cases where babies have been shaken are themselves complex, but we are also mindful of a number of key psychological and developmental indicators. Helen Dent's analysis of the impact of abuse and the implications of delaying protecting the child from harm, emphasises the overarching need to protect the child from harm, and to do so with all expedience.

14.13 From a theoretical and evidence-based position we might consider the influence of early trauma and neglect on the developmental capacity in middle childhood. Psychological evidence about developmental trauma[7] represents just some of the hugely influential research and discussion that has contributed our understanding of the impact of early trauma on the child.

---

[7] Golding and Hughes *Creating Loving Attachments* (Jessica Kingsley Publications, 2012); Van der Kolk 'Developmental trauma disorder. Toward a rational diagnosis of children with complex trauma histories' [2005] Psychiat Ann 35(5), 401–408; Perry and Szalavitz *The Boy Who Was Raised As A Dog. What traumatised children can teach us about loss, love and healing* (Basic Books, 2008); Schore 'Relational trauma and the developing right brain. The neurobiology of broken attachment bonds' in Baradon (ed) *Relational Trauma in Infancy: Psychoanalytic Attachment and Neuropsychological contributions to Parent-Infant Psychotherapy* (Routledge, 2010); Fonagy et al *Affect Regulation, Mentalisation and the Development of Self* (Karnac Books, 2004); Gerhardt *Why Love Matters* (Routledge, 2004).

14.14 Ward, Brown and Westlake[8] have undertaken extremely important research on the outcomes for children who do not receive adequate parenting and the impact on development. This research has produced some sobering evidence that suggests vulnerable parents with new born babies who do not show demonstrable change in their capacity to meet their child's needs with a 6 month period are likely to have placed their child at risk of significant harm. Interestingly, the follow-up of these children continues to demonstrate poor outcomes for the children into their middle childhood (Ward, personal communication, 2014). In other words the environment has an incremental influence on the development of, in this example, poor regulation of behaviour, attention and concentration.

14.15 Although the psychological literature provides very robust evidence concerning the impact of inadequate parenting and significant harm on the development of the child from the very start of life, some authors have been rightly cautious about having a blind adherence, almost evangelical belief about what the science tells us. Wastell and White[9] have been critical of the spin put upon the neuroscience and the impact that it has had on the decisions made about the welfare and needs of very young children, considering it excessive that the neuropsychological has been 'used', somewhat emotively, to foster a somewhat evangelical approach to the impact of early developmental trauma and the apparent irreversible effects on the child's well being. This is robustly refuted by Ward and Brown.[10]

14.16 There are other important risk factors for children being raised in an inadequate parent – child relationship. One particular concern is when the child is not only harmed, but finds themselves taking on the role of parent. Needing to be vigilant to their parents' vulnerability and adapting their behaviour and responses to stress, the child is placed in an invidious position. Crittenden[11] (2008) describes the child who is exhibiting over compliant or care taking behaviour towards the parent. We become curious about the impact of assuming this role in the parent – child relationship and need to observe how the child is learning self-regulation, especially when their role model for this important developmental task are poorly regulated in their own behaviour. When the child's emotional needs are being met they are comfortable, those whose needs are not, are vigilant. They lack connection to the relationship, but also to the things that should be preoccupying them.

14.17 The child needs the arousal of emotions to be moderated and well matched with their primary care givers. When we are assessing whether the parent can become attuned to their child and protect them from harm, we are

---

[8] Ward et al *Safeguarding Babies and Very Young Children from Abuse And Neglect* (Jessica Kingsley Publishers, 2012).

[9] Wastell and White *Blinded by neuroscience* (Families, Relationships and Societies Volume 1, Number 3, November 2012, 397–414(18).

[10] Ward and Brown *Decision making within the child's timeframe* (Loughborough University, 2013).

[11] Crittenden *Raising Parents:* Attachment, parenting and child safety (Willan Publishing, 2008).

really curious about whether the child's reactions moderate as the parent places themselves firmly in the position of being the adult, absolving the child of their 'parenting' responsibility. The reunion between the child and the parent, the separation and the experience of turn taking are essential markers. If these are poorly attuned and regulated, particularly following intervention, we have less optimism that the parent has the capacity to meet the needs of the child, or have the capacity to change within their timescales. The child's voice is important and we need to listen to what the child says. However, it is also important to be mindful of the child's attachment style. Some children who have developed in unpredictable environments use the escalation of negative behaviour to elicit care and support. This may give the immediate impression that the situation is worse than it is, whereas other children may minimise displays of distress giving the impression that things are better than they are. Although sometimes ignored in the process, we are always curious about the voice of the child and young person, a critically important subject covered in this book by Roger Morgan.

PARENTING AND CAPACITY

14.18 We are not social engineers, and take on board fully the words of Sir James Munby P when he says that families come in 'all shapes and sizes'. Within our formulation we seek to explore whether a parent has the capacity to meet the needs of the child, and able to meet the needs of the child where they may have previously failed. We also have to balance this against the risks associated with removing the child into a care system that might create its own risks. Remembering Horwath and Morrison's[12] 'ability and motivation' description of capacity, our assessment has to determine whether, first, that the parent has the skills to parent, and, second, has the motivation, intention and commitment to put the child first.

14.19 Parents have to be able to demonstrate that they are able to separate out their own needs, ideally address their own difficulties, in order to provide their child with a 'good enough' parenting experience. Sometimes because of the damage done to a child being 'good enough per se' might not be 'enough' because of the child's need for a reparative and restorative parenting experience.[13] The parenting role has to be 'good enough to meet the needs of the child'. We know that children can tolerate momentary stress, and indeed

---

[12] Horwath and Morrison 'Assessment of parental motivation to change, 2001 capacity' in Horwath (ed) *The Child's World, Assessing Children in Need* (Jessica Kingsley Publishers, 2001).

[13] Golding and Hughes *Creating Loving Attachments* (Jessica Kingsley Publications, 2012).

this may be expedient in acquiring developmental skills, however as discussed above, Perry & Szalavitz[14] and Schore[15] explain, how toxic and ongoing stress on the child is extremely damaging.

14.20 'Parent capacity' assessments are very complex due to the lack of clarity around what defines capacity or 'good enough parenting'. Jones[16] writes about the assessment of parenting capacity by telling the story of being in court and before being dismissed the judge asks one last question about 'parenting'. Parenting assessment tools and parent interventions are fairly consistent in approaching 'parenting' as a term to described a recipe of tasks undertaken by the 'parent' in order to benefit the 'child'. Building on the history of the developmental theorists such as Erikson and Piaget, parenting has been defined by marking the developmental needs of the child alongside the parenting role required to help a child achieve. Booth and Jernberg,[17] and Webster-Stratton[18] illustrate the parenting methodologies that are used therapeutically to help parents in need of help to move forward. The ingredients most frequently associated with 'good parenting' are:

- Providing basic care appropriate the child's developmental level.
- Ensuring the child's safety and stability.
- Providing emotional warmth to the child.
- Being attuned to the child and 'mindful' of them as an individual.
- Repairing ruptures in the relationship when they occur.
- Providing the children with stimulation, opportunities for learning, and challenging them.
- Offering guidance.
- Providing limits and boundaries.
- Offering a relationship to the child in which they can learn to trust themselves, explore the world, but know you will be there to help them regulate their feelings, thoughts and behaviours when they are lost or stressed.

---

[14] Perry and Szalavitz *The Boy Who Was Raised As A Dog. What traumatised children can teach us about loss, love and healing* (Basic Books, 2008).

[15] Schore 'Relational trauma and the developing right brain. The neurobiology of broken attachment bonds' in: Baradon (ed) *Relational Trauma in Infancy: Psychoanalytic Attachment and Neuropsychological contributions to Parent-Infant Psychotherapy* (Routledge, 2010).

[16] Jones 'The assessment of parenting capacity' in Horwath (ed) *The Child's World, Assessing Children in Need* (Jessica Kingsley Publishers, 2001).

[17] Booth and Jernberg *Theraplay: Helping parents and children build better relationships through attachment-based play* (Jossey-Bass (Wiley & Sons), 2010).

[18] Webster-Stratton and Reid 'The Incredible Years. Parents, teachers and children training series. A multi-faceted treatment approach for young children with conduct disorders' in Weisz and Kazdin (eds) *Evidence Based Psychotherapies for Children and Adolescents* (Guilford Press, 2nd edn, 2010).

14.21 Bentovim et al[19] provide a clear visual illustration of what are considered positive or harmful cycles of positive and harmful parenting linked to the dimensions described above. Critically in the assessment model they propose we make the connection between the parent and environmental influences and the outcomes for the child.

- A positive parenting experience and an adequate environment = good outcomes for children.

- A harmful parenting experience and an inadequate environment = poor outcomes for children.

At the heart of our formulation we need to explore the evidence about whether the parent has moved cognitively, emotionally and behaviourally from inadequate to adequate.

14.22 In reality we have found that these ingredients relate to the complex interaction between the ecological environment, what is an acceptable child developmental trajectory at any given time point, and how deficits in the adults ability to meet the child's needs are affecting that particular child. Such an assessment needs to consider not only imminent risk but also potential risk that may span the next 18 years. Therefore conceptualising 'good enough' parenting using a single definition is an almost impossible task. It is like a 'parenting' jigsaw puzzle that needs to be put together with care and respect.

14.23 One further issue concerning our understanding of the timescales for the child is whether the parent has both the skills and motivation to promote the child's well-being and to do so in such a way that is attuned and mindful of the developmental needs and stage of the child. We would not underestimate the value of all parents, including ourselves, having an opportunity to 'learn some parenting skills'. Rarely do the families we work with need a 6 week 'psycho-education' course about parenting. The Parent Assessment Manual System[20] is one such detailed parenting assessment and intervention tool used to assess knowledge, skills and parenting behaviours and is used widely with parents with learning difficulties.

14.24 By 'capacity to change' we set out to explore the interface between psychological models of change, evidence regarding known risk factors and bring together a wealth of multidisciplinary work and experience in the chapters, to disentangle the key themes that a parent needs to address in order to be able to meet the needs of a child. This varies greatly among the parents that find themselves within the legal system. Practically we have found that capacity to change often relates to how distorted the parents views and ability to perceive the child's actual needs are, how damaged or severe the child's needs

---

[19]   Bentovim et al *Safeguarding Children Living with Trauma and Family Violence: Evidence-Based Assessment, Analysis and Planning Interventions (Best Practice in Working with Children)* (Jessica Kingsley Publishers, 2009).

[20]   McGaw and South Coast Solutions *The Parent Assessment Manual Software (PAMS)* (St Austell Printing, 4th edn, 2012).

are and the level of unmet need that the child experiences. A powerful metaphor for our work is frequently captured in JM Barrie's *Peter Pan*[21] in when he says 'sometimes parents forget children', we would argue our task is to do all we can to ensure that whilst a momentary lapse might suffice, a long sustained childhood characterised by chaotic, abusive and frightening and forgetful parenting is harmful to a child and their psychological well-being throughout their lives.

14.25 An important part of our formulating 'capacity to change' is to consider the parent's ability to understand the needs of the child and to seek to understand cognitively and emotionally their experience of being exposed to harm. Golding and Hughes[22] provide an enlightened approach to helping children 'recover' from developmental trauma using what is called Dyadic Developmental Psychotherapy (DDP). Using a set of simple, but very powerful ideas, the approach asks us to be PACE. This refers to being playful with the child, whilst accepting of them, being curious about them, and having empathy for them and with them. Typically used in a therapeutic milieu, these ingredients are the ones that we also seek to foster in a parent who is capable of change.

14.26 For us, parents who are able to perceive or read fairly accurately the child's emotional and physical needs, without significant distortion, or separate these child's needs from their own needs and respond in a manner that was mostly consistent and timely, are more likely to survive their parenting experience. As David Howe[23] suggests that such parents see the child has having a 'mind' and treat them as such and the response from the child is usually comfort and joy within the interaction.

14.27 In our clinical work we came across a very good example of 'good enough parenting' in a young mother of two daughters who had been identified by health professionals as possibly 'neglecting' her children. The family were from a minority group, often perceived as being very private and avoidant. One of the girls was diagnosed as having a cerebral palsy and the mother was accused of not engaging with health services to support the child. In our assessment we learned that the mother felt that professionals did not listen to her, largely because every time she connected with services the personnel were different and they made her feel like she was stupid and did not find their support helpful. She cited an example of visiting an Emergency Department to seek help because she believed her daughter was aspirating and wanted her to have an x-ray. She said that the staff ignored her concerns and even tried to feed the child, until eventually decided on the x-ray and diagnosed aspiration, having made a bad situation even worse.

---

[21]   Barrie *Peter and Wendy* (Hodder and Stoughton, 1911).
[22]   Golding and Hughes *Creating Loving Attachments* (Jessica Kingsley Publications, 2012); Hatton and Simpson *Next Steps in Supporting People with Autistic Spectrum Conditions* (Sage, 2012).
[23]   Howe *Child Abuse and Neglect: Attachment, Development and Intervention* (Palgrave Macmillan, 2005).

14.28 However, in our direct observations with the family we witnessed a tremendous warmth between the mother and daughter, a high level of attunement and that the child was loved and cherished by all of the extended family, where she was stimulated and socialised. Whilst we recognised that the mother could perceive the needs of the child, at times she could not meet them because she herself was overwhelmed. Re-framing of the problem combined with correct support from services enabled her to do this task.

14.29 Equally, we have witnessed cases where parents had a highly sophisticated and manipulative way of avoiding, controlling and just keeping the social workers at the door. The family gave the social workers numbers, something we have seen more than once, in casting a rather cynical eye on the frequent change of case social worker. Having spent time in the home, observing day to day routines and the ways in which the parents managed, interacted and cared for their children, we found it hard to believe anyone would allow the children to remain in the home. The parenting was highly critical, emotionally cold, disconnected. All we could see was the parents being obsessed with money and benefits, new televisions, iPads, avoiding educational welfare officers and blaming social workers for not giving them what they needed. The difficulties in the family had been evident in the social work chronology for over 12 years.

14.30 Do not assume in anyway that the 'expert witness' is immune to these risks. We work hard to remain acutely aware of the risks of false positives. One assessment included work with a mother who was excellent at eliciting support from professionals, but not actually engaging in it. At one level we warmed to her and observed very good examples of her attunement with her children and her capacity to reflect on the difficulties in her parenting. We were hopeful, and remained really curious about the extreme behaviours displayed by her children. As our relationship with the family progressed, we became more concerned about the mother's attitude and intention towards her children. It became apparent that the mother's 'professional engagement' covered over the negative effects on the children. She significantly distorted the needs of the child and when placed in stressful situations it was apparent that her own emotional needs drowned the children. They were frightened, the boy angry and beyond her control, the girl timid, avoidant and placatory.

14.31 With less reliance on psychological assessment, and most worryingly in the haste to complete cases quickly and with limited assessment time, we risk making some enormous mistakes, both ways. Whilst we need to be expeditious, we also need to be able to do this job properly, ethically and really working in the best interests of the child. In this book Michelle Flynn and Siobhan Kelly provided a very clear summary of the legal framework used in England and Wales, and defines the roles and responsibilities of the expert witness.

14.32 It could be suggested that the psychological needs of children in private law proceedings including, as Ursula Rice indicated in her chapter, the forgotten ones. Although most families separate well, there is a minority of children who are exposed to the most horrific emotional abuse caused by parents whose own destructive attachment experiences become active against the child's other parent and the child themselves is left with their attachment security shattered. Ursula Rice quite rightly reminds us of the all too frequent tragedy that we fail as professionals to safeguard these children from emotional abuse. Our assessment process and the formulation of the child's needs is as important in private law as it is in public law.

14.33   In the formulation algorithm we need to consider all of this information and establish whether the parent has 'resolved' their difficulties, can put their child's needs first, and particularly when feeling threatened or overwhelmed, are able to recognise that their parenting can falter. This is referred to as 'reflective capacity'. Sarah Birch's exploration of reflective capacity appears as a critical ingredient in the analysis of the adequacy of a parent's ability to change.

14.34   In seeking to gain evidence as to whether the parent can develop an approach that puts the child first we are interested in the parent's response to the child's needs, for example the child's desire for comfort, protection, or the need to explore and have stimulation, as well as their need to separate from the parent. It also requires the parent to be aware of when and how the child is testing limits or even being manipulative. We are curious about the distortions that may exist in the parenting experience when interpreting the need and often use the assessment to test out whether the parent can be reflective about the child's behaviour. When parents respond to stress with their own unmet needs taking precedence, we become concerned that change is going to be harder to achieve. A good example of this is observing a mother shouting at her pre-verbal toddler during an assessment observation, 'oh that's it, you never want me in the play house with you, I don't know why I bother'. The mother found it hard to have either a cognitive understanding of the experience of the child, and saw both her child and the psychologist as punitive against her.

14.35   In our assessment of change we need to explore with the parent how such behaviour relates to their own early experiences. Kari Carstairs and Sarah Birch provided insights into some models for undertaking robust and quantifiable assessments of the adult's needs. We would be interested in whether for example the parent was themselves punished as a child for displays of attachment behaviour, or were they abandoned repeatedly and as such are fearful of developing independence in the child. It is typical for the decision makers to be guided by the recommendations regarding 'work' that needs to undertaken by the parent in order for a child to be safe in their care.

14.36   Taking a temporal view on case work, it is self-evident that a family who has been engaged with social workers for all six of the children age 2 to 8 years of age since the eldest child was themselves only 8, provides us with more material with which to explore patterns of behaviour. Compared to a teenage care leaver who becomes pregnant, the mother of six has a significant history.

However, we also need to be critical that for those parents who may have had children removed early in their lives, maturity and change happens. Inadequate parents can become good enough.

14.37 At the heart of what makes change possible is evidence that the parent has dealt with their trauma. Along with reflective function, we are interested in them having a coherent narrative about their own abuse experiences. In our work with parents we are curious about how they respond to alternative narratives about the child's behaviour, and whether they are able to offer more positive narratives about the child. Critically can they link the child's behaviour to mental states and consider their role in contributing adversely to the child's own behaviour and mental state. Triangulated with other evidence, particularly the observation of the parent and the child, and using other people's accounts of experiencing the relationship, we are interested in whether the parent can maintain a focus on the child's needs. Fonagy et al's[24] discussion of the importance of the parent's ability to mentalise about their child and to know their needs is also key in developing our formulation. In the algorithm we need to consider whether the parent has 'resolved' their difficulties, and as Slade[25] suggests, are able to recognise that their parenting can falter but they are able to recognise their own mental state, and that of their child.

14.38 As discussed by Sarah Birch we are of course interested not only in the parent – child relationship, but how functional the parent is in other relationships. We are curious about whether the insights into their previous, possibly destructive behaviour, enable them to make and sustain supportive relationships with partners, family members, friends, people in their community and the professionals involved in their child's life, such as teachers and social workers. We are equally interested as to whether, despite every best intention, they gravitate back to abusive, sometimes violent, relationships or, as John Castleton explored in his chapter, other adults with their own vulnerabilities with substance misuse. These 'adult' needs have to be weighed up alongside the functioning of the child. As we suggested, earlier experience for the child may have been so destructive that their needs are so substantial, even a therapeutic foster family is going to struggle to parent them.

14.39 Parenting behaviour can be deeply ingrained beliefs and desires, compounded by the adults' own battle with survival, perhaps whilst depressed, a victim of violence themselves, and self-medicating with prescription drugs. We are aware how their experiences are shaped by the interaction of internal and external factors. In order for us to gain confidence in their capacity to change it is typical for the issue of motivation to become central in our formulation. Prochaska and DiClements'[26] infamous model concerning motivation to change

---

[24] Fonagy, Gergely, Jurist, and Targe *Affect regulation, mentalisation, and the developmental of the self* (New York, Other Press, 2004).

[25] Slade *Parental Reflective Function: An introduction, Attachment and Psychopathology* (2005 7 (3): 269–281).

[26] Prochaska and DiClemente 'Transtheoretical Therapy: Towards a More Integrative Model of Change' [1982] *Psychotherapy Theory, Research and Practice*, 19(3).

depicts behaviour as arising from the interaction of external and internal factors, and shows how environmental supports and stressors interact with an individual's intellectual and physiological capacity, core beliefs, needs and desires. The likelihood of change occurring is strongly influenced by interpersonal interactions. Confronting interview styles therefore increase the resistance of service users to acknowledge their problems and think about change. Kathy Richardson and Caroline Pipe provided some interesting insights into 'change' moving beyond a cognitive shift in thinking and to a more meaningful, and ultimately sustainable and effective emotional, change in 'belief'.

14.40 Davies and Ward[27] were critical of professional 'over-optimism' about returning children home, highlighting the need for careful planning and support in cases of reunification. Boddy[28] places emphasises planning 'permanence' and recommends ensuring the qualities of 'best possible care' for the child. It is with this in mind that we have presented below an algorithm of factors that should be considered when asking the question 'does the parent have the capacity to change in the timescales of the child?'

14.41 In our assessment chapter, led by Emma Peart, we sought to highlight the process of how we approach our case work and sought to point out the blind spots and the challenges in holding in our minds the child's needs and undertaking a balanced analysis of whether the parent has the ability to 'change' and to do so in a way that is in a timescale that is in the best interests of the child.

14.42 The relationship between the two dimensions is orthogonal in nature with the child's development progressing horizontally and the capacity of the parent to meet the child's need cutting across vertically, as illustrated in the figure below. As the child develops into a self, the impact of the parent's role in enabling the emergence of a 'self' is measured through their ability to provide a good enough parenting experience.

---

[27] Davis and Ward *Safeguarding Children Across Services. Messages from Research* (Jessica Kingsley Publishers, 2012).
[28] Boddy *Understanding permanence for looked after children. A review of research for the care enquiry* (School of Education and Social Work, University of Sussex, 2013).

Figure 3: Algorithm of the parent's capacity in relation to the child's development journey

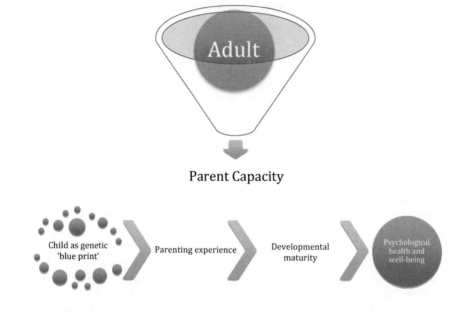

Child factors

- *The child is at a developmental stage where their development and long-term well being may be compromised if their parenting experience is not attuned to their needs and the tasks they need to accomplish at any given stage*

- *The context in which the child lives and the likely impact of removing or moving them at certain stages of development*

- *Understanding the child's attachment history and considering the impact of their earlier experiences on how they will relate to others in the future*

- *To what extent are the innate characteristics of the child, for example being hyperactive, influence the parent's ability to modify their parenting skills to meet the child's needs*

- *The child is reaching the appropriate developmental milestones with respect to self-regulation, physical and mental health, and the parent is able to attune to the child's needs and support them through these developmental tasks*

- *The child has been offered and will continue to be offered an environment that is free from violence, breakdowns in routine and continuity in care, exposure to the risks associated with substance misuse and mental illness*

Parent factors

- *Parents have the 'skills' and 'knowledge' to care, protect, nurture, stimulate and provide limits for the child*
- *Where parents are vulnerable, for example to mental health or learning difficulties, the child, other adults, the community and the resources are sufficiently 'present and robust' to meet the needs of the child*
- *The parent has the reflective capacity in order to understand and genuinely accept the impact of their role in harming the child*
- *The child's cognitive, emotional and behavioural response to being harmed by their parent is understood and the parent has the ability to repair any damage they or the circumstances have caused to the child*
- *The parent demonstrates a meaningful intention to change and have demonstrated they are motivated to change and have engaged in the process of change and there is both behavioural evidence (first order change) and psychological evidence (second order change).*
- *The parent has addressed their own developmental trauma through whatever means or there is evidence of the development of a consistent narrative about past trauma.*
- *Through a process of maturity, and over time, the parent is able to demonstrate that maladaptive behaviours and habits that compromised their parenting are no longer evident, or sufficiently minimised, (drug and alcohol, dysfunctional, perhaps violent relationships, mental health)*
- *The parent is able to demonstrate genuine effective attunement with their child, shows 'mindedness' for their child and has repaired*
- *The parent has learned that they are able to be sufficiently attuned to their child when their own attachment difficulties become activated*
- *The parent is able to have an open and transparent relationship with professionals*
- *Practical issues that undermine the parent have been addressed, such as addressing housing issues, poverty, employment and education for the parent and the child, and that community support is sufficient*
- *The protective factors are understood and assessed as being genuinely sufficient to mitigate future risk*

Service factors

- *Appropriate interventions have been offered or trialed with the family*
- *Goals have been set conjointly with the parent where possible*
- *The goals were time limited with appropriate methods of assessing change*
- *The service has not replicated unhelpful family patterns of interaction i.e. behaving in an ambivalent manner to an ambivalent family or behaving in a chaotic manner towards a chaotic family*

- *That the professionals remain able to consider alternative narratives about the family and respond in an empathic manner (indicating a workers capacity to remain reflective)*

INDEX

References are to paragraph numbers.

Self-harming
  consequence of abuse/neglect 3.20
Sensitive caregiving 2.13–2.17, 2.25
  attunement 2.14
  balance 2.15
  coherence 2.16
  contingent communication 2.17
Separation 2.4
  care proceedings, caused by 2.5
  extended, detrimental effect of 2.5
  infant behaviour during 2.8
Serious case review 3.18
Sexual abuse
  prevalence 3.14, 3.16
  psychological assessment 8.3
Sibling
  contact with 4.44–4.46
  unnecessary separation from 4.4
Significant harm 12.14–12.19
  future risk
    factors 14.2
  risk of 8.2, 8.3
    assessments for 8.1
    formulation for capacity to
      change 14.1, 14.2
Social worker
  contact with 4.9, 4.38–4.43
Strange situation procedure 2.8–2.11
Substance misuse *see* Alcohol abuse;
  Drug misuse
Suicide, attempts
  consequence of abuse/neglect 3.20

Timescales for child 4.1–4.5
  appearance in court 4.78–4.82
  assessments 11.5
  attachment functioning
    assessments 2.62–2.64
  care proceedings *see also* Care
    proceedings 11.1, 11.9–11.42,
      11.44–11.91, 11.101–11.103
    reforms 11.2–11.4
    twenty-six weeks limit 11.3–11.8
  complaints process 4.53–4.60
  contact with family 4.44–4.52
  delays 3.33–3.35

Timescales for child—*continued*
  development 14.3–14.11
  entering care 4.6–4.12
  formulation for capacity to change 14.1,
    14.2
  health care 4.69, 4.70
  inspection 4.71–4.77
  issues while in care 4.25–4.37
  leaving care 4.61–4.68
  placement in care 4.13–4.24
  private law proceedings *see also*
    Private law
    proceedings 12.1–12.49
    'intractable disputes' 12.20–12.31
    lawyer's role 12.32–12.39
    legal context 12.7–12.13
    parties to 12.8
    potential damage to
      child 12.40–12.49
    significant harm 12.14–12.19
  recovery from addiction 9.73–9.87
  reviews 4.38–4.43
  social worker contact 4.38–4.43

Views of child 4.1–4.3, 4.84
  appeals systems 4.4
  care proceedings in 4.4, 4.5
    appearance in court 4.78–4.82
    complaints process 4.53–4.60
    contact with family 4.44–4.52
    entering care 4.6–4.12
    health care 4.69, 4.70
    inspection 4.71–4.77
    issues while in care 4.25–4.37
    leaving care 4.61–4.68
    placement in care 4.13–4.24
    reviews 4.38–4.43
    social worker contact 4.38–4.43
  confidentiality issues 4.4
  long term plans 4.83

Welfare of child
  favouring parental care 3.26
  paramount consideration, as 3.32, 11.6,
    11.7, 12.13
  'rule of optimism' 3.26